I0813492

HOW TO BUILD AN INDIAN HOUSE

THE MUMBAI EXAMPLE

SAMEEP PADORA
NAI010 PUBLISHERS

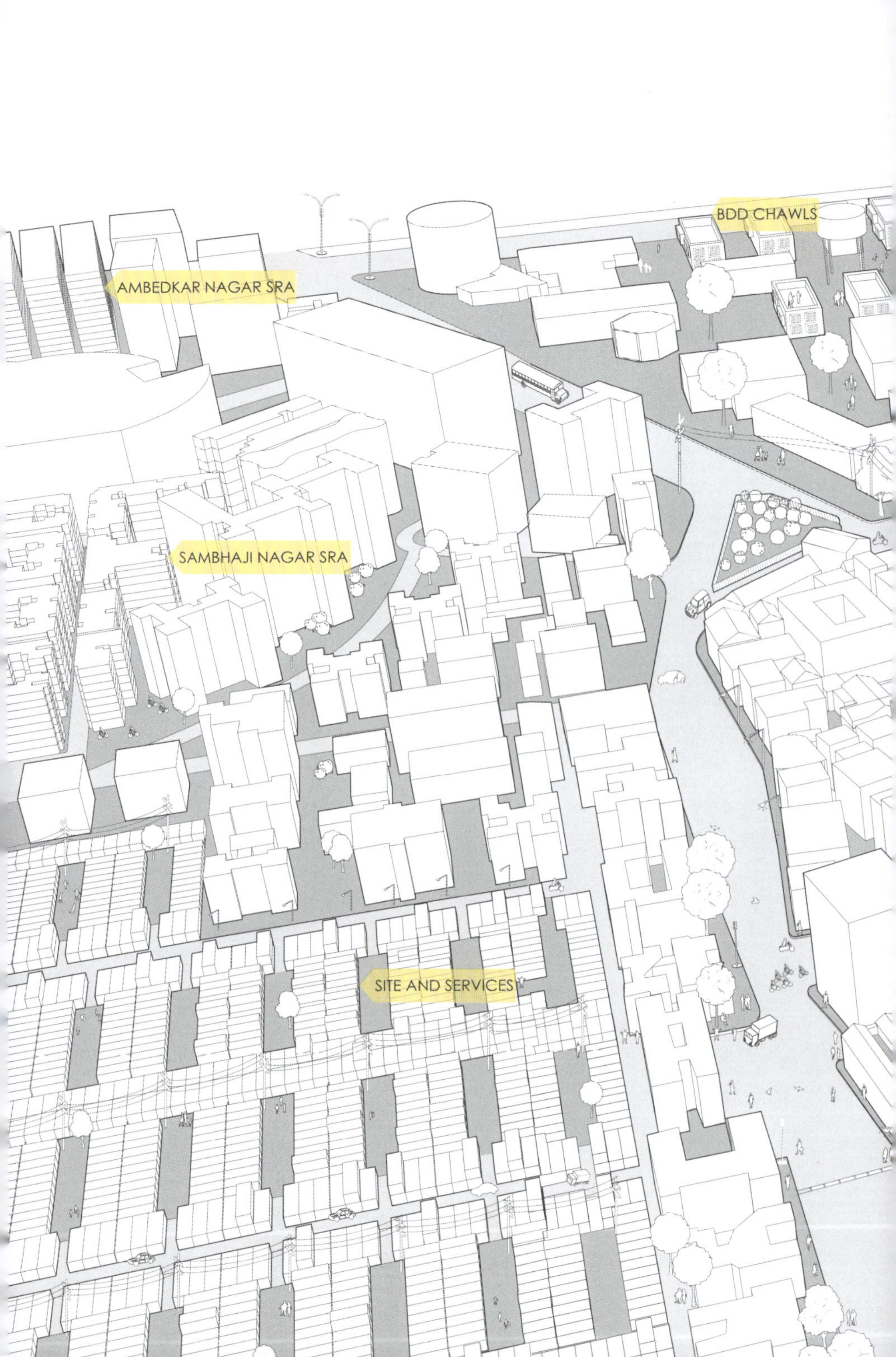
BDD CHAWLS
AMBEDKAR NAGAR SRA
SAMBHAJI NAGAR SRA
SITE AND SERVICES

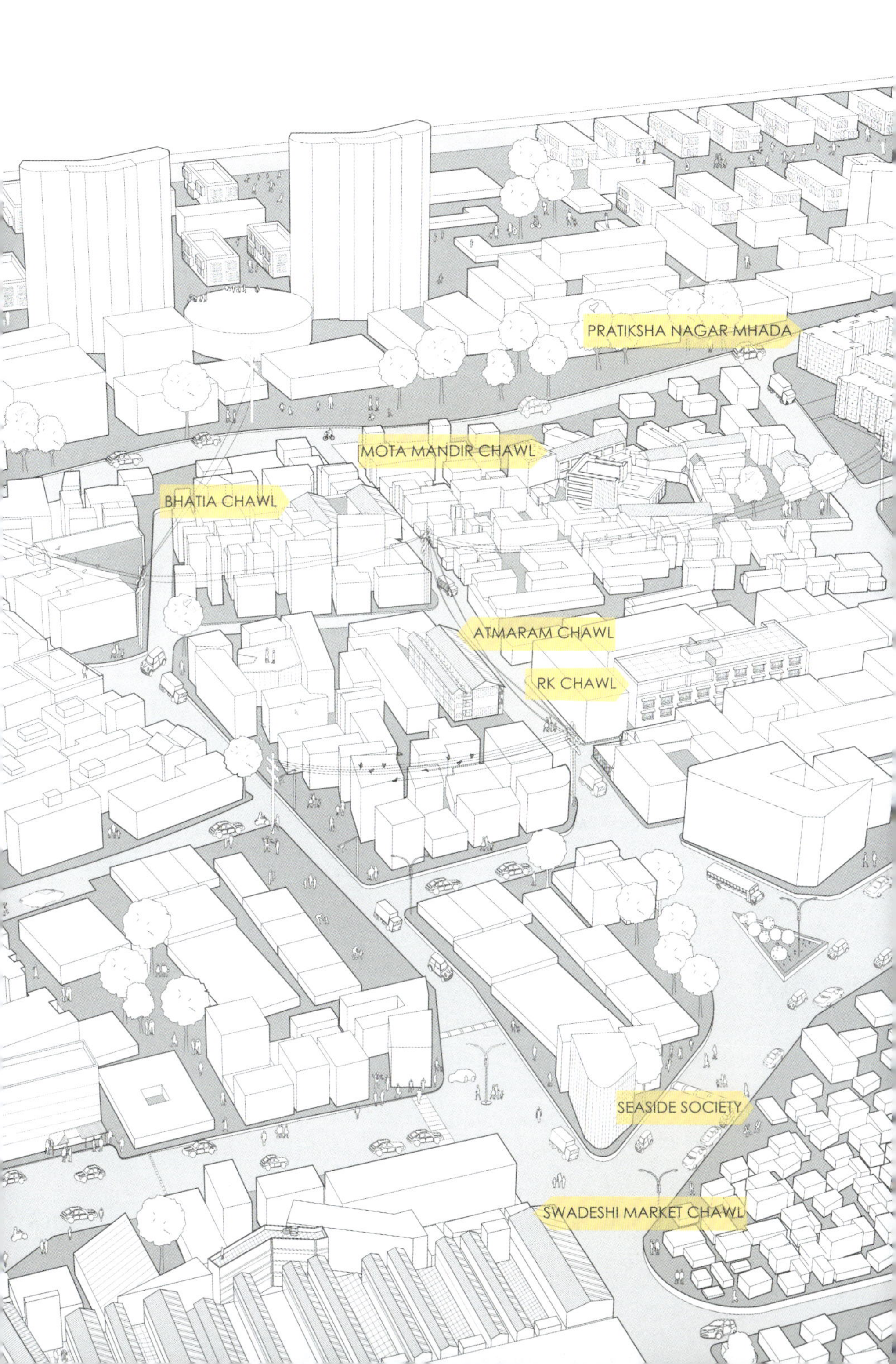
PRATIKSHA NAGAR MHADA
MOTA MANDIR CHAWL
BHATIA CHAWL
ATMARAM CHAWL
RK CHAWL
SEASIDE SOCIETY
SWADESHI MARKET CHAWL

CONTENTS

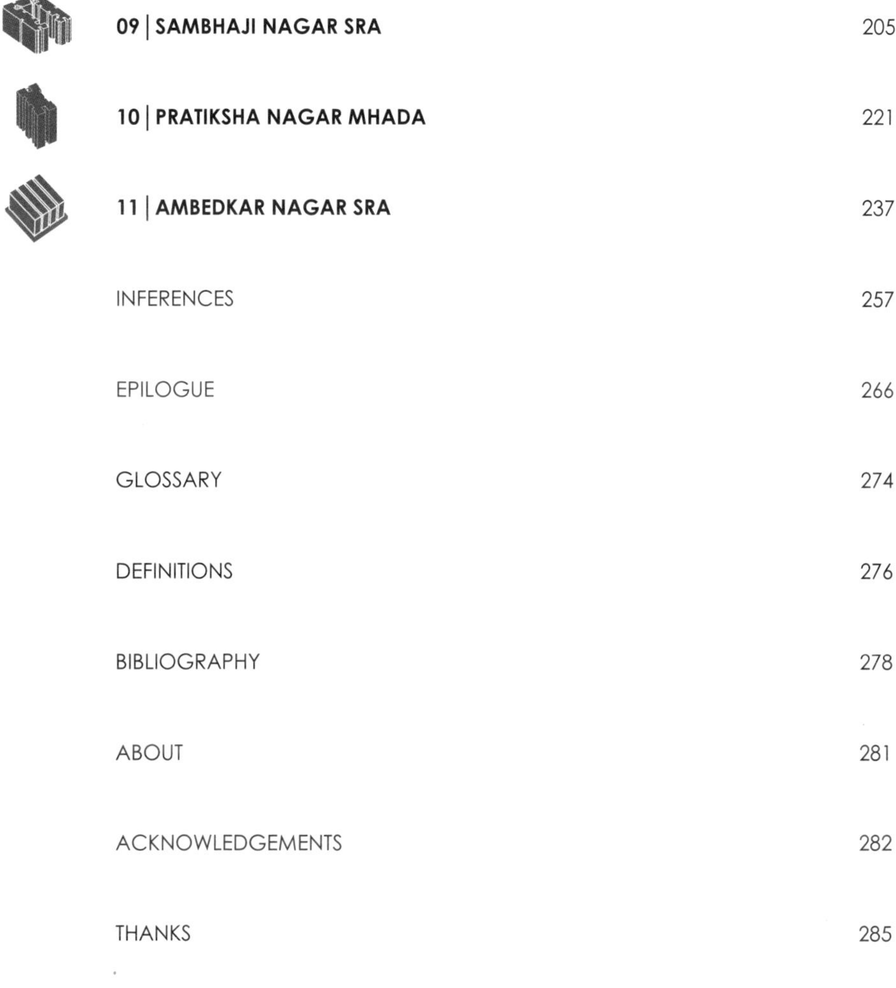

FOREWORD

How to Build an Indian House curated by the studio of architect Sameep Padora (sP+a) is a timely publication for global consumption. This book focuses on Mumbai's perennial and most daunting challenges, and discerns a sophisticated understanding of Mumbai common landscape of housing types. Mumbai is perhaps emblematic of the most extreme condition possible with regard to housing shortages. In Mumbai over forty percent of its population lives in what are auto-constructed dwellings often referred to as informal housing or slums! This acute shortage partly stems from the unidimensional imagination about housing typologies which revolve around the business as usual apartment type - albeit with a range of size configurations. This singular choice of typology has evolved from the impulse to maximize real estate values and efficiencies. In the process an entire spectrum of potential housing types that could address an array of living configurations have been eliminated from consideration for addressing the housing crisis in Mumbai. It is in this context that this book is timely for It most critically reminds us of other ways in which housing has been and can be imagined and configured. In fact , the book adds a new dimension to the many research projects, publications and books, that have attempted to document, analyze, and represent robust examples of different housing typologies globally. Along with the documentary drawings and photographs, sP+a has developed a series of analytical models, to understand issues of space organization and infrastructure in residential building typologies that they have documented with great care. In fact, one would describe their methodology as a process of decoding the DNA of traditional housing typologies in Mumbai!

This book is particularly pertinent today given the critical need to add valuable knowledge to the discussion of housing globally in that it is more than just a mere 'documentation or Mapping' of housing but rather discerns and articulates the protocols and processes for the making of appropriate housing in a highly contested urban context. In addition, this catalogue propels us to think about housing in the broadest sense – of a range of typological solutions that make any city. In today's world the singular imagination of housing as stacked single family apartments undermines potential solutions for housing in contexts like India that are experiencing urban flux. Here housing , or the act of dwelling more broadly, takes on many different forms ranging from temporal dwelling to shared configurations of space that challenge the designer to imagine new typologies. This valuable documentation, from a slice in Mumbai's history, shows us how a range of housing types in fact serve societies in ways beyond just dwelling but also in the formation of communities that are critical in these conditions of flux.

The cases studied range from typologies in Mumbai like the *chawls* (originally workers' housing that have morphed into vibrant communities) to more hybrid examples such as the Swadeshi Market, which demonstrates an interesting multiuse building. Here housing is stacked above a textile market and where the ground itself is re situated on the upper floor to replicate plazas and courtyards as a communal space. In both these cases, the notion of community is critical. Furthermore, these cases also transcend the question of housing to address more expansive challenges of urban design and the very making of the city's fabric. Questions of urban form, circulatory systems that ensure privacy gradients and a host of spatial configurations critical for community interactions. Thus, these Mumbai typologies challenge contemporary architects, planners and designers to push their imagination in thinking about affordable housing for the emergent landscapes in many parts of the world. To challenge ourselves in the design of housing beyond the contingences of investments and returns but rather see housing as the fundamental building block for the city itself.

This publication, sets an admirable precedent in that a professional design studio, sP+a, used research as an instrument to inform their own commission for designing a mass housing project. The effort that the sP+a team have taken to collate and represent these examples ensures that the present publication could function as a handbook for academics as well as practitioners: for example, designers could use it to compare and discern efficiencies and various ratios which can inform the process of their design exercises. And more importantly learn about how housing is embedded in the larger fabric of a city.

In a broader historic context , the catalogue is a refreshing look at our recent past. More often than not architects tend to look to a more distant past for inspiration in housing or urban types. This connection to the recent past is often more critical as it makes for an easier transition into the future. Thus, the selection of the case studies captured in this publication will I believe help the present generation of architects be inspired by crucial link to what preceded its generation in thinking about solutions for housing. In that sense this publication is a housing primer for the architect and urban practitioner in Mumbai and India and an important housing manifesto for us all globally.

Rahul Mehrotra
Chair of the Department of Urban Planning and Design and the John T. Dunlop Professor in Housing and Urbanization Harvard Graduate School of Design.
GSD, Harvard University

INTRODUCTION

The search for new models for affordable housing in the world's ever-growing cities has never been more urgent. Good, affordable housing is needed to confront the still accelerating growth of urban populations and the challenges of urban segregation. Also, to enable those with little or no means to access and inhabit the cities, which hold the promise of providing a better future.

Despite India's recent economic success, the state's inability to actively and effectively deal with the country's rapid urbanization has led to megacities such as Mumbai and New Delhi that continue to be crippled by the unrelenting pressures of migration. At the same time, there has been an exponential growth of several smaller cities that are growing at an even faster rate than the large metropolises. So, while India remains a predominantly rural society with only a little over 30 per cent (about 385 million people) of its entire population living in urban areas, it is expected that an additional 500 million people will be living in its cities by the year 2050. However, as urban India propels forward, construction and planning have been unable to keep up with demand, leading to a situation where large informal settlements or slums have become an inevitable consequence of this rapid growth. Today, in India, the enormous task of providing housing for both the new migrants as well as improving the conditions of those living in the already existing self-built informal settlements has never been more acute.

Designing affordable houses in large numbers is a constant process of balancing opposites. The way people can live in the city is a key factor in the transformation of a traditional rural society into a modern urbanized economy. Should affordable dwellings be designed to accommodate a traditional rural way of life, or should they aim immediately for a future urban lifestyle?

The opposites of rural versus urban, of tradition versus modern, local versus global played a key role in the formation of a new and independent India. Mahatma Gandhi, for example, always stressed the origins of Indian society. 'India is to be found not in a few cities, but in its 700,000 villages' is a famous quote of his from 1936. On the other hand, India's first Prime Minister, Jawaharlal Nehru, was a firm advocate of the modernization and urbanization of India. Chandigarh, the new state capital designed by Le Corbusier in the 1950s and 1960s came to symbolize Nehru's visions for a new, free and modern India.

It was in this context that the first generation of modern Indian architects found the patronage to address the issue of large-scale affordable housing design and production. Since the country's independence in 1947, these architects produced some wonderfully inventive housing designs that still inspire but also clearly demonstrate the near impossibility of finding successful and lasting solutions, as they remain incidents, and have difficulty surviving the impact of real estate speculation in a housing market characterized by extreme pressures.

One city where the effects of relentless growth and an unbridled free-market economy are overwhelmingly visible is Mumbai – the largest city of India and its economic capital. At first glance, the megalopolis of Mumbai seems to know only two housing conditions: freestanding apartment blocks and towers, and informal settlements scattered throughout the formal city, finding an existence in often hazardous areas such as marshlands or on the fringes of the city's overcrowded road and railway infrastructure.

There hardly seem to be any rules, whether one is confronted with extremely dense and large slums—such as Dharavi, which houses nearly a million people and 30.000 enterprises on a mere two square kilometre site—or with the very opposite condition: glass-clad high-rise towers, some bearing Trump's name, or the Ambani house, a 30-storey high-rise tower built as a single-family home.

Most extreme, however, are the attempts of the last twenty years to reconcile the need for slum rehabilitation with the forces of real estate, leading to projects that create extreme densities and rather inhuman living conditions for the original slum dwellers in order to create space for high-end profit-making commercial developments.
Within this urban chaos, one can find still find other places, neighbourhoods, and residential buildings that show that alternatives do exist. Well-documented are the projects of leading Indian architects such as Charles Correa, most famously his incremental housing scheme located in Belapur in Navi Mumbai, which is based on the spatial layering of Indian villages, or Raj Rewal's reinterpretation of traditional urban structures of India, as can be found in his CIDCO Housing project, also located in New Mumbai.

There are, however, other survivors, equally threatened, of much older generations of housing provided for working class people that also show us valid and inspiring alternatives for the current housing production.

How to Build an Indian House provides beautiful and carefully made documentation and thorough analysis of these unknown projects, called *chawls*, positioning them in a chronological time frame, followed by an equally precise documentation of both informally built housing and current mass-scale projects for affordable housing and slum rehabilitation. In between the *chawls* and the present-day projects stands an intriguing example of another mode of production: the Charkop sites and services project, developed in the 1980s in collaboration with the World Bank.
The *chawls*, the working-class housing projects mostly built between 1865 and 1940, are a unique case in the global history of housing design. As a typology, they are most of all characterized by

the connection of quite minimal private living units to collective spaces of various scales, both in the interior and the exterior. The *chawls* show an amazing variety in organization of spaces, urban structures, materiality and craftsmanship, and together form a rich catalogue of typological figures for collective housing.

The earliest *chawl* documented here, the Mota Mandir Chawl, built around 1865, shows how in a simple but at the same time very effective way the private living units, arranged in a beautiful section, can be opened up to one another to create a continuous collective space for communal celebrations. Another example, the Atmaram Chawl, stands out for the adaptability of its units. But perhaps the most extraordinary project is the Swadeshi Market Chawl of 1909, where linear clusters of stacked dwellings are positioned on a two-storey covered market, creating a second residential 'ground level' in one of the densest pockets right in the heart of Mumbai. Easily fifty years ahead of its time, Swadeshi Market is a hybrid megastructure and an unknown precursor of many post-war modernist projects in Europe and elsewhere that experimented with elevated pedestrian networks and mixing of programmes and functions.

For these *chawls*, but also for all the other studied projects, changes and interventions over time by the residents form an essential component of the documentation. This in addition to the original inventive typological solutions, an aspect that provides today's designers with important insights and lessons. These appropriations range from very small changes in the internal layout and the addition or removal of partitions and window boxes to very drastic extensions such as the entire rebuilding of the original units. Particularly striking are the cases of the apartment buildings of the BDD Chawls, and the low-rise sites and services project at Charkop. These changes over time together form the best brief a designer can have when designing optimal solutions for affordable housing.

In the chronological ordering of the projects, the final ones confront us with the realities of either commercially driven or state-initiated large scale (re)housing projects of the last 15 years in Mumbai. They show how, inevitably, the focus on numbers fails to address those aspects that the study brings forward so strongly; the necessity of social spaces in a dense and crowded city, the importance of community, which is lost in endless repetitions of identical units, and finally the possibilities and beauty of interventions by the residents themselves.

Most of all, the comparisons of projects, in numbers, drawings, and photography vividly describe what can happen if housing is imagined solely as a commodity, and not as a social right and expression of culture and everyday life.
The research can help us understand and find directions for how the architectural project for affordable housing can and should be used as a vehicle to investigate alternative possibilities to current financial models, land policies, systems of ownership, modes of delivery, and typological solutions not only in India but in all places affected by the global housing crisis.

The amazing range of typologies and architectural proposals for affordable housing in Mumbai represented in this research has fascinated me since Sameep Padora, the book's author, took me on an evening expedition to some of the documented chawls, on the initiative of our mutual friend Monika Correa. The introduction of his study—a unique example of research from practice—to students in both Delft and Mumbai made a huge impact on their thinking. More recently, an exhibition of the research material in Delft drew interest from all disciplines within the faculty of architecture: urban planners, housing policy researchers, engineers, and architects. The exhibition also showed the author's project for affordable housing that is currently being built in Mumbai, and briefly introduced in the book's epilogue.

The clear connection between the new project and the research is possibly the best proof of the importance and relevance of this publication. The book is at the same time a guide to housing in Mumbai, a designers' toolbox, and an inspiration to continue studying that most urgent question: how to design a house, in India and elsewhere, a house that addresses the needs of its inhabitants, of the community they are part of, and of the city as a whole.

Dirk van Gameren
Dean Faculty of Architecture and the Built Environment
Delft University of Technology

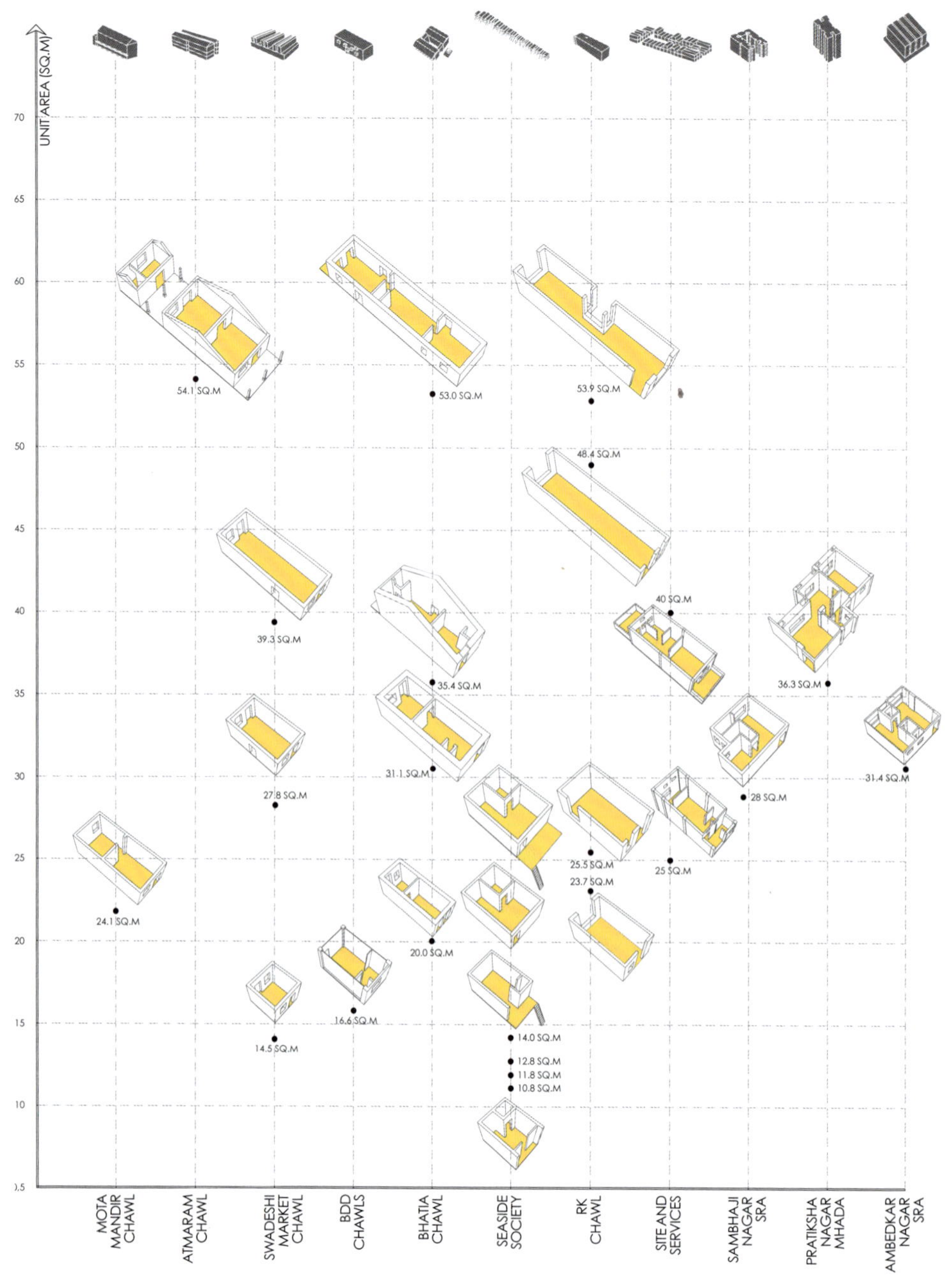

UNIT AREA (SQ.M)
70
65
60
55
50
45
40
35
30
25
20
15
10
),5
54.1 SQ.M
53.0 SQ.M
53.9 SQ.M
48.4 SQ.M
39.3 SQ.M
40 SQ.M
35.4 SQ.M
36.3 SQ.M
31.1 SQ.M
31.4 SQ.M
28 SQ.M
27.8 SQ.M
25.5 SQ.M
25 SQ.M
23.7 SQ.M
24.1 SQ.M
20.0 SQ.M
16.6 SQ.M
14.5 SQ.M
14.0 SQ.M
12.8 SQ.M
11.8 SQ.M
10.8 SQ.M
MOTA MANDIR CHAWL
ATMARAM CHAWL
SWADESHI MARKET CHAWL
BDD CHAWLS
BHATIA CHAWL
SEASIDE SOCIETY
RK CHAWL
SITE AND SERVICES
SAMBHAJI NAGAR SRA
PRATIKSHA NAGAR MHADA
AMBEDKAR NAGAR SRA

READER'S GUIDE

Premise:

The alarming deficit of affordable housing in the country has received a fair amount of attention in current and preceding governments. The latest central government mandate of *Housing for All* finds impetus in the 2016 budget, backed by a slew of fiscal incentives to promote the building of affordable homes.

In the city of Mumbai, burgeoning real estate prices have further exacerbated this shortfall. To ameliorate this bottleneck the state government recently announced the construction of 1.1 million affordable homes over the next four years in the city alone. While all of these policy mandates speak of well-intentioned bureaucratic and political machinery, there is absolutely no imagination of what the physical form of this housing is to be. So despite there being strong government will and frameworks, there is a danger that real estate pressures will eventually subvert the intent of this policy and consequently, the quality and diversity of life and livelihood within these projects.

In the Name of Housing attempts to provide a framework to question this approach to housing, where the top down prescription of policy has in the past, resulted in models like the Slum Rehabilitation Authority (SRA). On paper they offer parity of space for residents but actually result in inhuman and apathetic living conditions, devoid of socio-cultural fabric.

This research attempts to sieve through the fabric of Mumbai, excavating historical and current models of affordable housing sutured deep within the city. It compares 11 housing projects in Mumbai through metrics of open space, social space, circulation space, built areas and densities, using drawings, sketches and models to highlight and illustrate their projective capacities. Its focus is to document the potential of existing and emergent architectural types native to our context, as a means to inform new or hybrid models for the design of affordable housing. This research argues that once ascertained, it is critical for architectural proclivity to inform regulatory mechanisms, which in turn should then feed into policy frameworks, in addition to considerations of tenure, occupancy and equitable allocation. As a result, the desired built and spatial form influences the framing of housing policy from the bottom up, rather than the other way round.

Selection Criteria:

State policy on affordable housing is based on the metric of unit size, ranging from 250 sq.ft (23.23 sq.m) in the early SRA projects, to 300 sq.ft (27.87 sq.m) area as per national policy. This numerical range of unit size hence became the qualifying criteria for the inclusion of most of the projects in the study. The intent of this study is to analyse the specific spatial and formal architecture that allows people to inhabit these tight interior spaces.

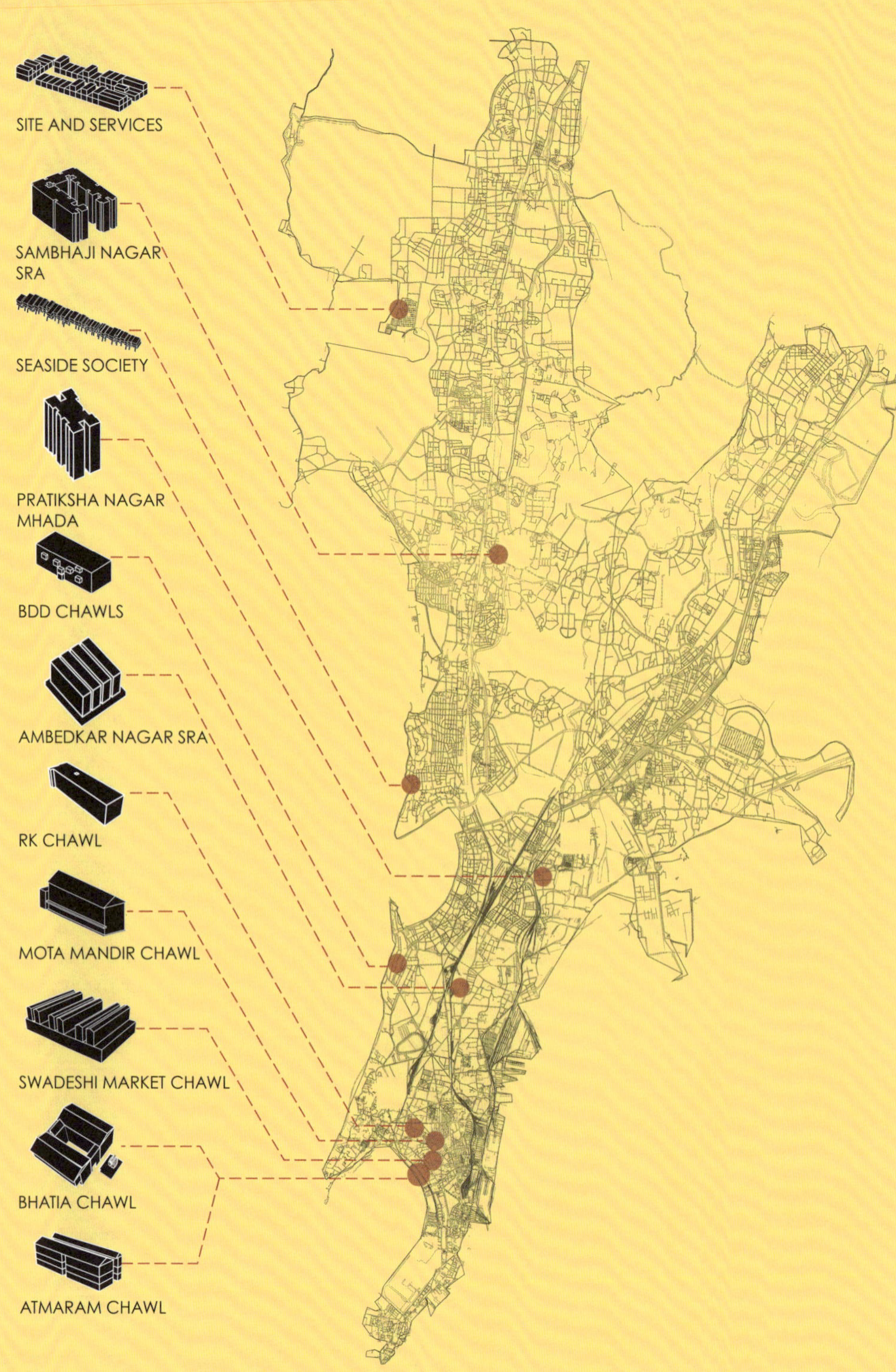

SITE AND SERVICES
SAMBHAJI NAGAR SRA
SEASIDE SOCIETY
PRATIKSHA NAGAR MHADA
BDD CHAWLS
AMBEDKAR NAGAR SRA
RK CHAWL
MOTA MANDIR CHAWL
SWADESHI MARKET CHAWL
BHATIA CHAWL
ATMARAM CHAWL

Method:

The data for this study was collected through fieldwork that entailed measured drawings, interviews with residents and observations at each of the sites. The format of the exhibition allowed for each project to be compared across ten metrics that included Location, Building Form, Circulation, Programme, Tenure, Community, Floor Plans, Envelope, Unit Plans and Analysis. In a departure from the structure of the exhibition, this catalogue presents the research of the projects as individual case studies.

Projects:

The broad categorisation of the case studies of affordable housing projects is as follows:

1. Chawls

Most of the chawls we studied (except the state-owned BDD Chawls) lie in C-ward of South Mumbai and are privately owned. Contrary to the singular image of the chawl in popular imagination, we found many variants of the standard chawl within this small geographical area.

2. Pavement Dwellings

These *slim cities* unlike aggregated slums do not enjoy the benefit of being addressed by state and private mechanisms in situ. They are slivers of mixed use that inhabit thin interstitial spaces in the formal city based on a symbiotic economic network that binds them to their particular location.

3. Site and Services

The Site and Services project at Charkop marks an alternative approach to housing for the poor and is spatially the most impressive of all the state-built projects. Closest to the high density low rise models of slums or urban villages in Mumbai, it displays a distinct character and scale that is fast disappearing in lieu of the singular high rise format of the city fabric today.

4. Maharashtra Housing and Area Development Authority (MHADA)

Being the state authority responsible for providing housing, a project by MHADA is also included in the study. Recently MHADA announced collaborations with landowners and developers to provide housing for Economically Weaker Sections and Low Income Groups, raising questions on the further dilution of the state's mandate and quality control of these built environments.

5. Slum Rehabilitation Authority (SRA)

Two extreme variants of housing under the aegis of the SRA are included in the study – one, a project of intense vertical compression on a limited site with no open space, and the other with a fairly good proportion of built to open space.

We hope to expand this ongoing research – of which the exhibition and catalogue are the first part – vertically by looking at regulations and policy, and horizontally by looking at housing models in other cities. We do hope this catalogue will prove to be useful for academicians, practitioners and state officials to inform housing policy, projects on ground and further research on the subject.

01

MOTA MANDIR CHAWL

01 | MOTA MANDIR CHAWL

THE SOCIAL INTEGRATOR

1865
BHULESHWAR

The chawl documented in this study is a part of the Mota Mandir precinct, located on a 6685 sq.m land parcel. The nucleus of this development was a Vaishnavite temple built in 1801 and dedicated to the Hindu deity Krishna and his elder brother Balarama. It was built by the Goswamis – descendants of Vallabhacharya and founders of a staunch Vaishnavite sect.

In addition to the temple, there is a winding public pedestrian street connecting the city fabric through the land. In 1865, housing for the Girnara Brahmins working in the temple was planned and a residential block was wedged between the plot boundary on the southwest and this pathway on the northeast. To satiate the demand for more facilities, there has been intermittent construction of chawls and administrative buildings going on from the 1800s till as recent as 2007.

The Mota Mandir precinct was owned by a private trust headed by the Goswamis, who managed the temple until 1958. Following a dispute, the administration of the temple precinct was transferred by a high court order to a public trust, specifically set up for its management.

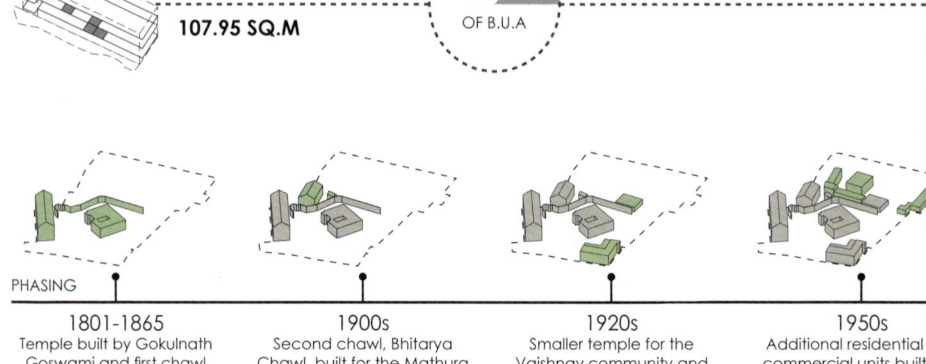

LOCATION

The Mota Mandir precinct is located in Bhuleshwar, a part of Mumbai's inner city fabric – an area with several temples, many of them centuries old. It is flanked by Panjarapole Road on its north and 3rd Bhoiwada Lane on its south.

Within the compound, the chawl which is the focus of this chapter, fronts the public pedestrian pathway with the verandah and corridors aligned parallel to it, as well as to the temple façade.

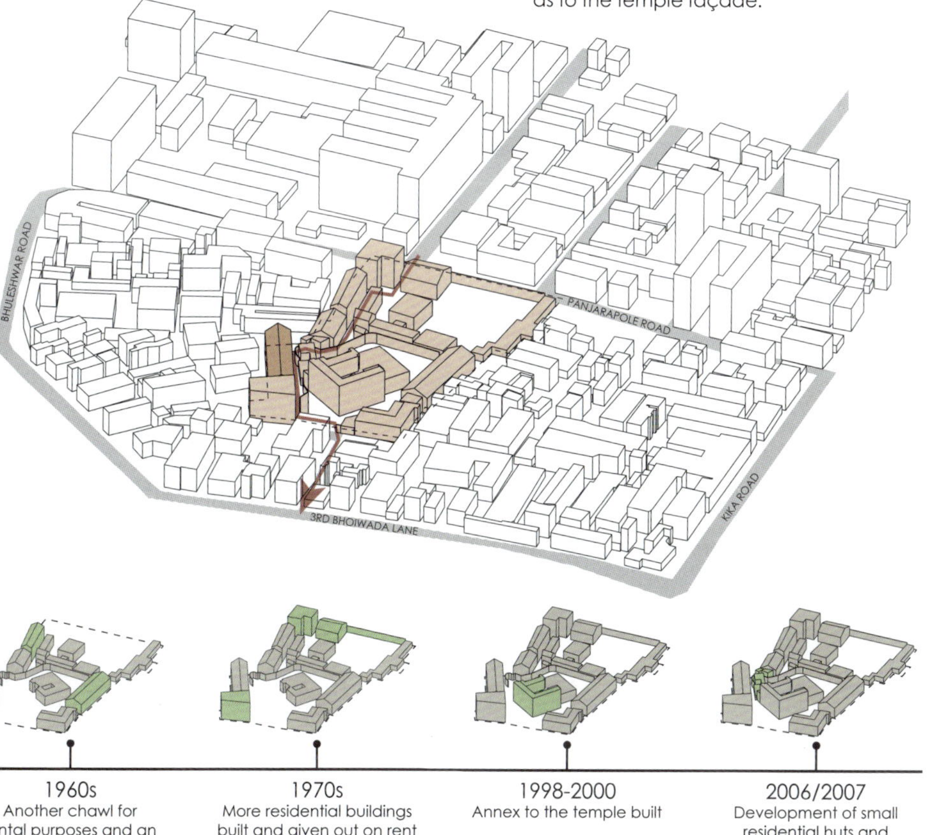

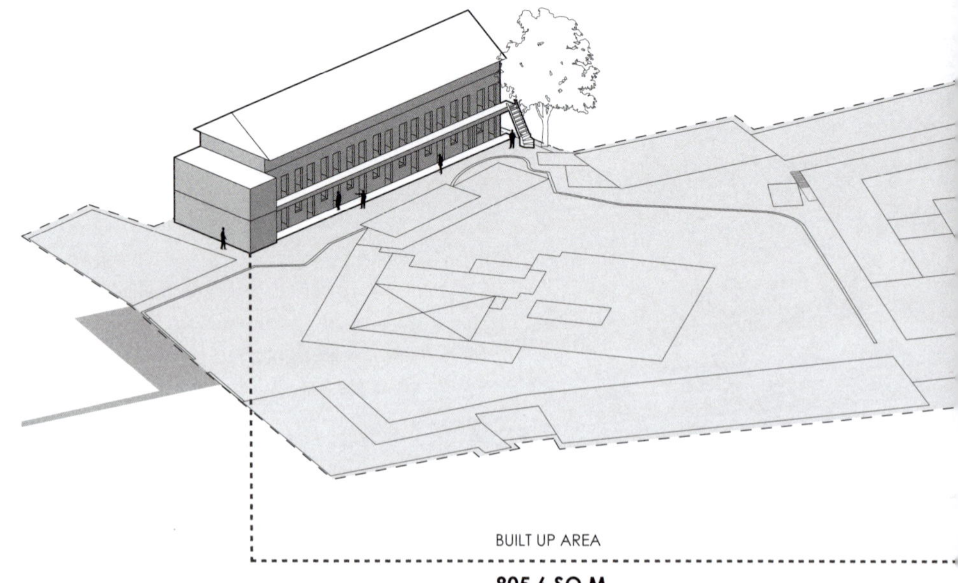
BUILT UP AREA
805.6 SQ.M

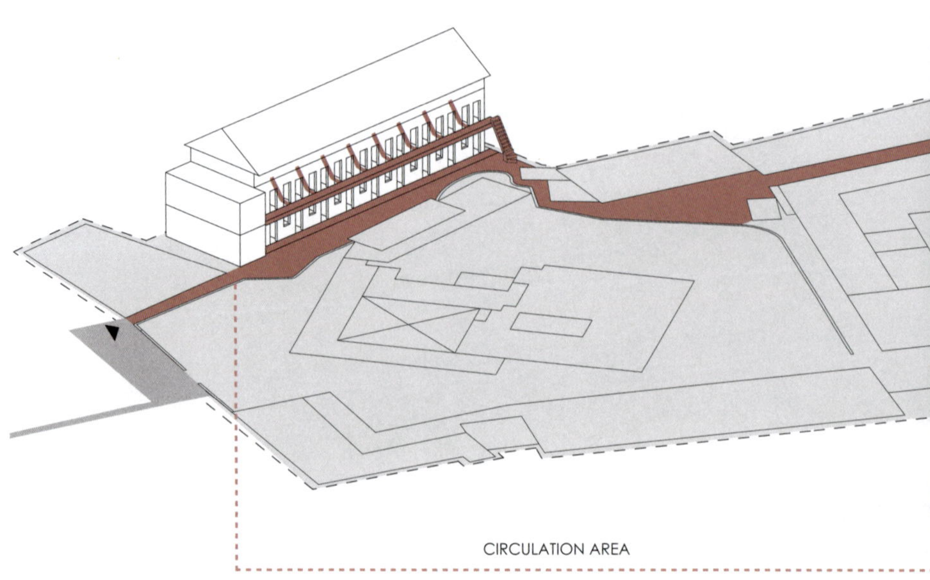
CIRCULATION AREA
105.1 SQ.M

BUILDING FORM

The building is a three tiered linear block aligned northwest-southeast, with each level consisting of nine residential units of standard size, and topped by a pitched roof. Access to the ground floor units is from a verandah, and for the first floor units, from a common corridor.

Each second floor unit is accessed from a small lobby containing an independent staircase adjacent to the corresponding first floor unit. This unique arrangement has resulted in maisonette-like structures on the first floor, differing drastically from the ground floor units. Common toilets, located towards the southeast end of the building, are accessible from only the ground and first floors.

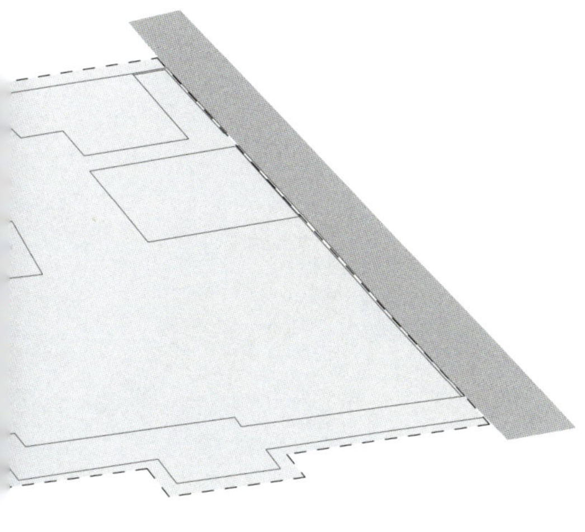

BUILT UP AREA PER PERSON

4.97 SQ.M
CONSIDERING 6 PEOPLE PER UNIT

CIRCULATION

The pathway connecting Panjarapole Road to 3rd Bhoiwada Lane winds along the chawl, providing the residents access to city roads on both sides of the precinct.

Within the building, on the ground floor, wooden posts form a permeable boundary between the walkway and the verandah linking to the units. An external staircase towards the northwest end of the verandah connects to the first floor where a corridor runs along the length of the building, leading to small foyers. Each of these foyer spaces in turn connects to the first floor unit, or to a stair leading to the unit on the second floor.

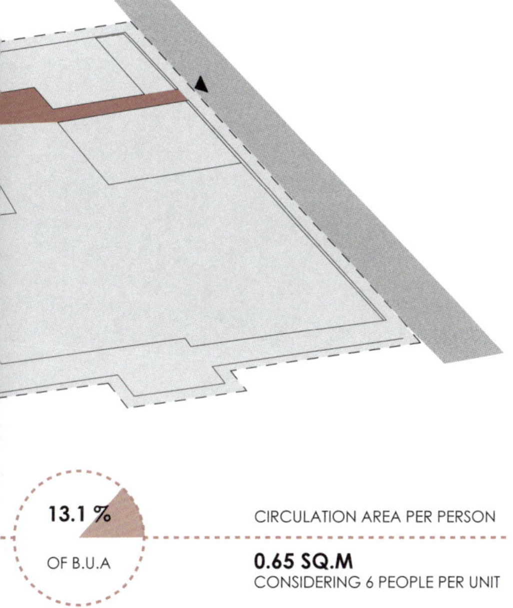

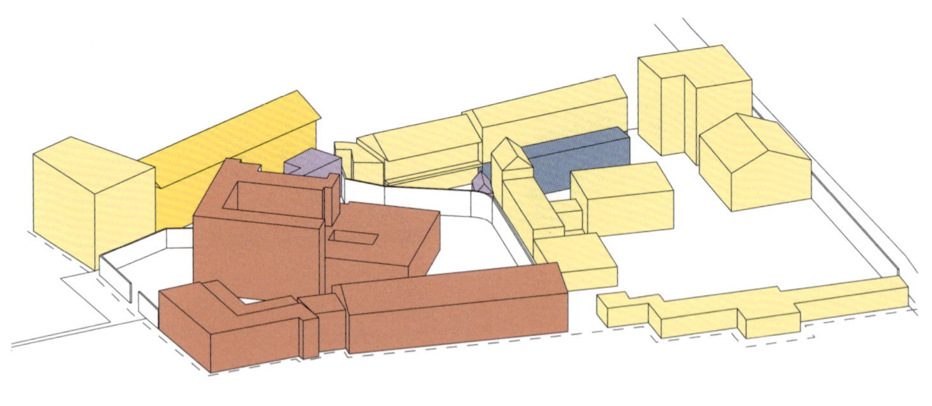

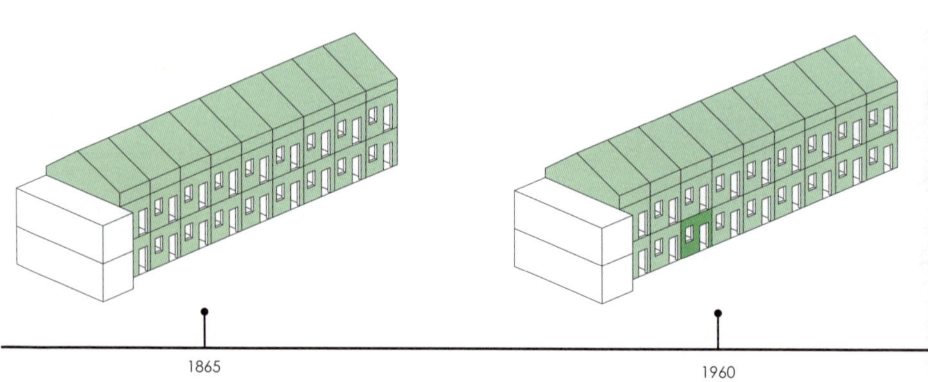
1865
1960

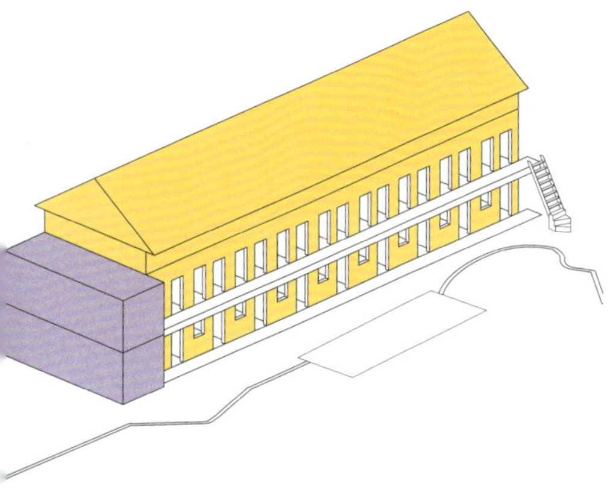

PROGRAMME

The chawl is part of a complex of mixed-use buildings spread across the precinct. These consist of various housing blocks built over 200 years along with smaller temples and administrative buildings for the trust. There also exist facilities of a common kitchen and toilets on the site, as well as commercial units on the ground floors of some residential buildings.

Within this chawl – as is typical – services are common, although the uppermost level has no access to these shared facilities. So while on the ground floor, approximately 54 people share one bath and four WC units, above, the number doubles.

4.11 SQ.M
27 NOS = 651 SQ.M

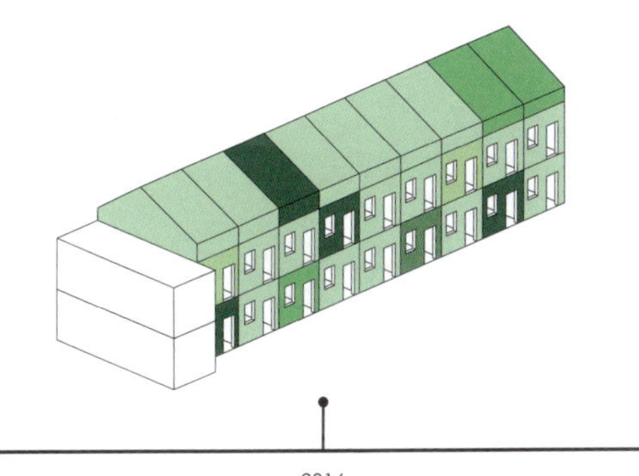

COMMUNITY

As the built environment of the complex has changed, so has its social fabric. What started out as a solely Gujarati Brahmin habitation has through the years acquired a limited diversity, new residents being from Kutchi, Maharashtrian, Marwadi and Jain communities. This diversity is a result of the original temple workers and their children having sub-let their rooms and moved away for employment opportunities.

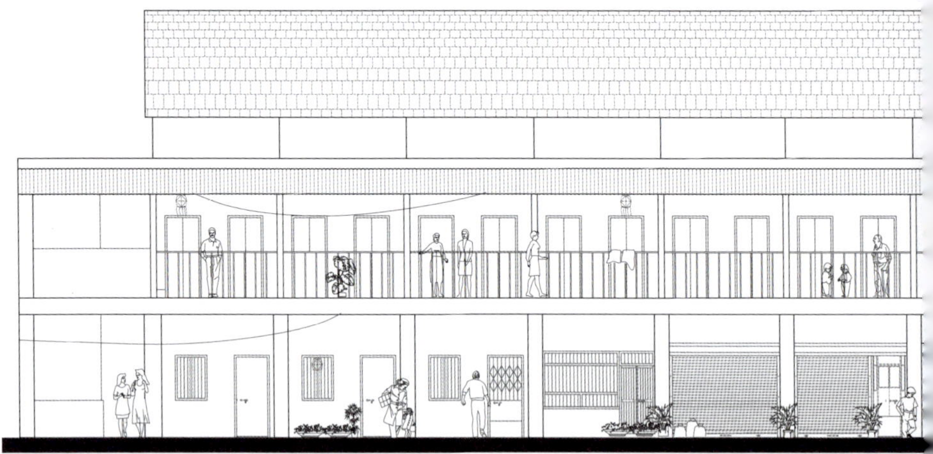

NORTHEAST SIDE ELEVATION

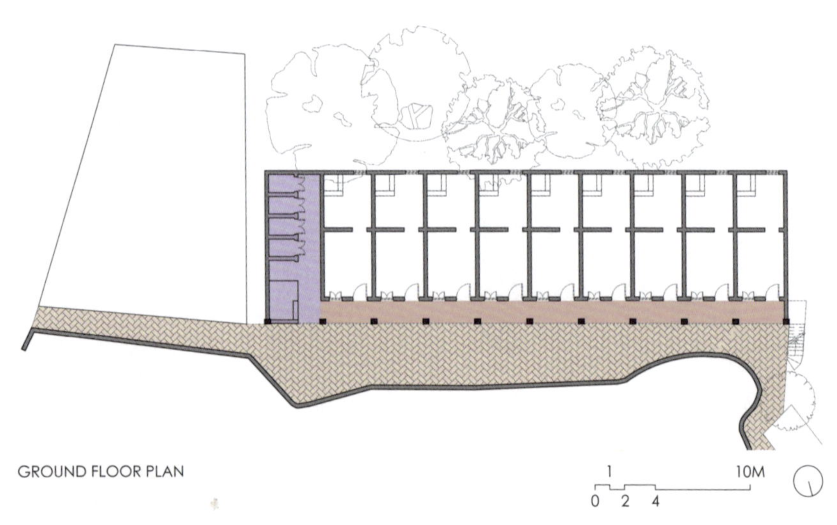

GROUND FLOOR PLAN

OPEN SPACE
2118 SQ.M

32.64 %
OF B.U.A

OPEN SPACE PER PERSON
2.5 SQ.M
CONSIDERING 6 PEOPLE PER UNIT

SHARED SERVICES AREA
61.7 SQ.M

7.66 %
OF B.U.A

ENVELOPE

The chawl is a timber framed structure set within a repeating grid, resulting in identical unit sizes. Despite the overall structural order, the façade has variations of insets and projections; a row of posts on the ground floor supports the first floor balcony that is covered by a lean-to roof, and the residential units above are hybrid maisonettes topped by a pitched roof, setting them apart from the level below.

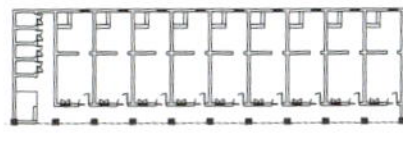

1 4

0 2 15M

FLOOR PLANS

Every level consists of nine units, each of 24.11 sq.m. All units are identical in layout, the front portion being a living and sleeping space and the rear, a kitchen and services space.

The first floor units are interconnected through doors that would allow the entire floor to be used as a common public realm in the case of festivals or weddings. The second floor units are accessed by individual staircases located in first floor foyers; thus the corridor on the first floor services two levels.

COND FLOOR PLAN

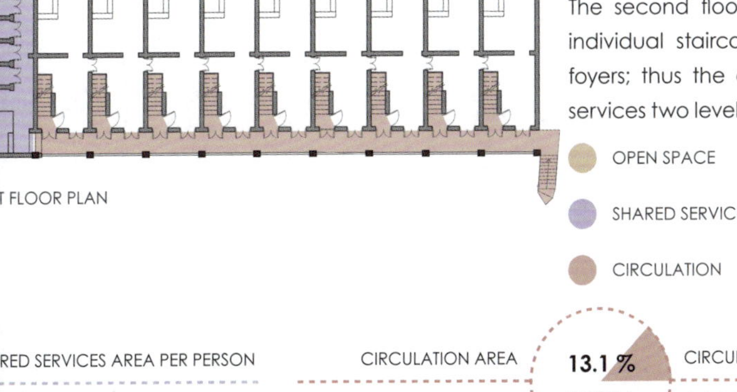

ST FLOOR PLAN

RED SERVICES AREA PER PERSON

38 SQ.M
NSIDERING 6 PEOPLE PER UNIT

CIRCULATION AREA

105.1 SQ.M

13.1 %
OF B.U.A

CIRCULATION AREA PER PERSON

0.65 SQ.M
CONSIDERING 6 PEOPLE PER UNIT

UNITS

Unit types 1 and 2 share access through a small common foyer. In terms of configuration, a wall divides Unit 1 so that its rear is used for services and storage. While in most cases *moris* have been converted into bath areas, here it has also been enlarged so that both a bath and WC are accommodated.

Unit 2 is a large multipurpose space which originally had a partition dividing it into two parts. The extra volume of the pitched roof accommodates a storage loft.

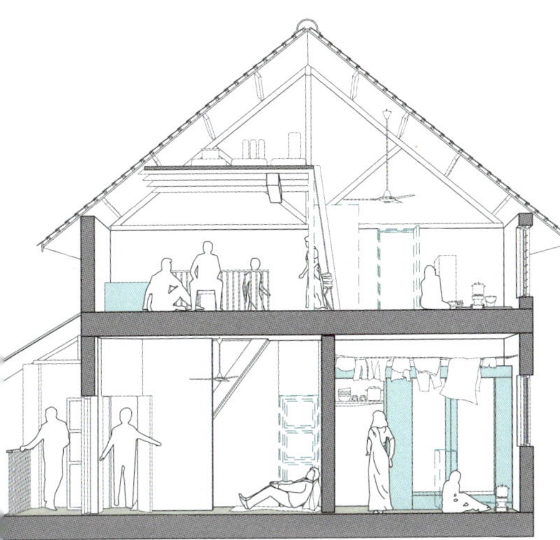

SECTION A

APPROPRIATIONS

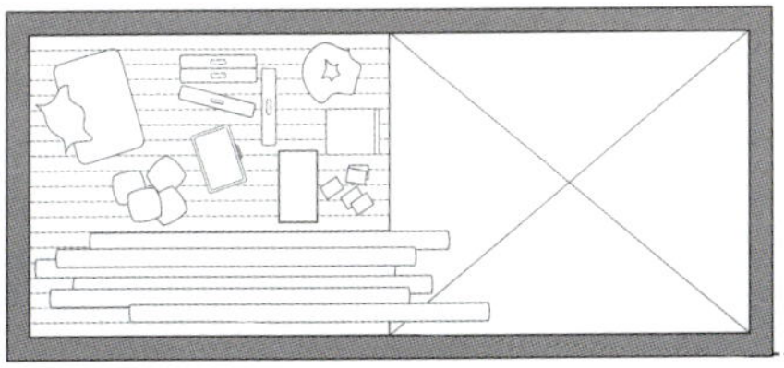

UNIT TYPE 2 - LOFT PLAN

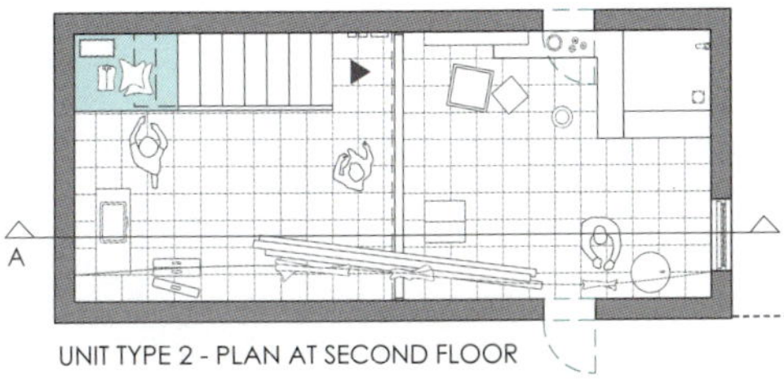

A

UNIT TYPE 2 - PLAN AT SECOND FLOOR

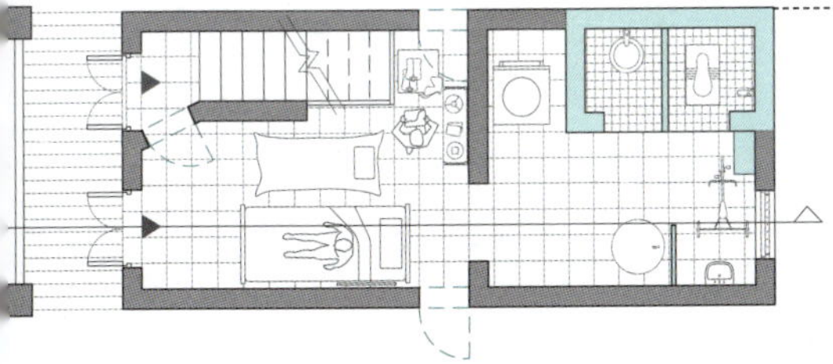

UNIT TYPE 1 - PLAN AT FIRST FLOOR

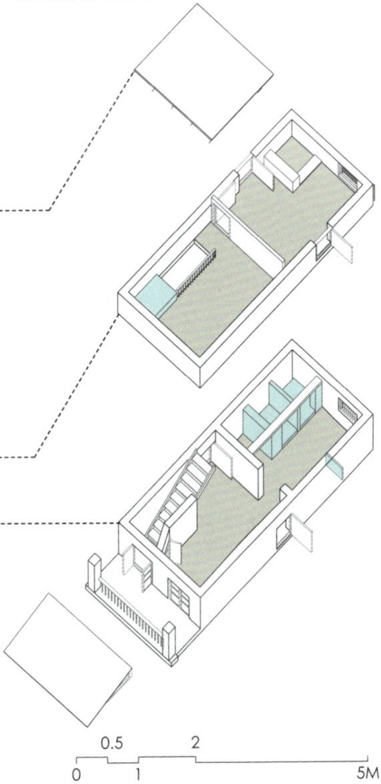

0 0.5 1 2 5M

SECTION 1

SECTION 2

SECTION 3

KEY PLAN

ANALYSIS

Mota Mandir is an example reminiscent of medieval towns where despite sporadic development over 200 years, the private temple precinct even today retains a connection to city streets on either side, allowing for an extension of the city fabric. In what is a constant conversation between the public and the private, the architecture of the chawls along with the other buildings negotiates the presence of the public street through elements of staircases and verandahs.

The development has also been impacted by the extant freestanding wall that separates the temple from the other programmes on the site. The temple is situated within the fold of this wall while other structures like residences and commercial units line its periphery across the internal street.

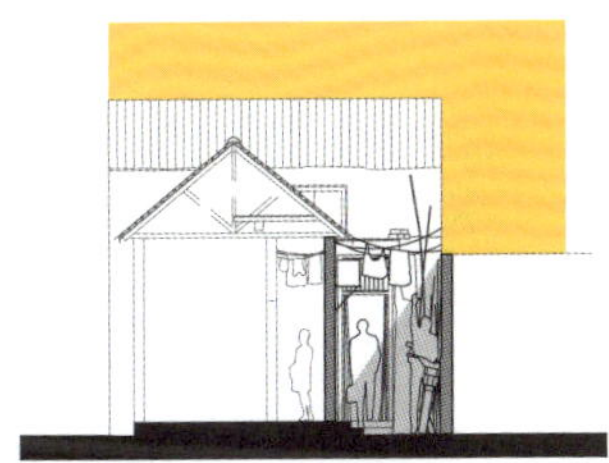
SECTION 4

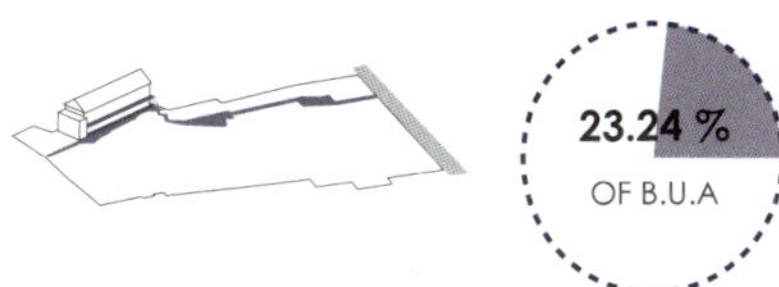

SOCIAL SPACE

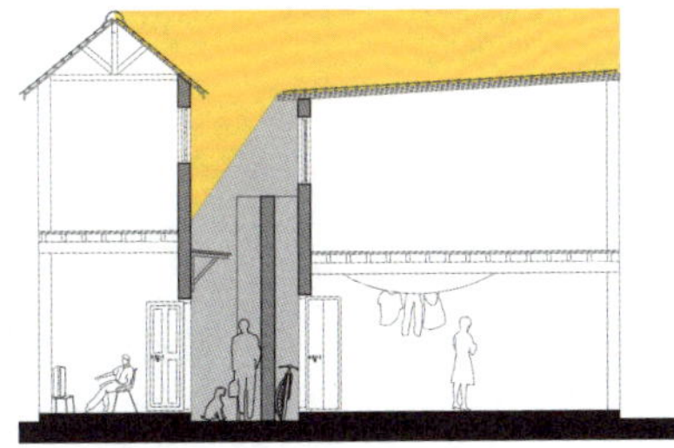
SECTION 5

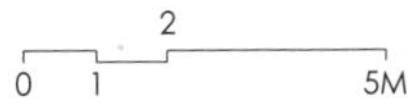

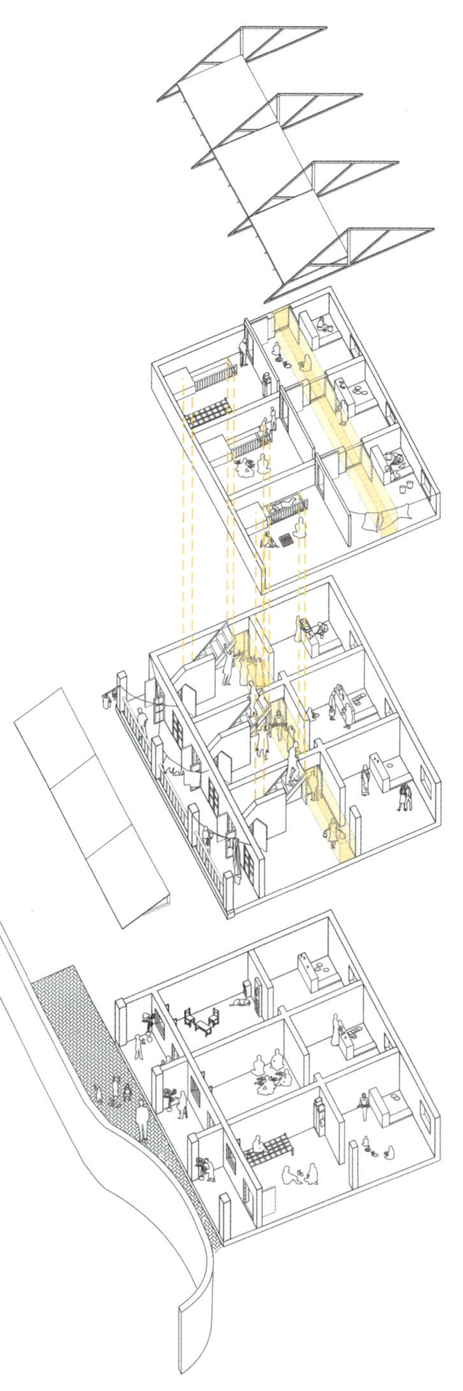

ANALYSIS

Every floor of the chawl has a distinct quality of social space – at the ground level, the verandah extends into the internal street, facilitating interaction between inhabitants and passersby, and at the first floor level, is a corridor connecting the entrances to the foyers of the typological hybrid of the *maisonette chawl*. Even though the floors are simply stacked one above the other, sectionally spatial interaction differs. Standing in the verandah, ground floor residents engage with people in the street while the entrances to the first and topmost level houses being shared, nodes of communication are inevitably created between first floor residents and those of the units directly above them.

Consequently, social interaction is not facilitated by larger spaces of congregation alone, but also by the articulation of the unit plan and its mode of access.

OM JEWELLERS
ॐ ज्वेलर्स

Shah & Associates

02
ATMARAM CHAWL

02 | ATMARAM CHAWL

TWO FRONT YARDS

1866

KALBADEVI

Atmaram Chawl, built by the Chowgules in 1866 was originally housing designed specifically for the Parsi community. Its unique layout is possibly a reflection of the community's living habits. When the Parsis moved out, the landlord made a bid to position the chawl as a predominantly Christian habitation, so as to attract a certain market segment. It is now inhabited by Christians and Hindus.

Flats were rented out till 1947, after which the introduction of the Rent Control Act meant that the informal *pagdi* system became the modus of operating these tenements. In this system tenancy is transferred at rates a little below market rates.

The chawl probably derives its name from that of the ascetic Atmaram Baba, who built the Thakurdwar temple in the same area.

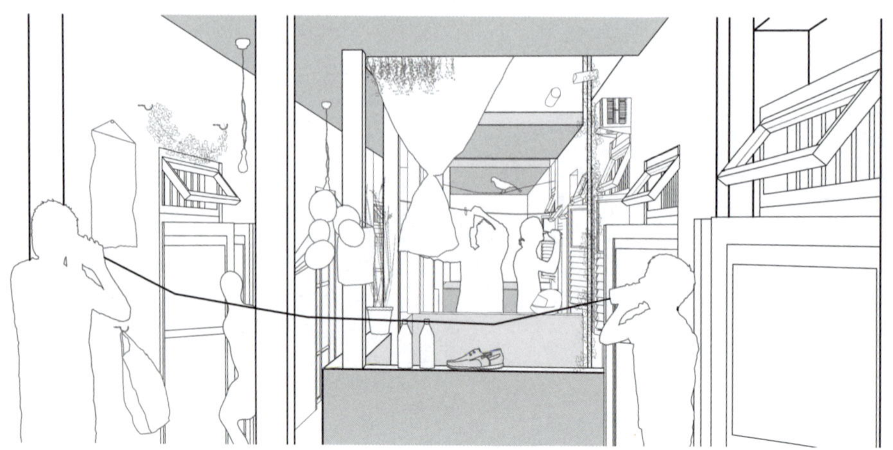

BACKYARD VIEW

LOCATION

The front façade of the chawl abuts St Francis Xavier lane in Kalbadevi. In the vicinity of the chawl lie the St Francis Xavier church, a convent school and a Catholic community centre – all markers of the Christian socio-cultural fabric of the area.

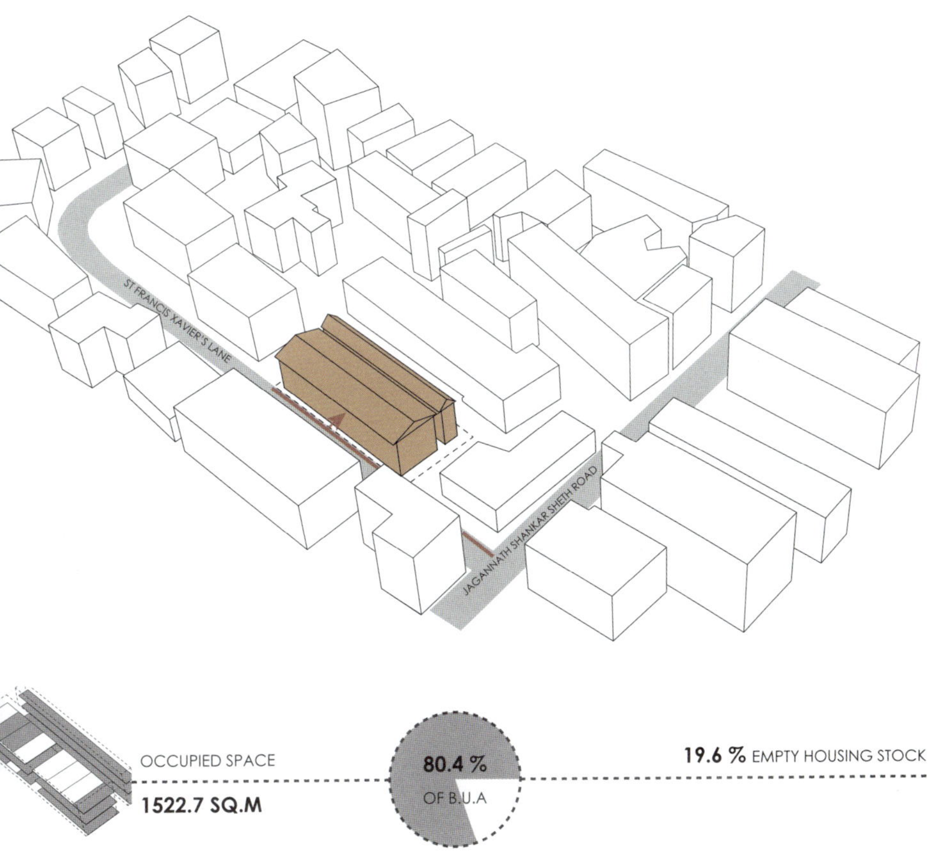

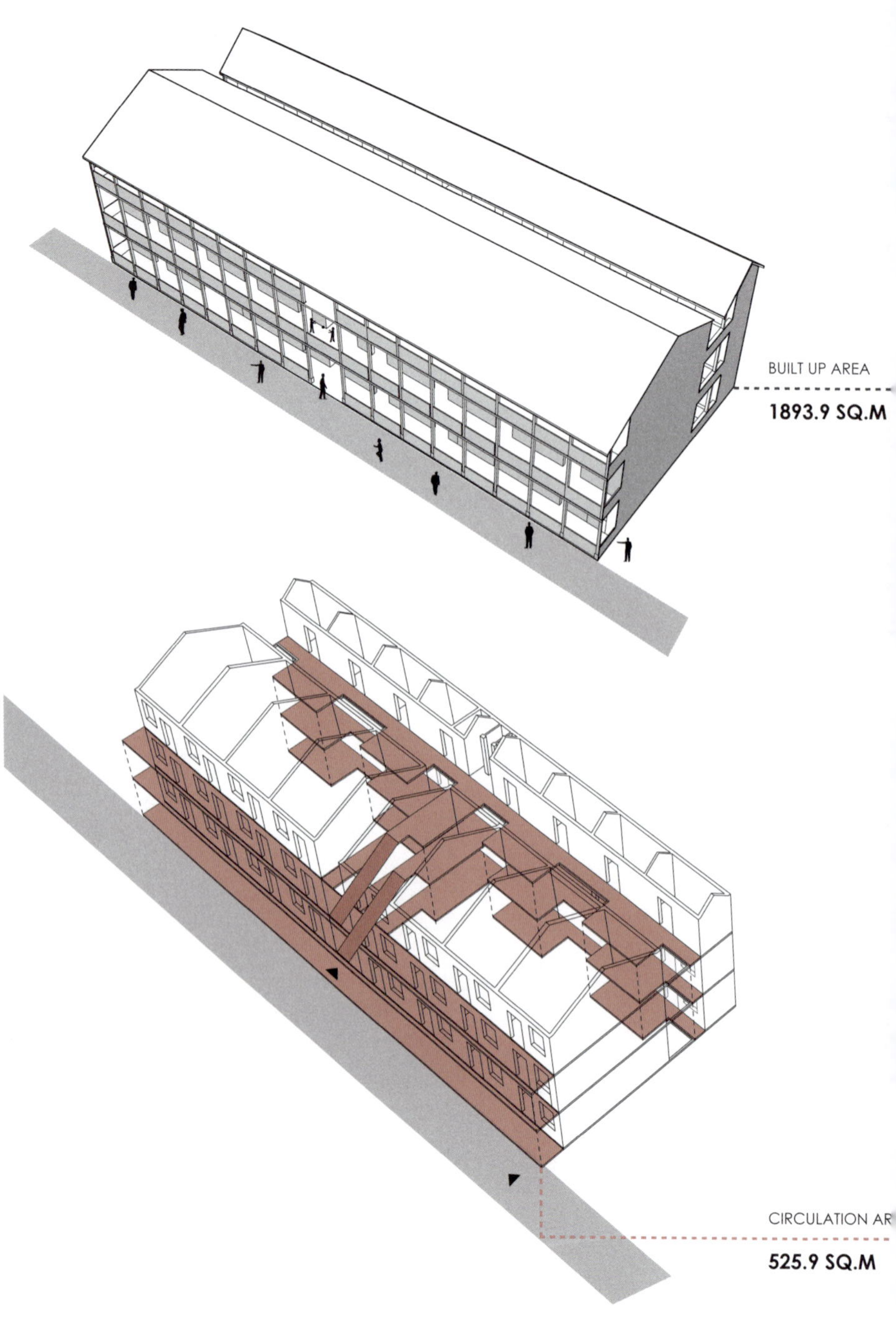
BUILT UP AREA
1893.9 SQ.M
CIRCULATION AR
525.9 SQ.M

BUILDING FORM

The form is a set of two clearly differentiated rectilinear parallel blocks with pitched roofs, oriented with their longer sides along the northeast-southwest axis. The form of the building is a product of all the living and bedroom functions being clubbed together in the block towards the road, and with every unit having its kitchen separated by a common corridor in the second block.

BUILT UP AREA PER PERSON

13.15 SQ.M
CONSIDERING 6 PEOPLE PER UNIT

CIRCULATION

There are two circulation corridors within the structure. The one towards the northwest is wedged between the living and kitchen units and is amply lit and ventilated by light wells and open-to-sky courtyards. This corridor, originally intended to separate living spaces from kitchens, is semi-private and now populated by furniture, as the space is used commonly by all the residents. The other circulation path is road facing, and doubles up as a means of access to the units.

The circulation format of Atmaram Chawl and its separation of internal functions by a common corridor set it apart from other structures in the chawl typology, the design strategy prevalent at the time being corridors loaded with independent units on one or both sides.

27.7 %
OF B.U.A

CIRCULATION AREA PER PERSON

3.65 SQ.M
CONSIDERING 6 PEOPLE PER UNIT

ESTD. 1926.
TEL: 22012421.
B.F. MARTYRES
OFFICIAL UNDERTAKERS & SCULPTORS

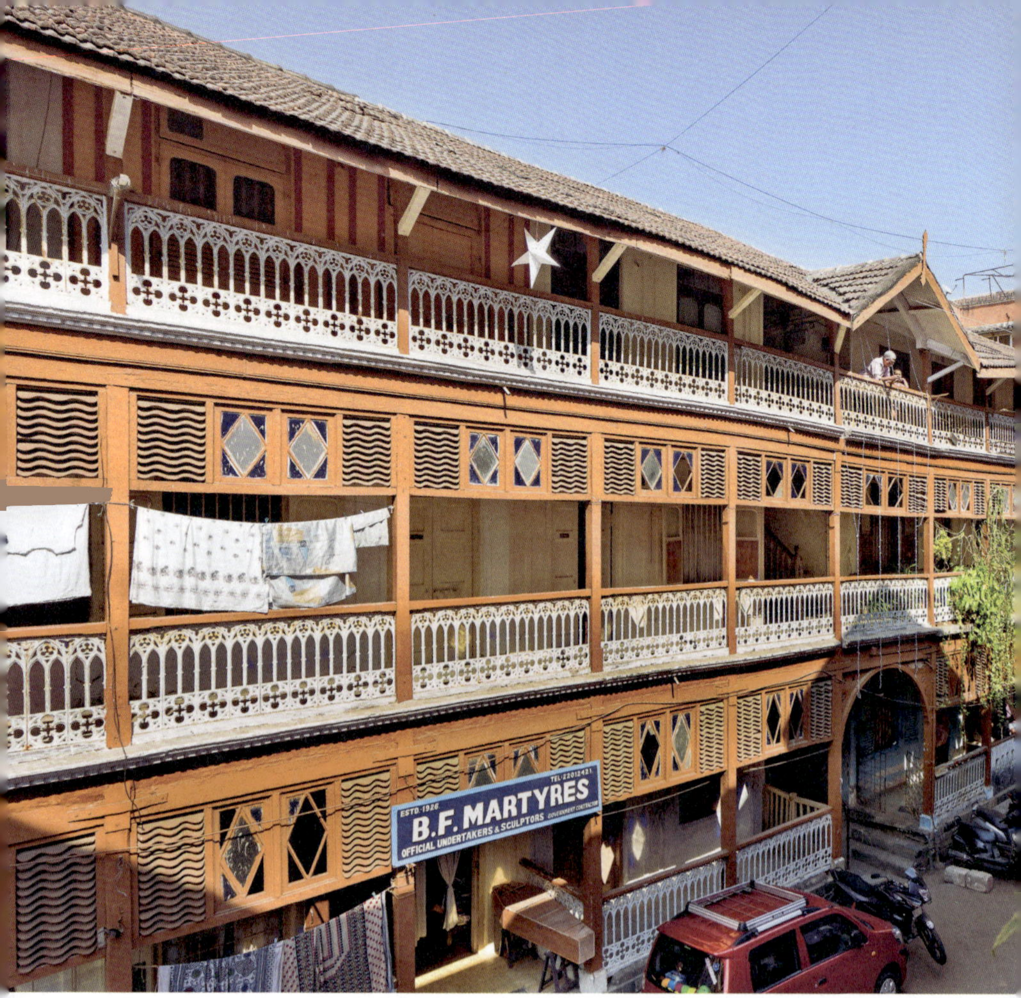

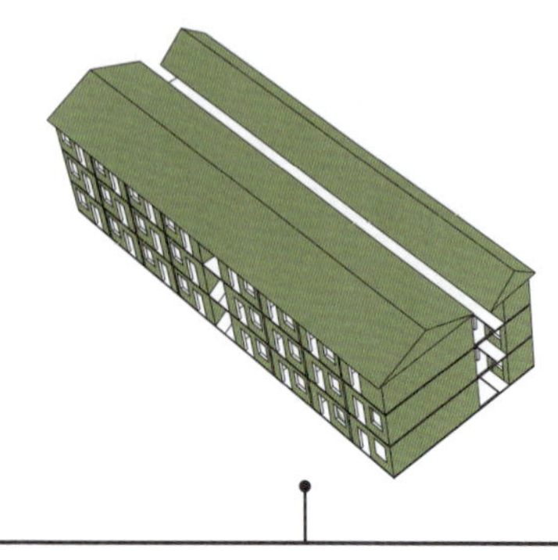

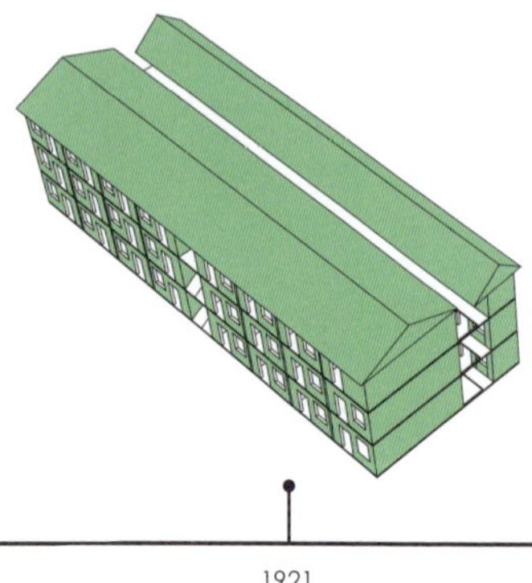

1866
1921

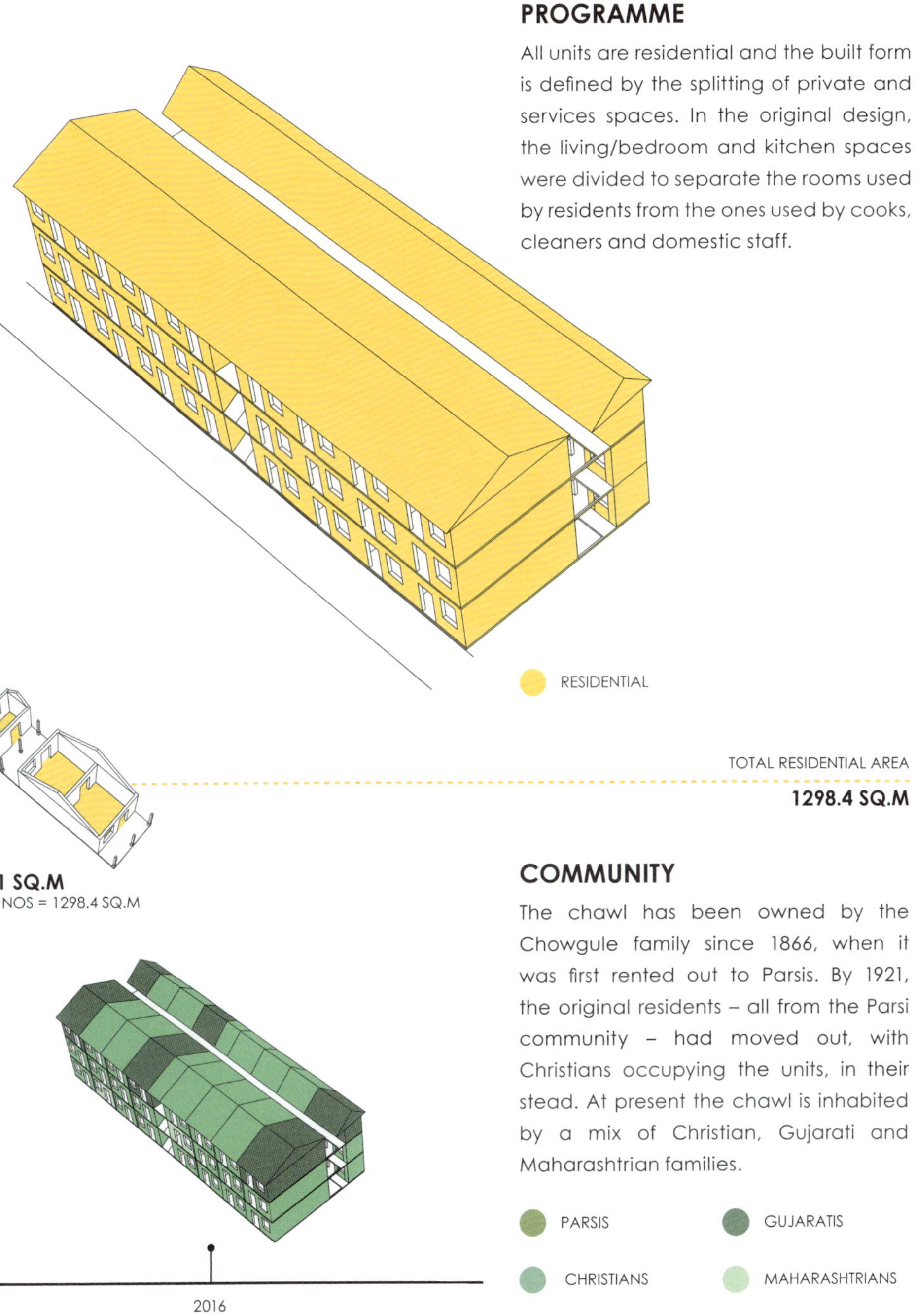

PROGRAMME

All units are residential and the built form is defined by the splitting of private and services spaces. In the original design, the living/bedroom and kitchen spaces were divided to separate the rooms used by residents from the ones used by cooks, cleaners and domestic staff.

COMMUNITY

The chawl has been owned by the Chowgule family since 1866, when it was first rented out to Parsis. By 1921, the original residents – all from the Parsi community – had moved out, with Christians occupying the units, in their stead. At present the chawl is inhabited by a mix of Christian, Gujarati and Maharashtrian families.

OPEN SPACE
66.1 SQ.M

3.49 %
OF B.U.A

OPEN SPACE PER PERSON
0.46 SQ.M
CONSIDERING 6 PEOPLE PER UNIT

SHARED SERVICES AREA
20 SQ.M

1.06 %
OF B.U.A

FLOOR PLANS

The standard unit living type measures 41.3 sq.m and the standard kitchen is 12.8 sq.m in area. The separation of the kitchen – in addition to segregating access – was meant to keep smoke resulting from wood-fired cooking away from the main unit. At the centre of the row of kitchens is a block of common toilets.

Natural light and ventilation is introduced through courts and light shafts that puncture the slab of the northwest corridor at every level. The eight living units that make up every floor benefit from the verandah acting as a buffer against the south sun.

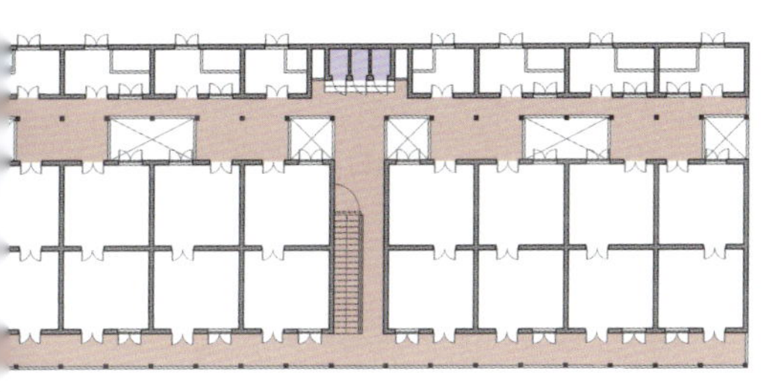

ICAL FLOOR PLAN

OPEN SPACE

SHARED SERVICES

CIRCULATION

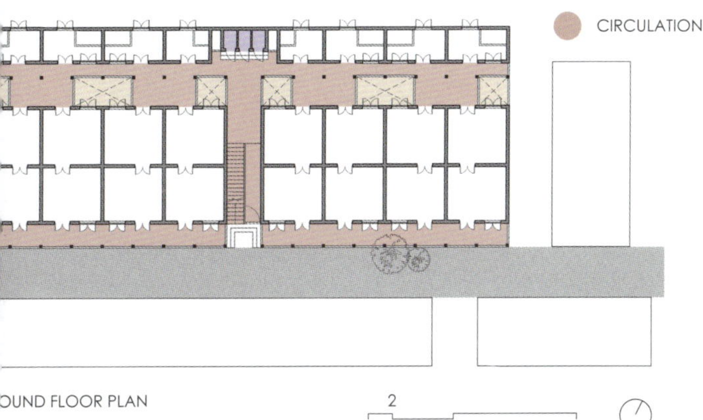

OUND FLOOR PLAN

0 2 5 15M

RED SERVICES AREA PER PERSON

4 SQ.M
NSIDERING 6 PEOPLE PER UNIT

CIRCULATION AREA

525.9 SQ.M

27.7 %
OF B.U.A

CIRCULATION AREA PER PERSON

3.65 SQ.M
CONSIDERING 6 PEOPLE PER UNIT

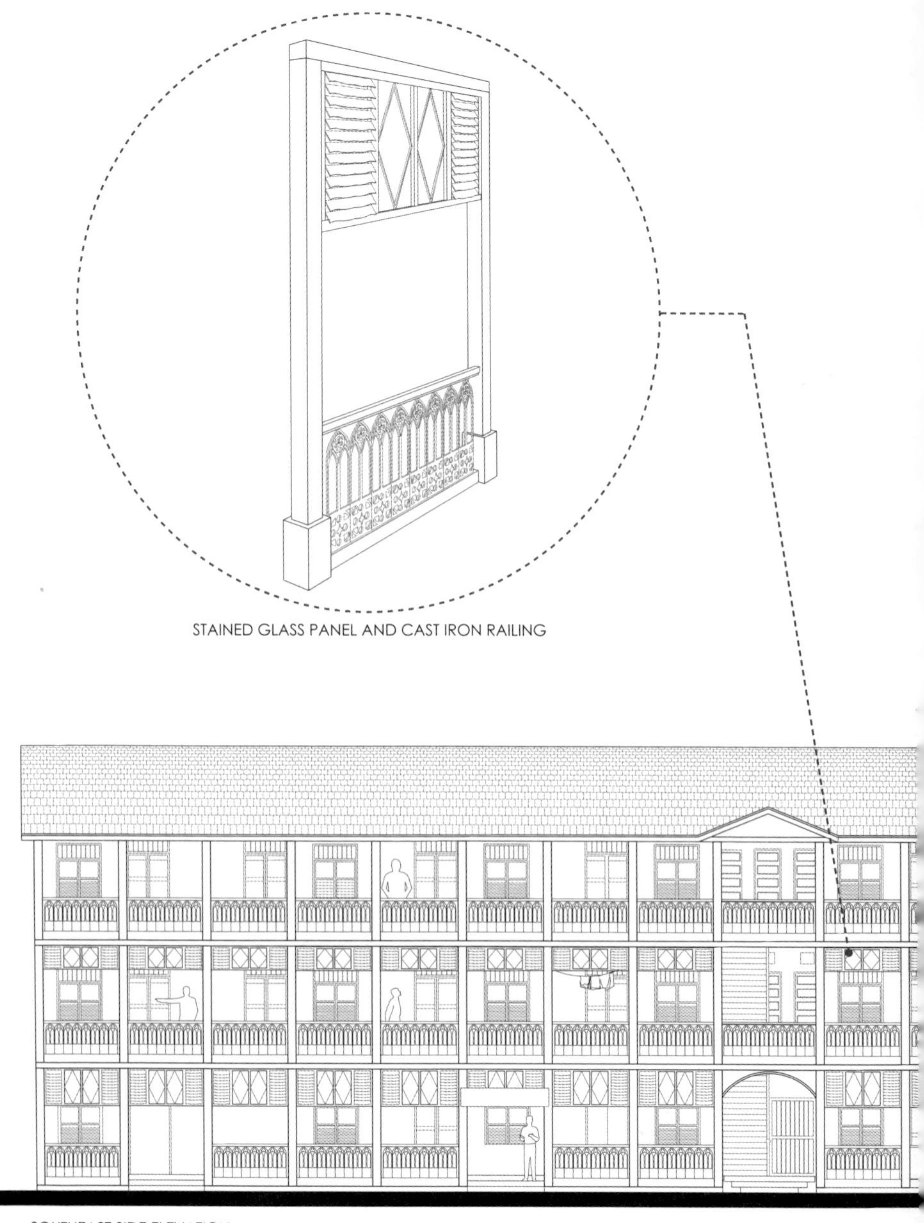

STAINED GLASS PANEL AND CAST IRON RAILING

SOUTHEAST SIDE ELEVATION

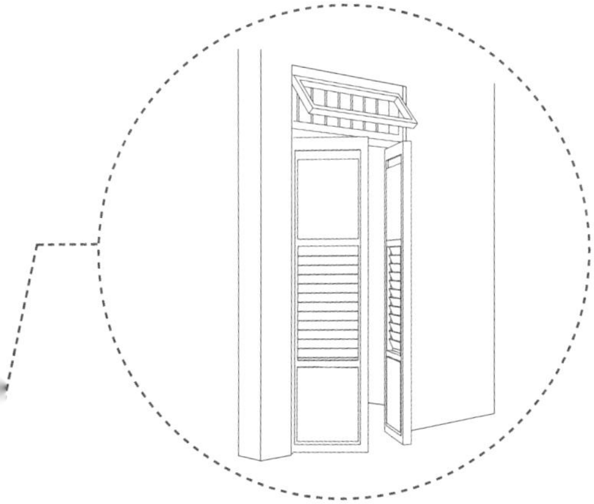

LOUVRED DOOR

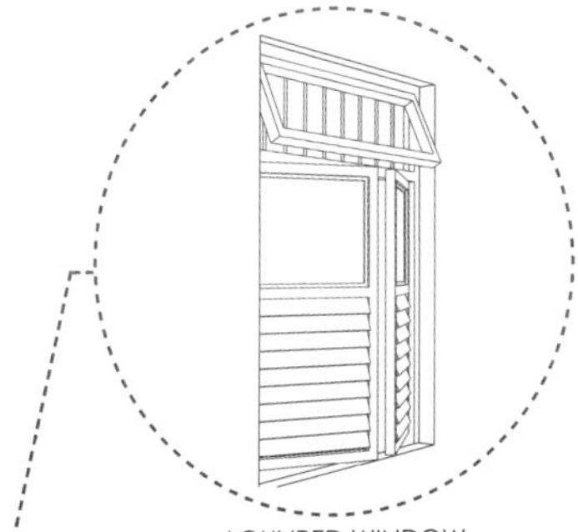

LOUVRED WINDOW

0 1 2 5 10M

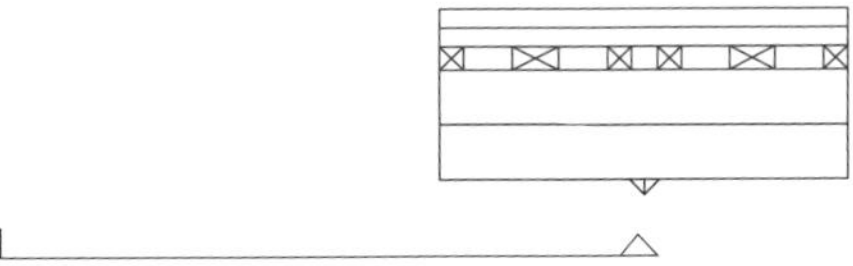

ENVELOPE

The road facing elevation of the chawl is intricately put together with design elements that are indicative of an era of fine workmanship and hand-crafted details. On each of the upper floors, ornate cast iron railings and a combination of patterned louvred ventilators and stained glass fixed windows frame the external façade of the corridor. Road facing window shutters are louvred too. The door to the external corridor from every unit is equipped with a ventilator above and louvres within its shutters. These design details allow cross ventilation and ample air passage between the exterior and the open shafts of the northwest corridor, across the house.

Apart from a few broken window panes, a slightly sagging roof and a reconstructed portion of the ground floor parapet, the façade gives an authentic indication of what the chawl must have looked like in its original state. It remains largely free from appropriations and extensions, most of them manifesting as interior modifications.

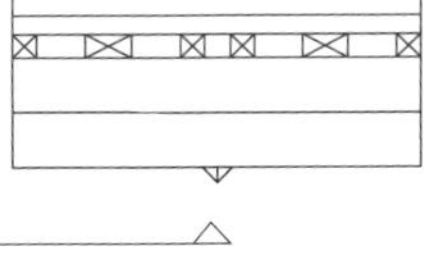

UNITS

Unit 1 is typical of the modifications made by residents whose houses do not have openings on the northeast or southwest. Here, aside from adding bathrooms and kitchen counters, the owners have also converted the kitchen across the corridor into an extra bedroom to be potentially rented out, separate from the main unit. Other appropriations are in the form of subtle additions of plants and seating in the building passage.

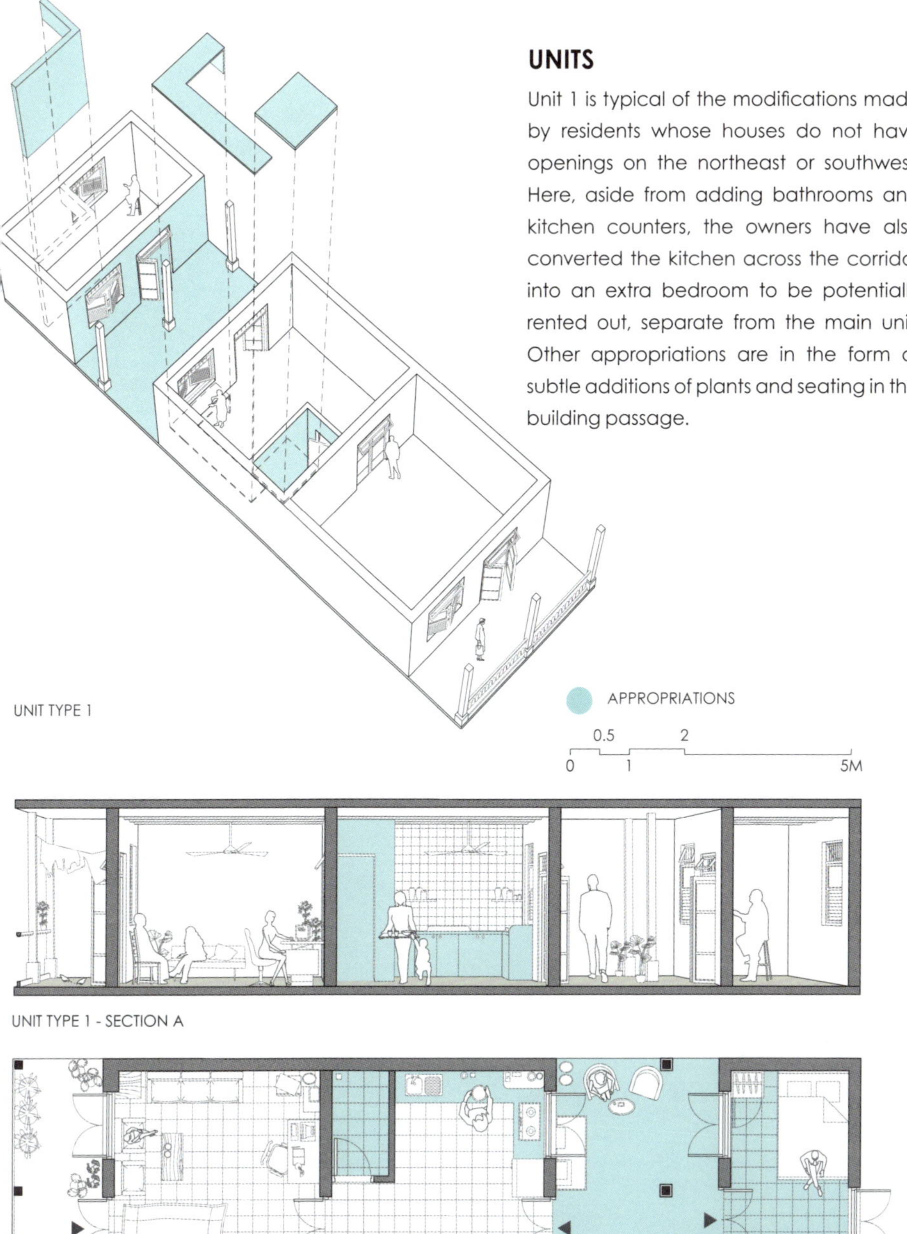

UNIT TYPE 1

UNIT TYPE 1 - SECTION A

UNIT TYPE 1 - FIRST FLOOR PLAN

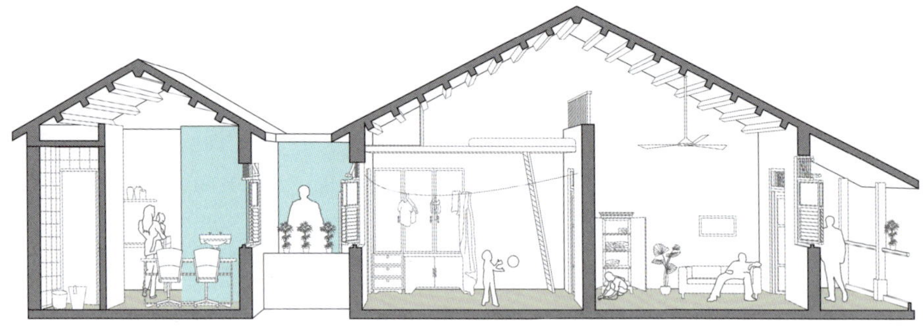

UNIT TYPE 2 - SECTION A

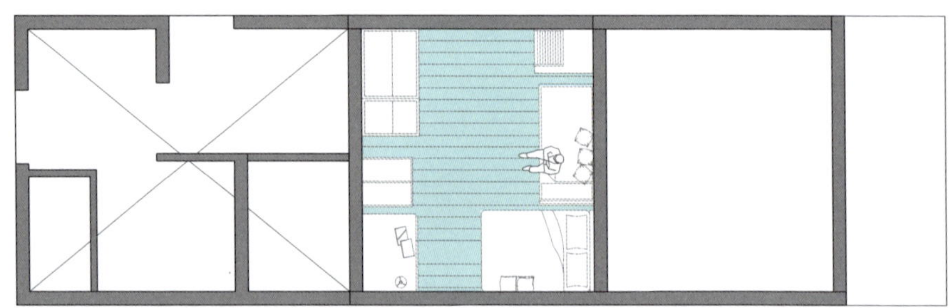

UNIT TYPE 2 - LOFT PLAN

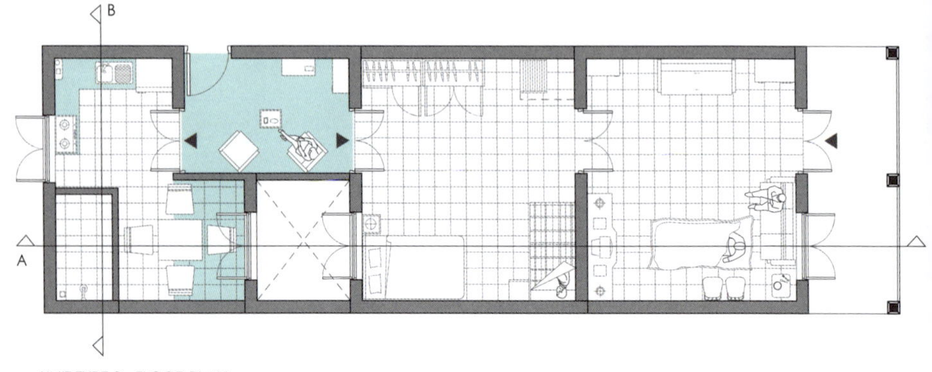

UNIT TYPE 2 - FLOOR PLAN

UNITS

Unit 2 is representative of second floor houses at the far ends of the corridor. These residents have integrated the ends of the passage into their living rooms and as a result, have also acquired a large skylight in their houses. Not only are the formerly separate living and kitchen spaces used as one consolidated unit, but the additional space allows for a dining area too. Kitchen counters and a loft have been built, in addition to the construction of a complete bathroom unit.

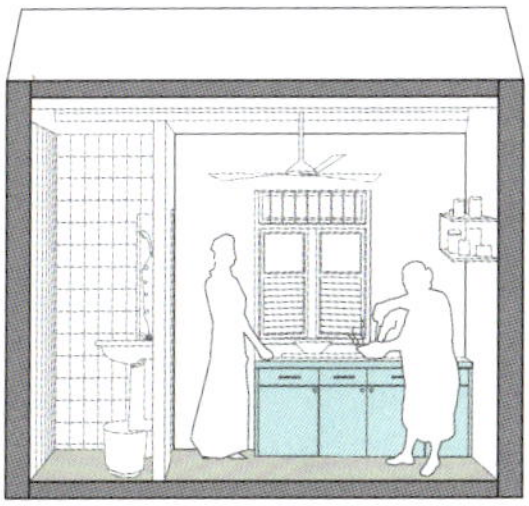

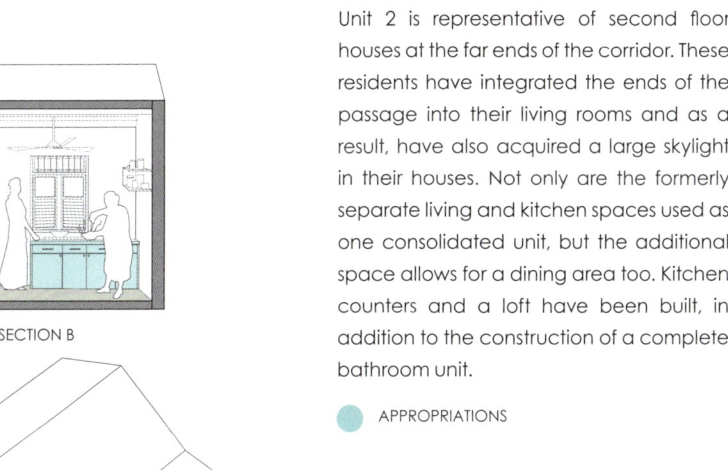

UNIT TYPE 2 - SECTION B

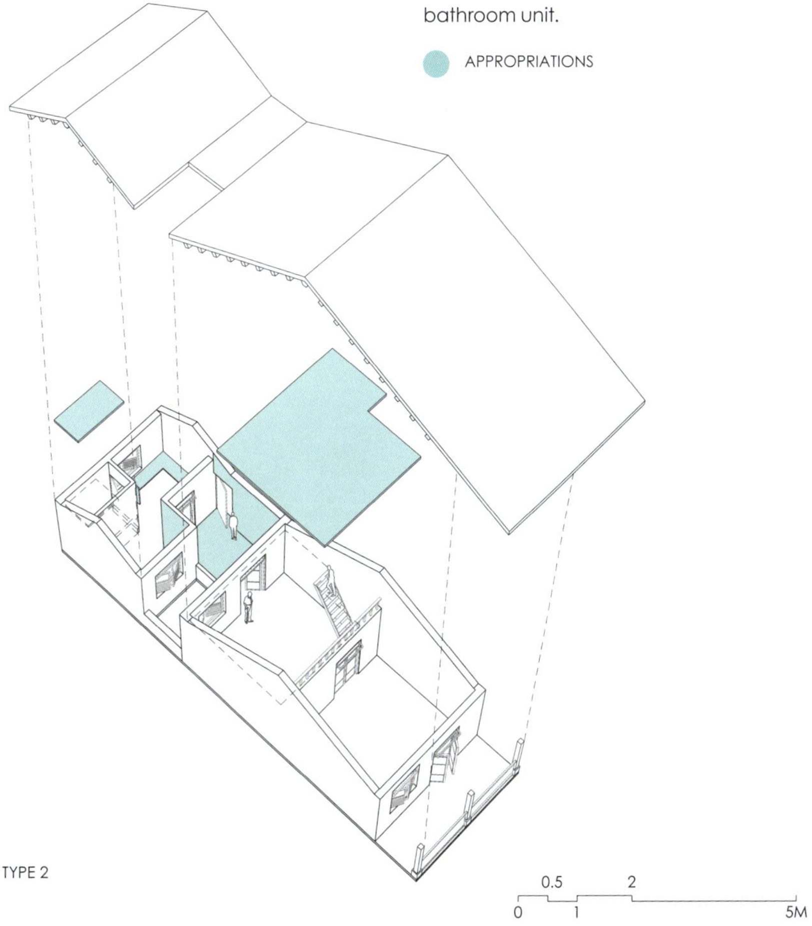

APPROPRIATIONS

UNIT TYPE 2

0.5 2
0 1 5M

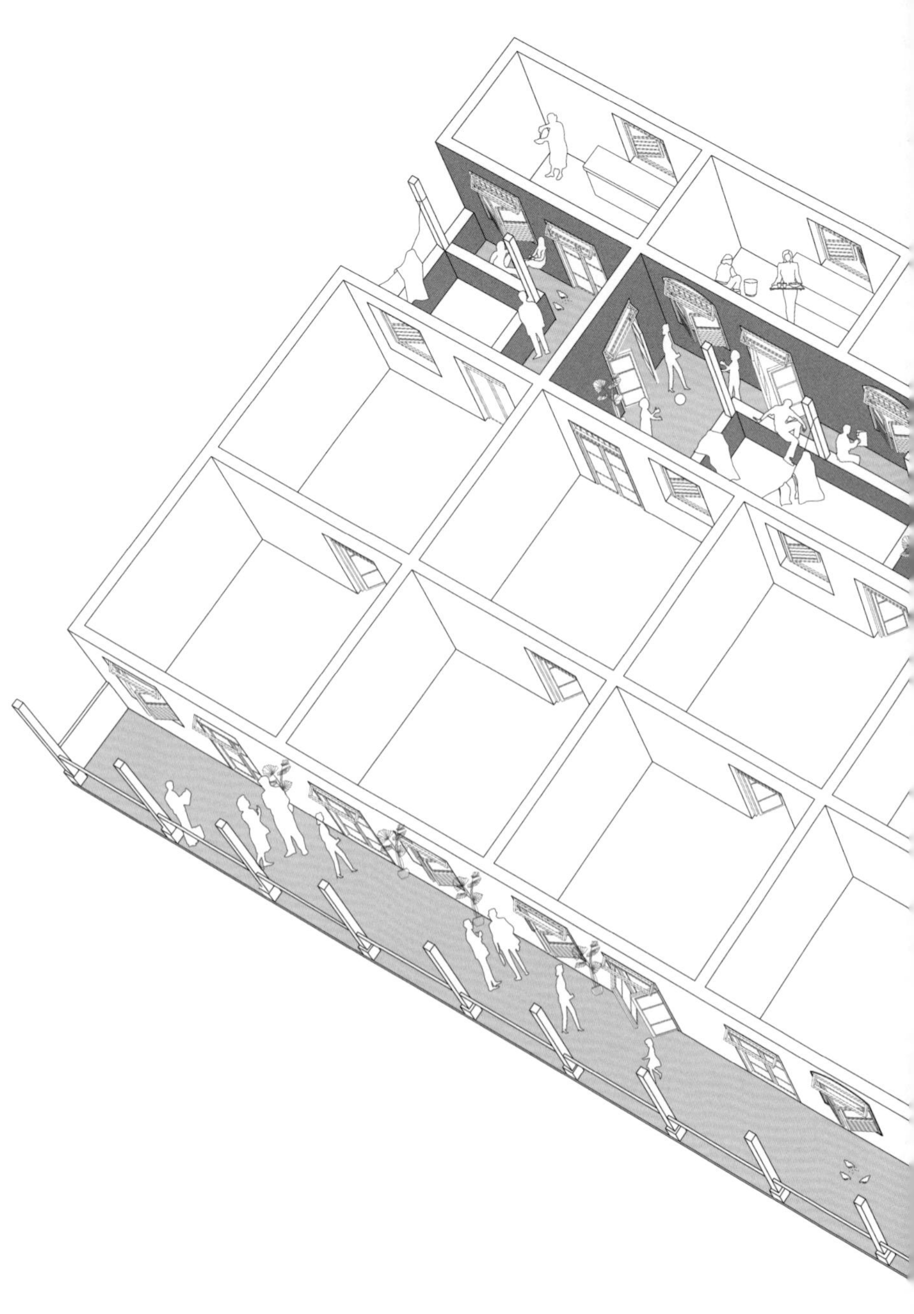

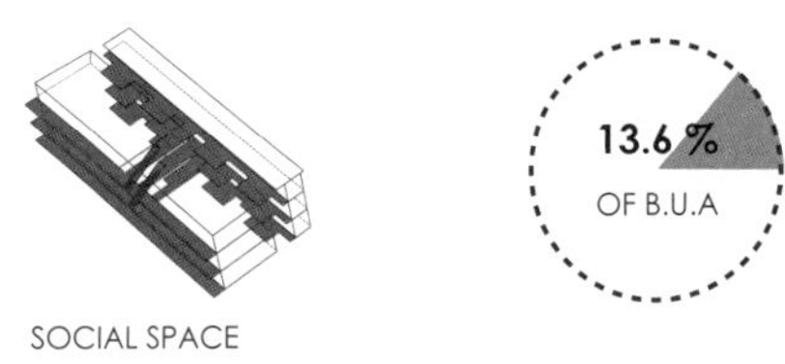

ANALYSIS

The plan type of Atmaram Chawl is a unique variation of the typical chawl and is probably based on the borrowed configuration of the bungalow type, with kitchen and services spaces removed from the main living quarters. Irrespective of its origin, the positioning of the corridor results in the splitting of the traditional consolidated plan of the house and opens up new potential community spaces.

The northwest corridor is a vital social space since residents constantly use it to navigate from one part of their houses to the other. In contrast is the passage on the road face which sees little activity, despite running continuously in front of all the units.

Also of note are the internal windows that open out from the units on either side of the northwest corridor, enabling cross ventilation as well as visual connection through units. The repeated pattern of private space with public circulation allows for an open structure that makes it possible for the kitchen space to be converted into an independent room for sub-letting to paying guests, or be used to accommodate the needs of growing families.

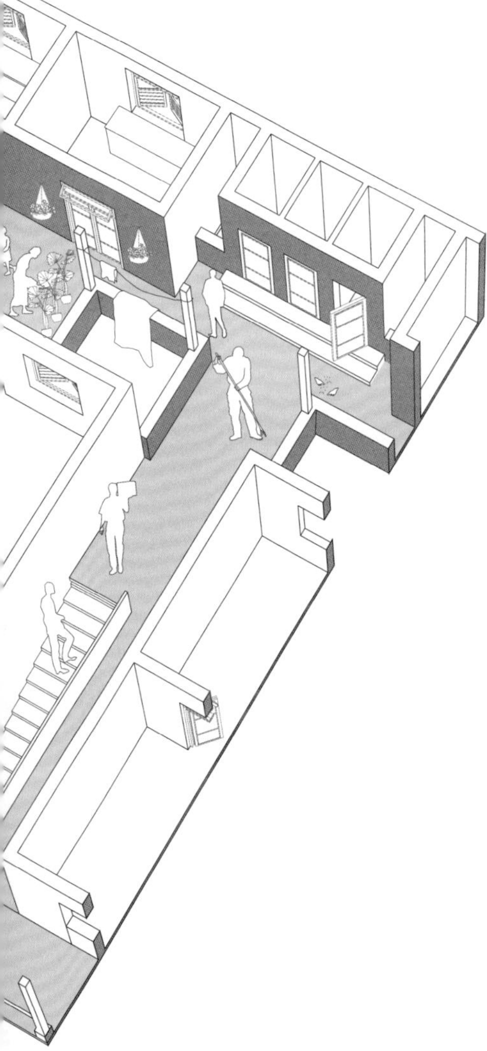

03
SWADESHI MARKET CHAWL

03 | SWADESHI MARKET CHAWL

ELEVATED GROUND

1909

KALBADEVI

Swadeshi Market Chawl is a monumental construct, a mixed-use building constructed in phases, the first of which started in around 1909 and involved the construction of the ground and first floor cloth trading wholesale market. Subsequent phases involved extensions to the market as well as a podium or upper ground with residential chawls. It is one of the oldest cloth markets in the city and its narrow double height streets are crowded with thousands of shoppers and traders on any given work day.

For all the vitality of the market however, parts of the structure are in a dilapidated condition. One of its century-old staircases, and part of the elevated ground floor slab recently collapsed. Swadeshi, listed as a Grade II A heritage structure, is cessed, and under the jurisdiction of the Maharashtra Housing and Area Development Authority (MHADA).

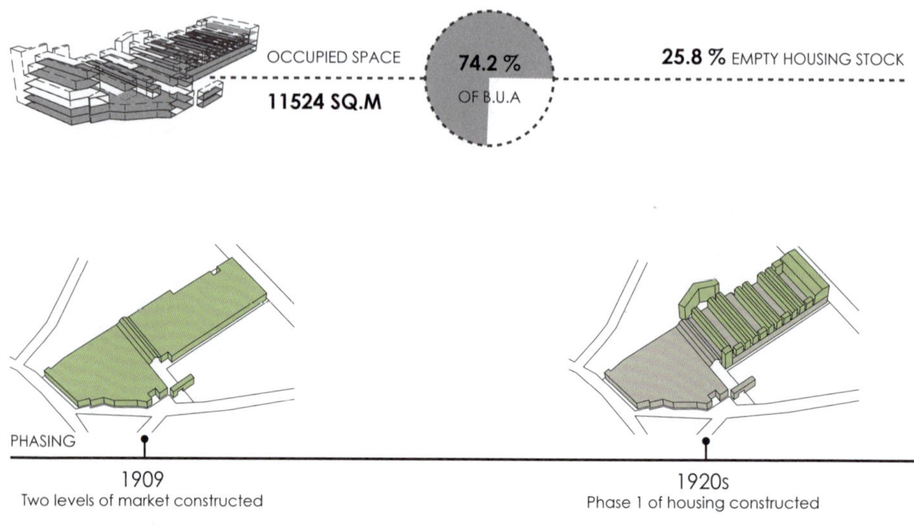

LOCATION

Swadeshi Market Chawl is situated in Gaiwadi, Kalbadevi. Owing to its scale and length, the complex opens out on to numerous streets but has its main entrance on the main Kalbadevi Road. Other roads that flank it are NJ Acharya Marg and Old Hanuman Road.

1940s
Phase 2 of housing constructed

1950s
Phase 3 of housing constructed

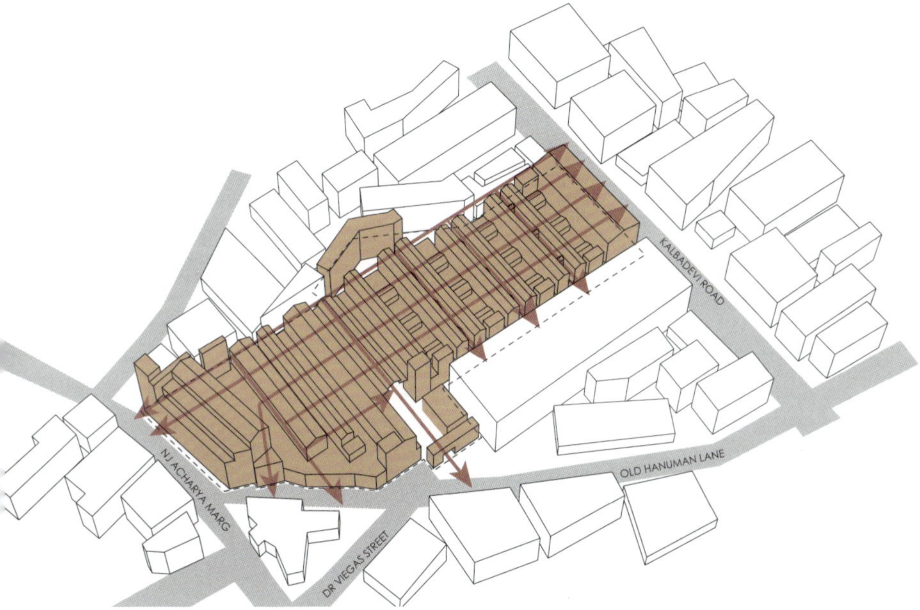

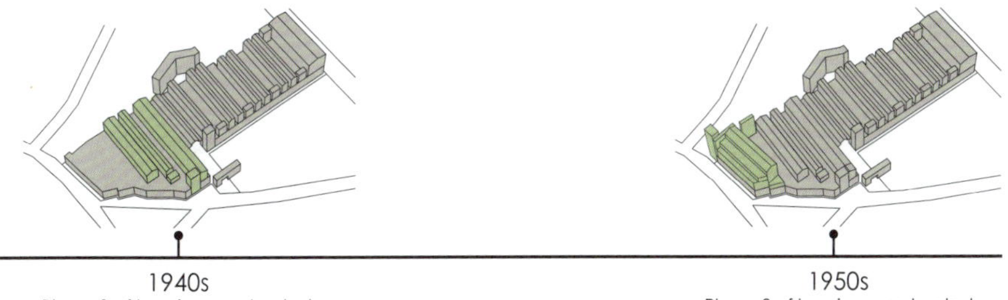

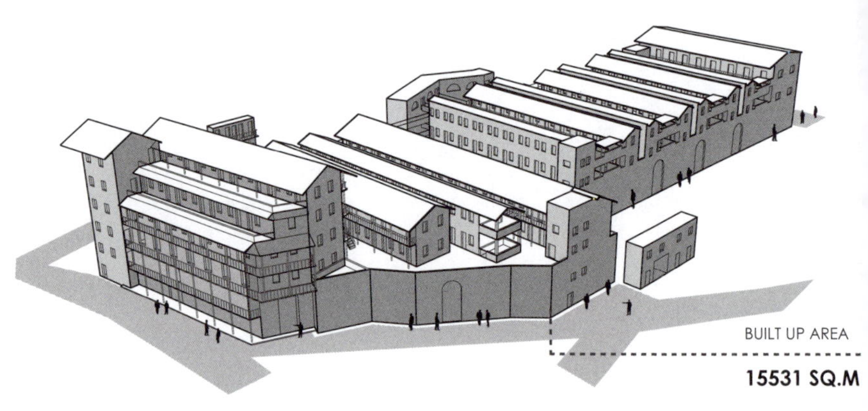

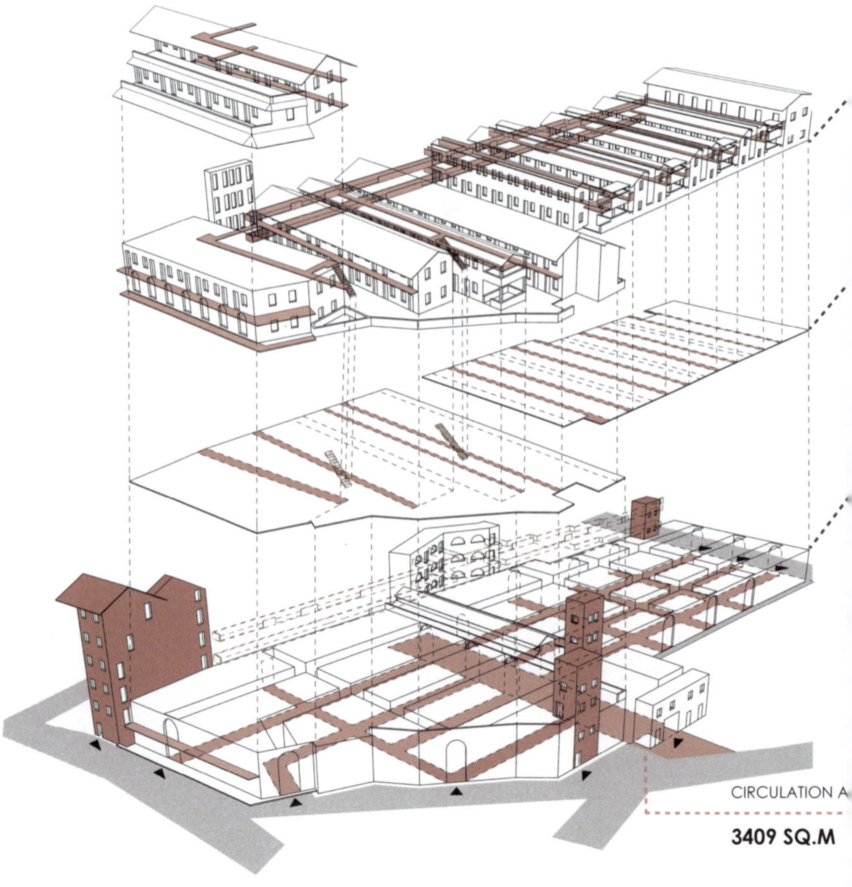

CIRCULATION A

3409 SQ.M

BUILT UP AREA PER PERSON

6.24 SQ.M
CONSIDERING 6 PEOPLE PER UNIT

CHAWL CIRCULATION

PODIUM LEVEL

MARKET STREETS

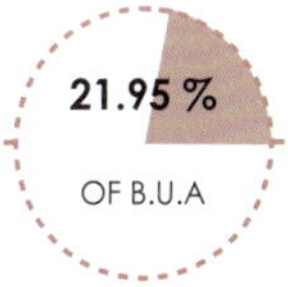

21.95 %
OF B.U.A

CIRCULATION AREA PER PERSON

1.21 SQ.M
CONSIDERING 6 PEOPLE PER UNIT

BUILDING FORM

A mix of commercial and residential programmes, the building has a single footprint measuring roughly three-fourths the size of a typical Manhattan block. At the first two levels, the structure covers the entire plot, accommodating within its shell, market streets and shopping units. Despite being a mass that covers the entire plot, it is characterised by its porosity, drawing in people from the surrounding roads. The internal streets – some of which stretch for up to 120 m – together with the shops are covered by a slab that forms the podium for the chawls above.

A sophisticated structural system organises the residential chawls on the podium, perpendicular to the east-west market streets. This produces voids within the structural grid that light and ventilate the ground floor markets.

CIRCULATION

Primary and secondary north-south passages and three east-west passages run through the structure at the ground level and are used not only by shoppers but also for navigation between the two main roads on either side of the precinct.

The north-south axes lie parallel to the corridors of the residential level above. The east-west axes are double height and at certain points, their roofs break out of the surface of the residential courtyards allowing the commercial corridors to be ventilated. While the commercial area is abuzz with activity, the residences are isolated, their elevation affording them spaces for relatively peaceful habitation.

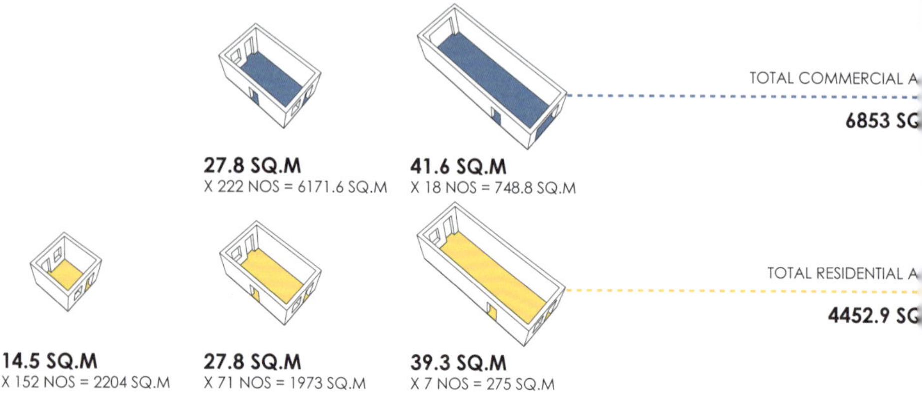

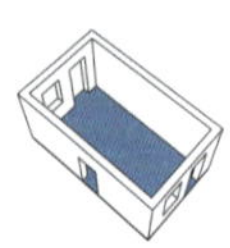

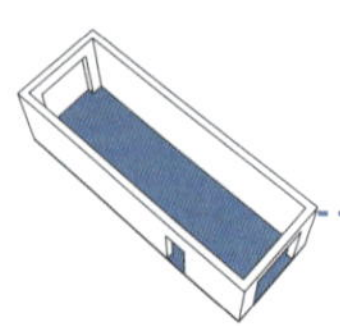

27.8 SQ.M
X 222 NOS = 6171.6 SQ.M

41.6 SQ.M
X 18 NOS = 748.8 SQ.M

TOTAL COMMERCIAL A

6853 SQ

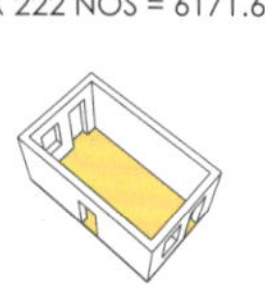

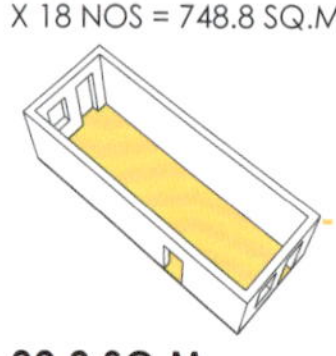

14.5 SQ.M
X 152 NOS = 2204 SQ.M

27.8 SQ.M
X 71 NOS = 1973 SQ.M

39.3 SQ.M
X 7 NOS = 275 SQ.M

TOTAL RESIDENTIAL A

4452.9 SQ

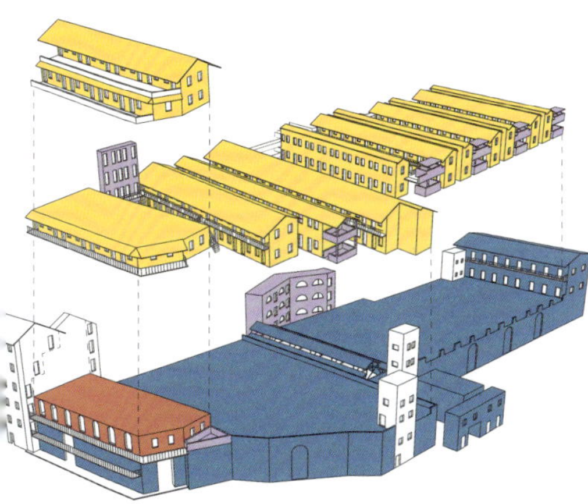

PROGRAMME

The first two levels and the road facing block in the east are purely commercial while the rest of the units were designed to be residences. Many of them now house commercial programmes.

The second floor in the west wing of the complex also accommodates a now defunct *balwadi*.

1909
First two levels and road facing block in the east dedicated to market activities.

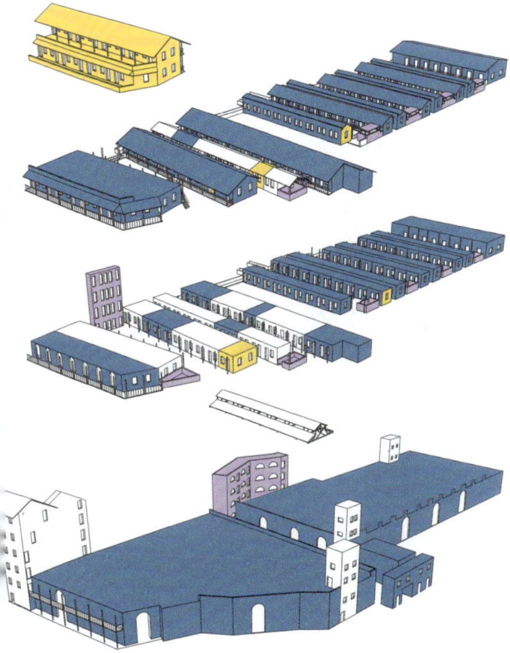

2016
About 10% of the original housing component remains residential, the rest having been taken over by market activities. 25.8% of the residences are unoccupied.

RESIDENTIAL

COMMERCIAL

SHARED SERVICES

INSTITUTIONAL

સ્વદેશી માર્કેટ
स्वदेशी मार्केट
OPTICIANS
Nilesh Optic
HEMA OPTICS
PRADHUMAN KHIMJI
(MULLS, DORIYA, CAMBRICS)
NILESH OPTICS

SECOND FLOOR PLAN

GROUND/FIRST FLOOR PLAN

0 1 2 4 15M

OPEN SPACE
2355 SQ.M

15.16 %
OF B.U.A

OPEN SPACE PER PERSON
0.84 SQ.M
CONSIDERING 6 PEOPLE PER UNIT

SHARED SERVICES AREA
737 SQ.M

4.8 %
OF B.U.A

RTH FLOOR PLAN

FIFTH FLOOR PLAN

FLOOR PLANS

The entire ground floor consists of shops, each having internal access to the level above. This level – essentially a store – cantilevers out above the lower level, into the internal passage, marking out a foyer space (*otla*) in front of each shop.

The second floor is the first residential level where an alternative ground or podium connects all the houses. Here repeating rows of houses are laid out fronting a common corridor. Each row is repeated on the third floor and in one case, fourth and fifth. The entire spread is a complex of chawls, two rows paired together to front each other while still connected with other chawls through courtyards or a series of intermittent bridges.

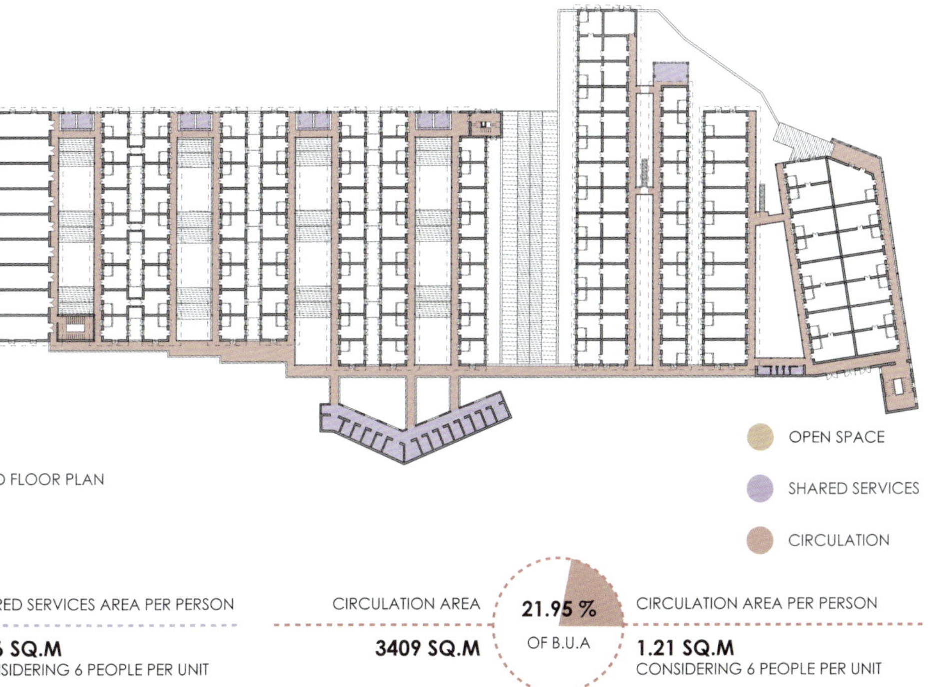

D FLOOR PLAN

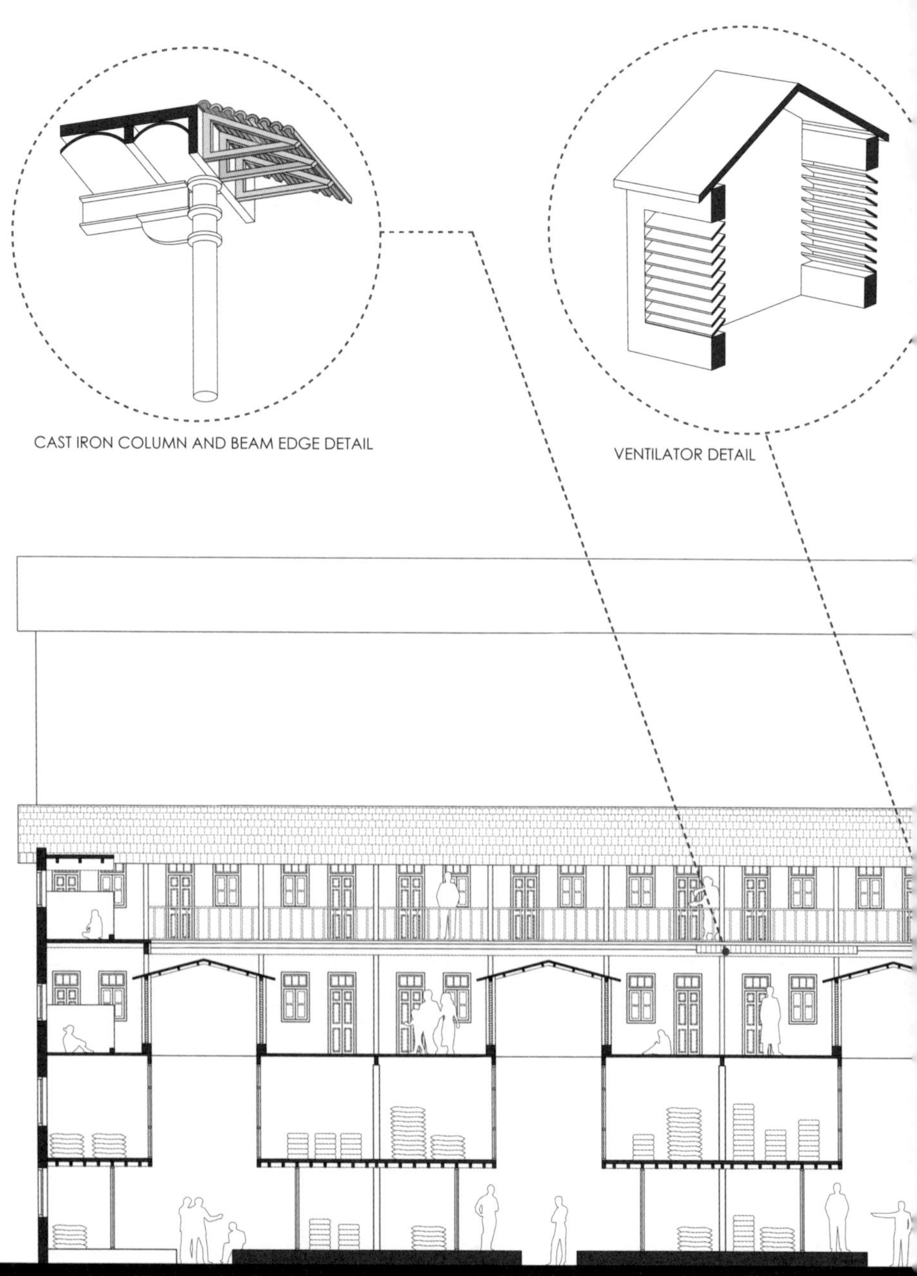

CAST IRON COLUMN AND BEAM EDGE DETAIL

VENTILATOR DETAIL

TYPICAL COURTYARD SECTION

ENVELOPE

Swadeshi Market Chawl's structural sophistication carries through to the finer grain of its detail. Houses lining each courtyard are inset, their private verandahs separated from it by a row of cast iron columns that support the corridor above by means of I-beams. To protect against rain, some residents have fastened *chajjas*, in the form of lean-to corrugated sheets held up by brackets.

The double height commercial corridors running through the ground floor are ventilated by means of louvred ventilator shafts that open into courtyards at the podium level. These have pitched roofs and metal louvres on their sides. They repeat in every courtyard and though they serve a functional purpose, they also break the length of the courtyard into smaller, more intimate spaces.

The bridge connectors between the third floor residential units in the east wing connect the rear sides of adjacent chawl rows. Mosquito mesh screens now cover their sides. The bridges form a point of contact between houses that do not have podium level access and also allow for the amalgamation of two units into one.

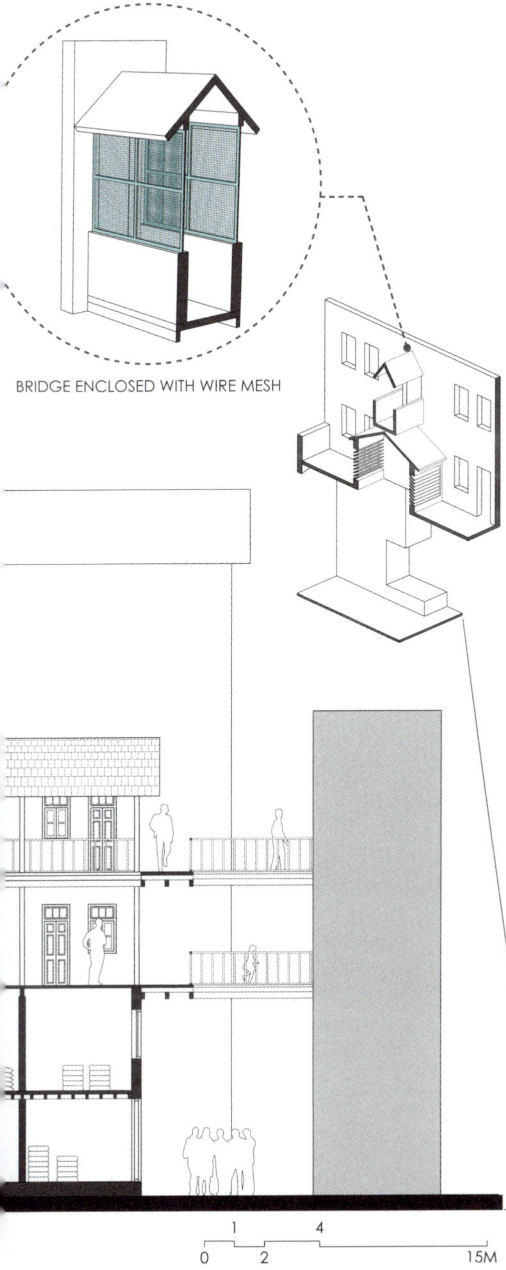

BRIDGE ENCLOSED WITH WIRE MESH

APPROPRIATIONS

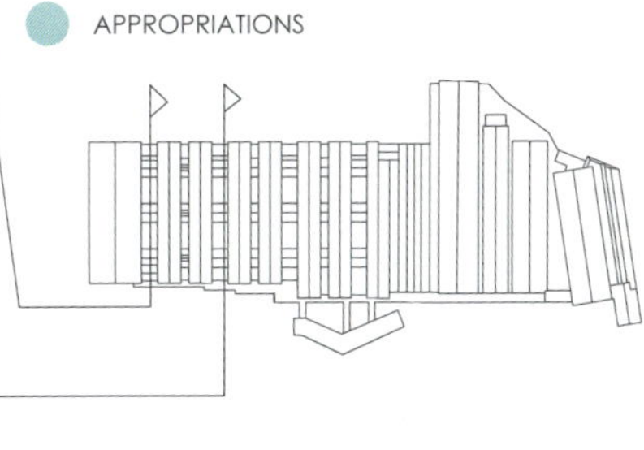

0 1 2 4 15M

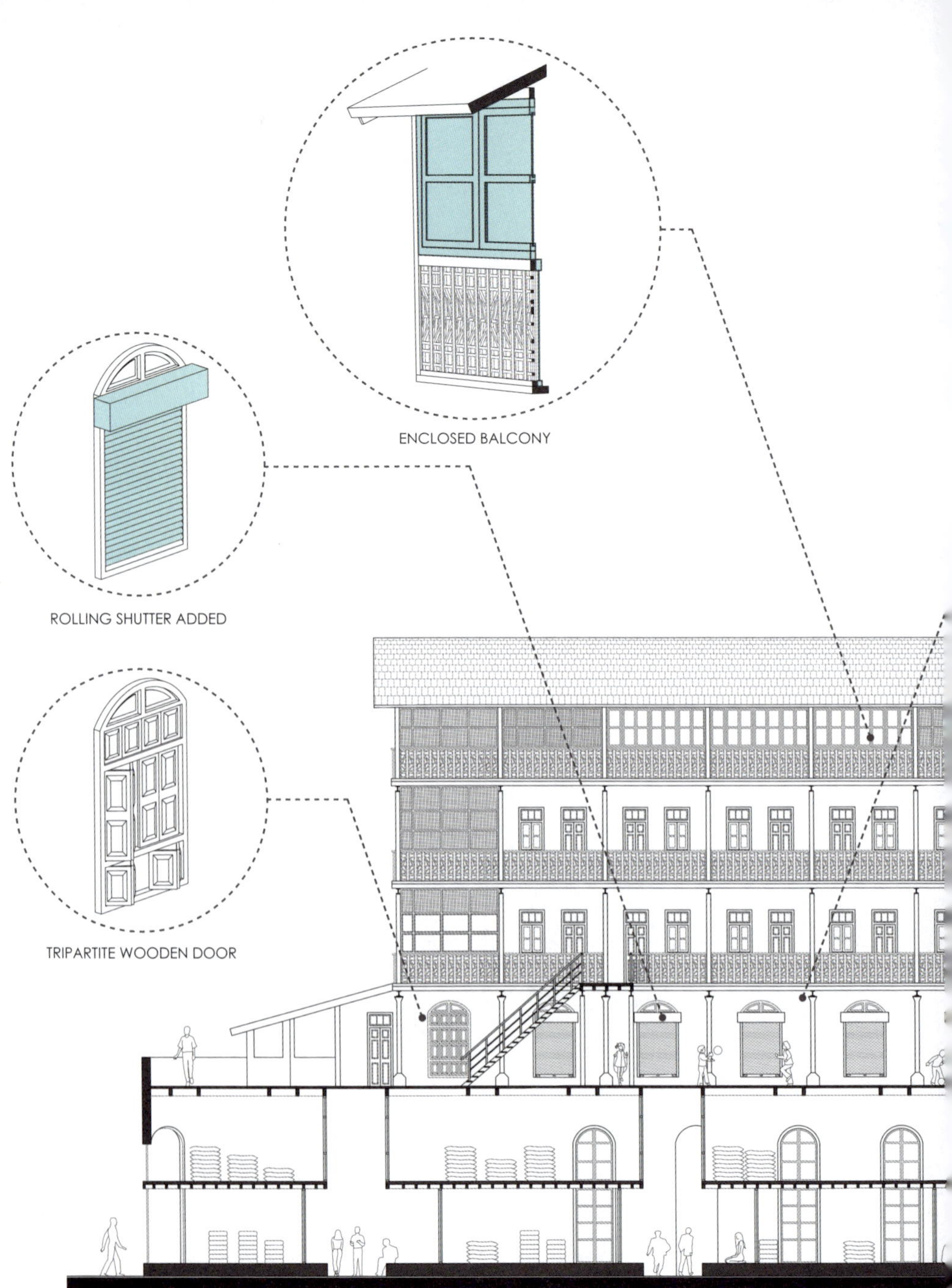

FAR WEST COURTYARD SECTION

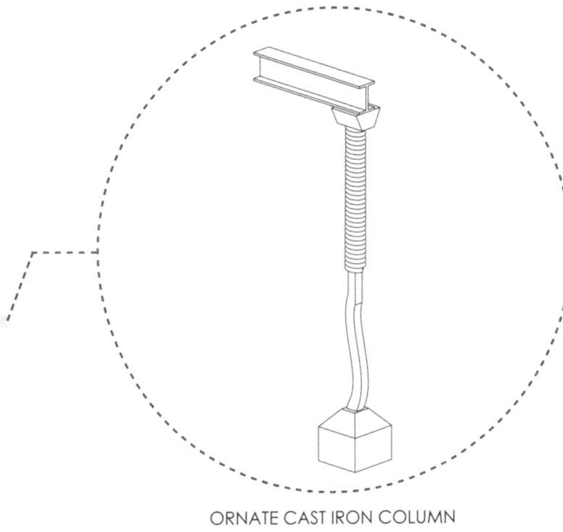

ORNATE CAST IRON COLUMN

ENVELOPE

The fenestrations in the chawl block at the far west of the plot have been modified to accommodate the changing function of the space. What was earlier a *balwadi* at the podium level is now a commercial space and as a result, many of the large openings that were once doors, have been covered by rolling shutters. The tripartite doors that remain in their original form are panelled and split into several shutters.

The upper three levels in this block have similarly designed corridors and railings; however the corridors at the uppermost level have been taken over as kitchens, storage spaces or additional bedrooms. As a result, what manifest on the courtyard facing façade are opaque window shutters or mosquito screens, the only indication of a once homogeneous façade being the presence of identical, jagged railings on each of the three levels.

The level above the *balwadi* is supported by a set of unique cast iron columns, twisted, set in concrete pedestals and bright green in colour. These columns were possibly imported as was the case for most such construction of the time.

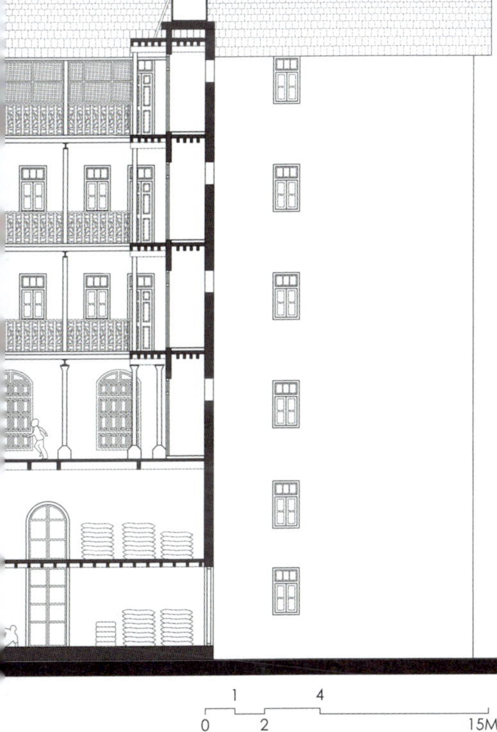

APPROPRIATIONS

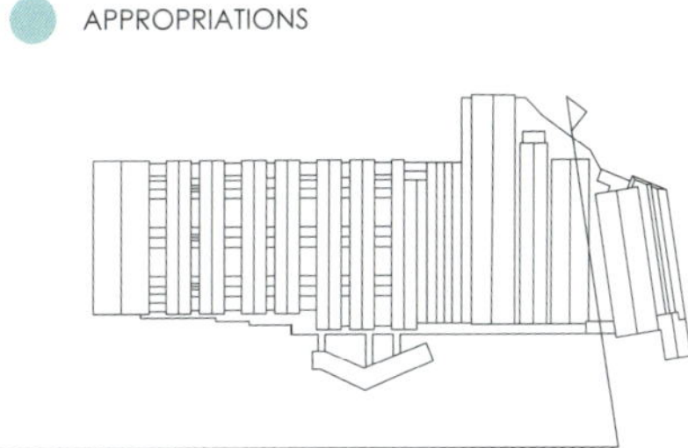

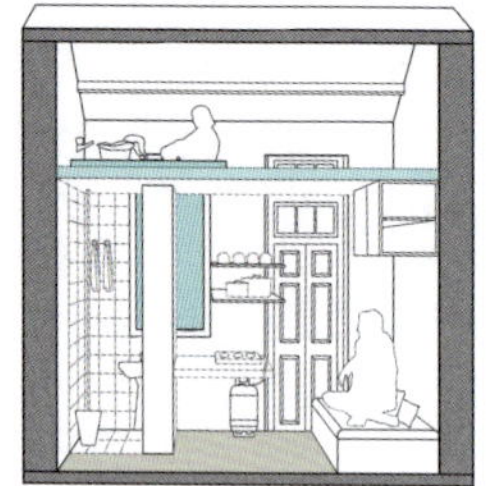
UNIT TYPE 1 - SECTION A

UNIT TYPE 1 - SECTION B

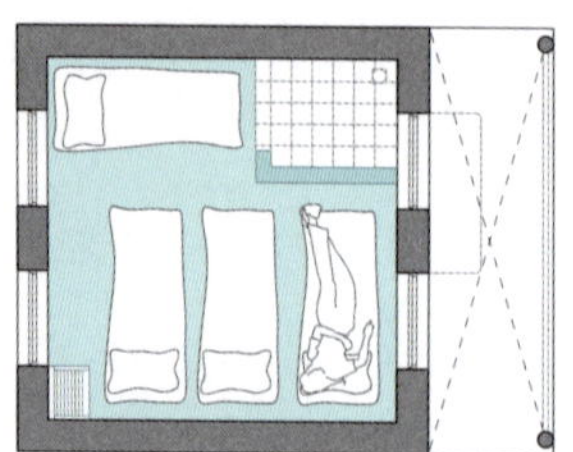
UNIT TYPE 1 - LOFT PLAN

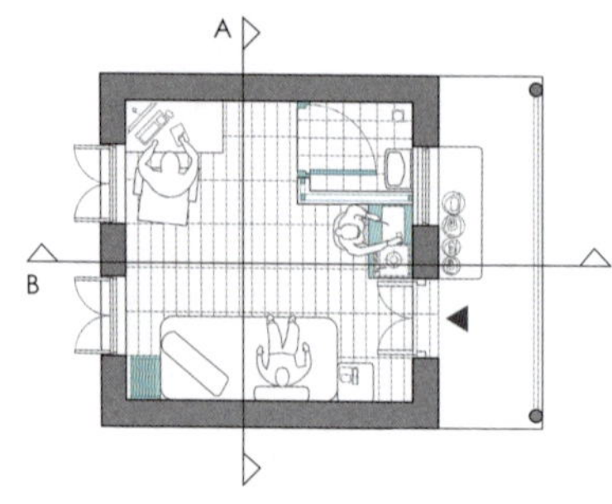

UNIT TYPE 1 - FLOOR PLAN

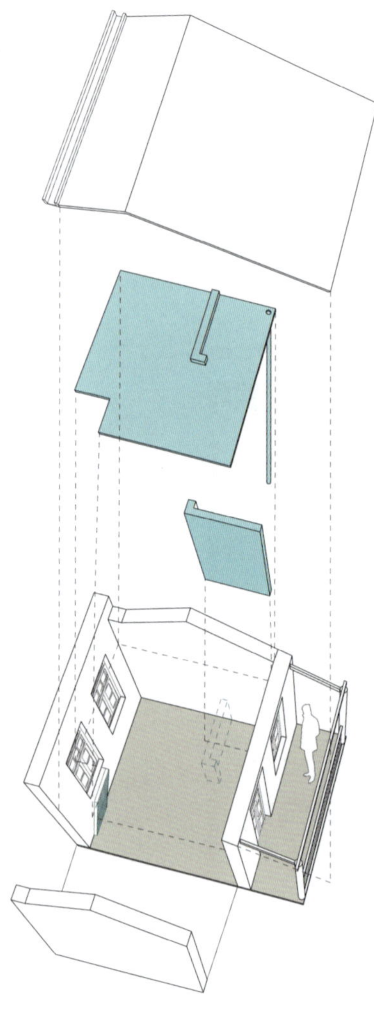
UNIT TYPE 1

UNITS

The modifications in Unit 1 include the insertion of a loft and the walling up of the *mori* on the lower level. The loft level has a *mori* too, with an accompanying drainpipe.

As in the case of Unit 1, the residents of Unit 2 have also constructed a loft for storage, and a bath area in the space originally designed as a *mori*. Here though, the expansion is less contained, for the owner has enclosed the end of the corridor, using this space as a kitchen. Additionally, the open-to-sky backyard portion of the house has been partly covered by a bamboo pergola.

The original area of both units was 14.5 sq.m.

UNIT TYPE 2 - SECTION A

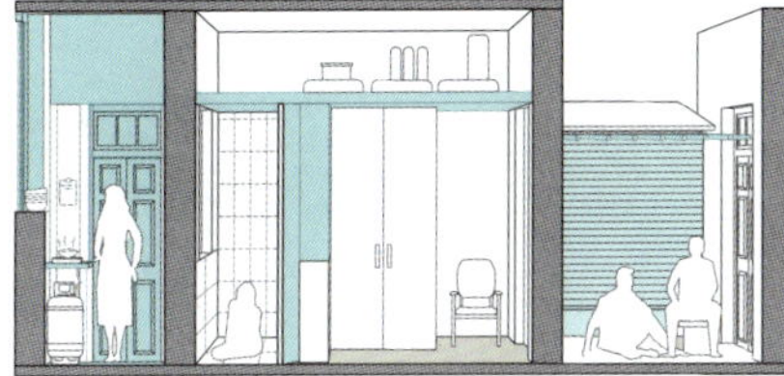

UNIT TYPE 2 - SECTION B

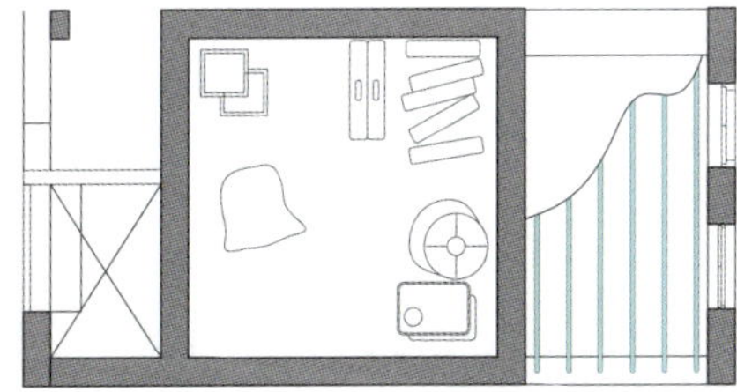

UNIT TYPE 2 - LOFT PLAN

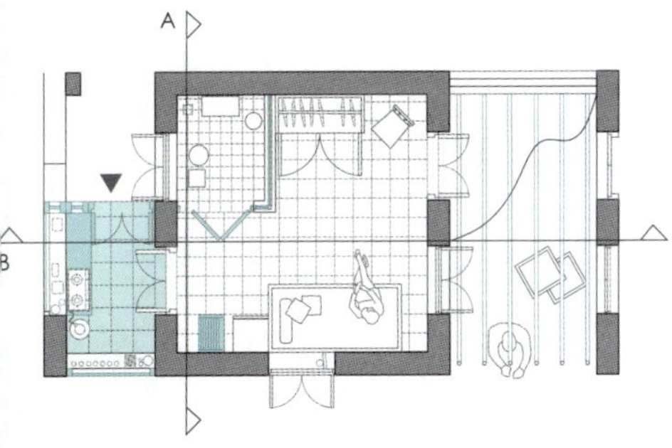

UNIT TYPE 2 - FLOOR PLAN

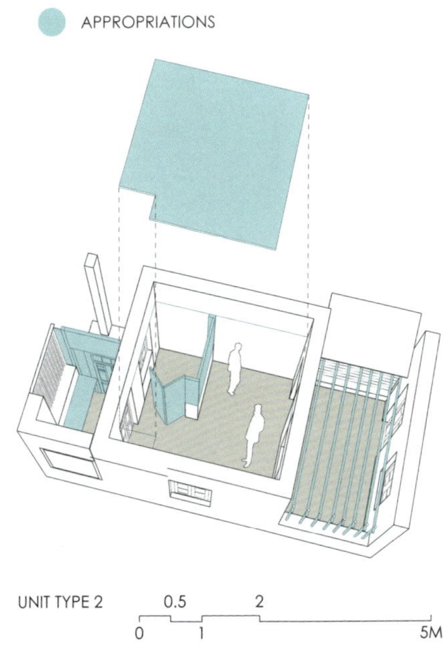

UNIT TYPE 2

GUINEA
15.5
SWITCH OFF
REGULATOR
WHEN NOT IN USE

UNITS

Unit 3 – on the fifth floor of the west block – measures 39.3 sq.m in area and its residents use the enclosed corridor as a kitchen. Their loft covers about a fourth of the floor plate and is used for storage. Outside the main entrance, like many of the other units, a swing has been installed, and also a *chajja* projection above it.

APPROPRIATIONS

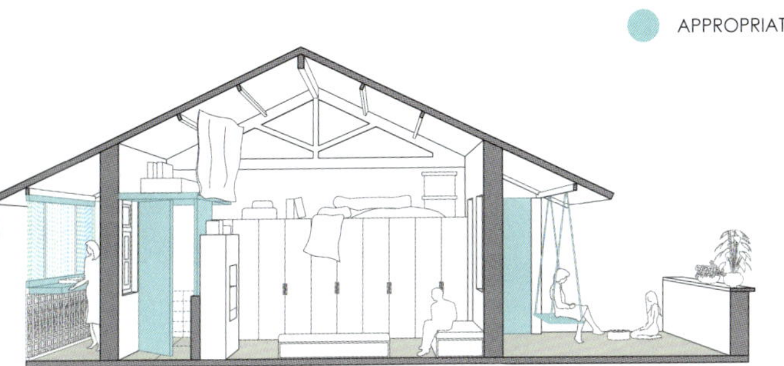

UNIT TYPE 3 - SECTION A

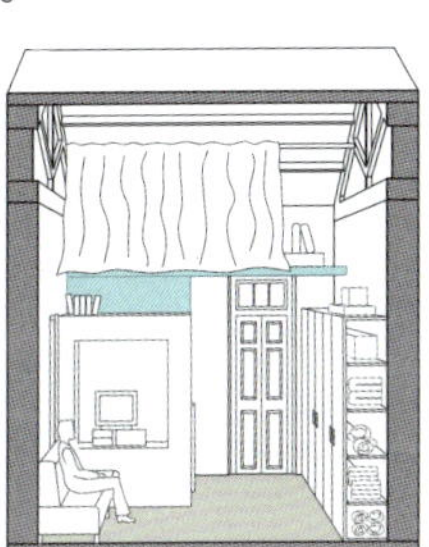

UNIT TYPE 3 - SECTION B

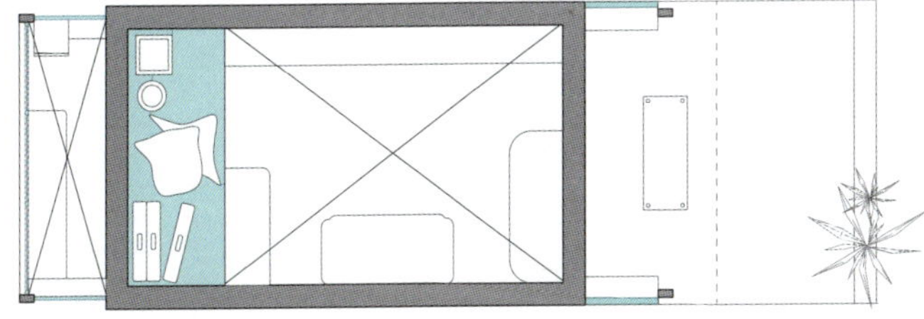

UNIT TYPE 3 - LOFT PLAN

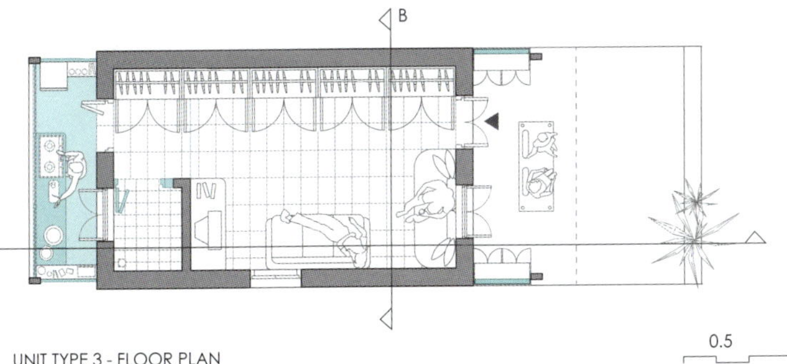

UNIT TYPE 3 - FLOOR PLAN

1

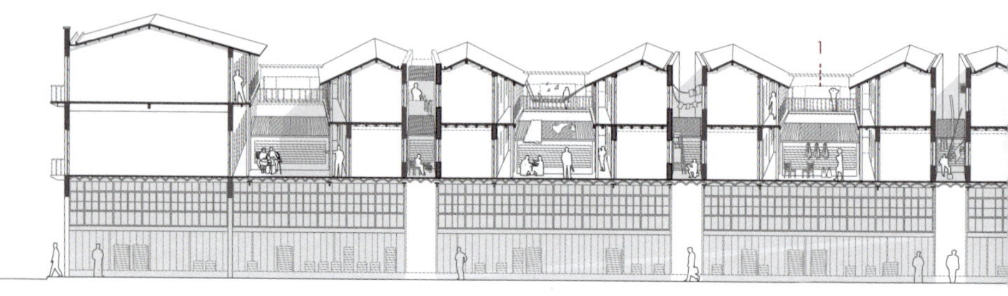

ANALYSIS

The structure and design of Swadeshi Market Chawl exhibit an articulation of form and space that is inventive and unique, and could be considered as a typological model for mixed-use development in the city. The nature of activity through the building is clearly a result of its built form – at the ground level, the narrow streets and tightly packed shops create a bazaar receding from the activity of the main public streets, while still allowing the city fabric to connect through. Above, the broad courtyards and connecting corridors allow for the potential generation of a neighbourhood social fabric.

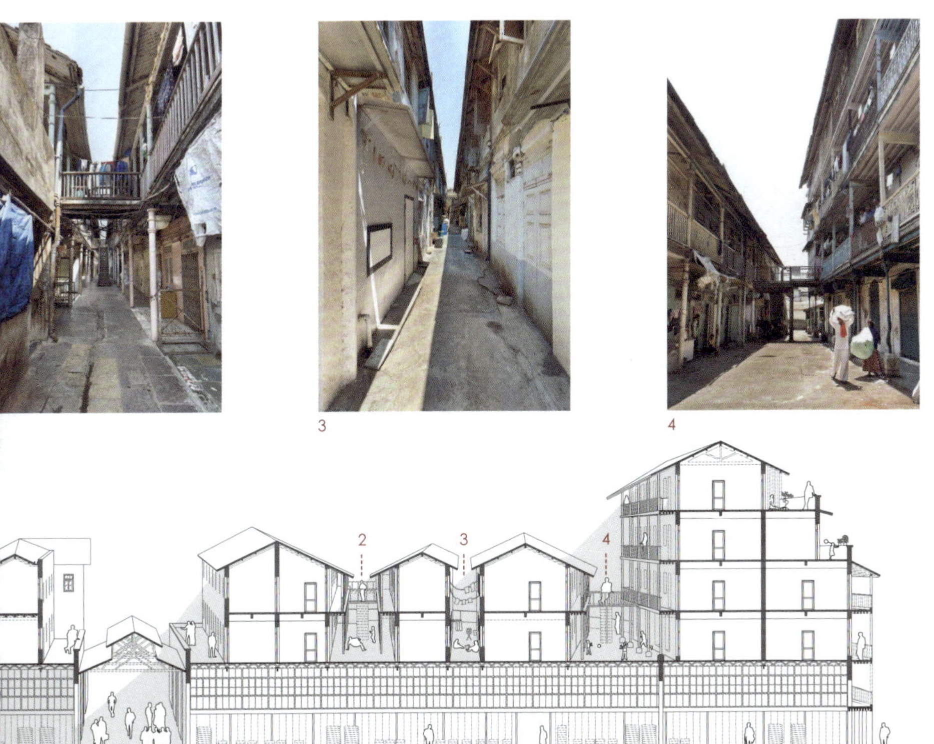

लिमिटेड
डिविजन
HIGH PERFORMANCE YARN

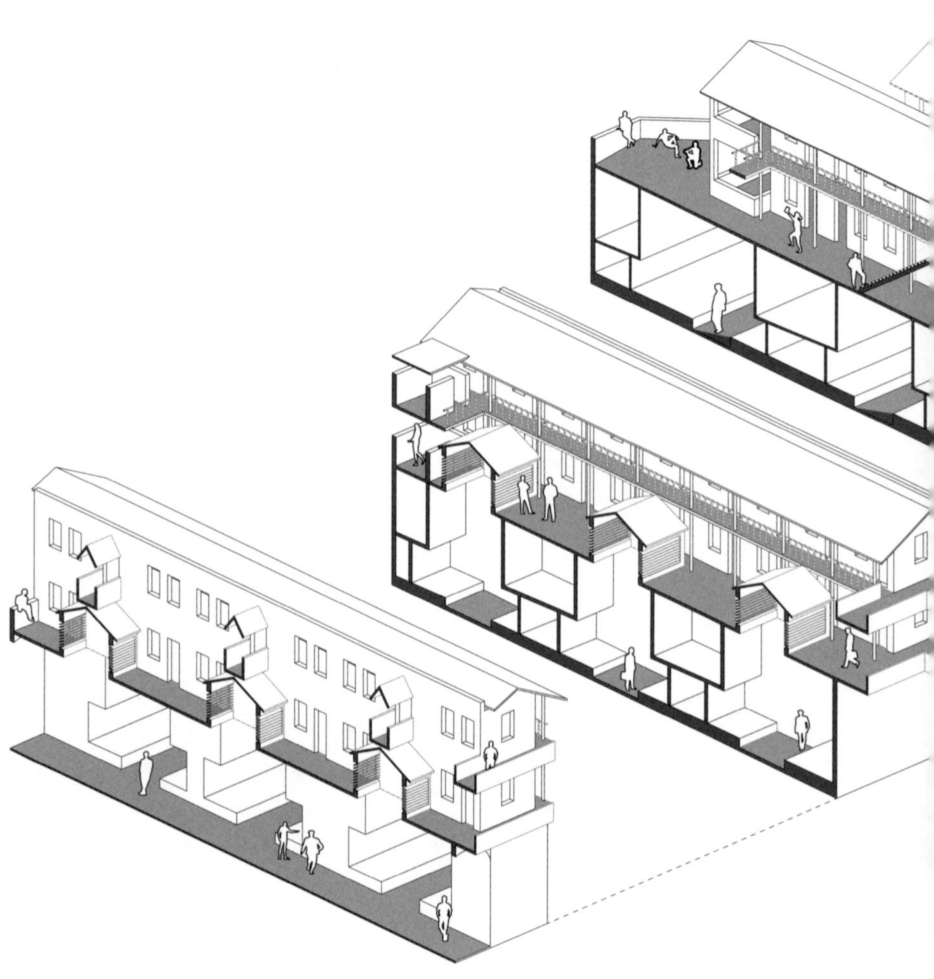

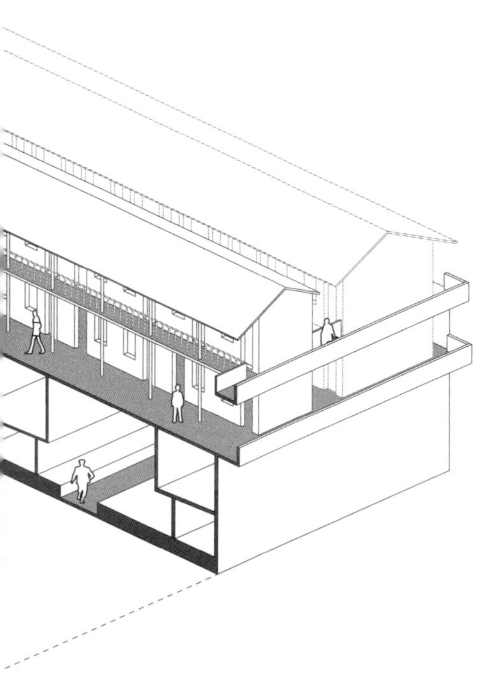

ANALYSIS

Swadeshi Market Chawl is an interesting model of a mixed-use project distinguished by its vertically segregated layers of programme that sit on an elevated ground plane. Residents interact with one another on the podium level, disconnected from the shops below. Currently however, due to a range of reasons, many of the erstwhile residences have been converted into commercial units, contributing to a lack of social activity on these floors.

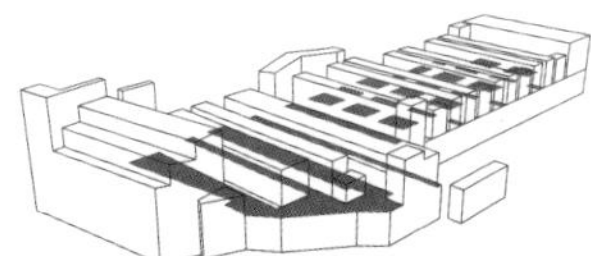

SOCIAL SPACE

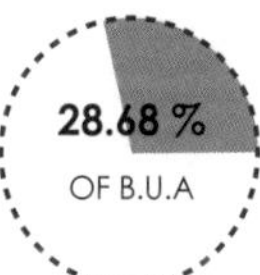

04
BDD CHAWLS

04 | BDD CHAWLS

OUT OF THE BOX

1925
WORLI

The BDD Chawls mark the British colonial authorities' first intervention in Bombay's public housing supply. They did so first through the Bombay Improvement Trust (BIT), established in 1898 to provide hygienic accommodation in the aftermath of the bubonic plague, and later through the Bombay Development Department (BDD), established in 1920. The BDD was set up with the aim of constructing 50,000 houses to ameliorate the housing crisis – a condition the colonisers saw as a cause of the social and political unrest in the city. The chawls were constructed between 1921 and 1925 and were home to nearly 16,500 families.

As of 2016, all 207 chawls are slated for redevelopment due to their supposed poor condition – crumbling structure, corroding reinforcement and leakages. Additionally, due to low rents and the Public Works Department's (PWD) inability to recover even half of the maintenance costs, a redevelopment strategy has been devised by the Maharashtra Housing and Area Development Authority (MHADA) in conjunction with private developers to provide free housing to existing inhabitants and also a free sale component.

Currently 78% of the households in Worli pay a monthly rent less than Rs. 100. 21% of the original occupants have transferred their tenements to others with or without PWD consent, and many have done so through the *pagdi* system.

In the 1930s, the chawls in Worli became a hotbed of political movement, as the high percentage of non-Brahmins and 'untouchables' were galvanised into fighting for their civil rights. The large numbers of Scheduled Classes in the chawls can be attributed to the difficulty these communities faced in finding private sector accommodation.

The original inhabitants were largely from the Satara-Sangli-Karad-Sangola belt and even today 90% of the residents are from Maharashtra. In terms of religious distribution, the majority is neo-Buddhist, followed by mostly Hindu and Muslim state government employees.

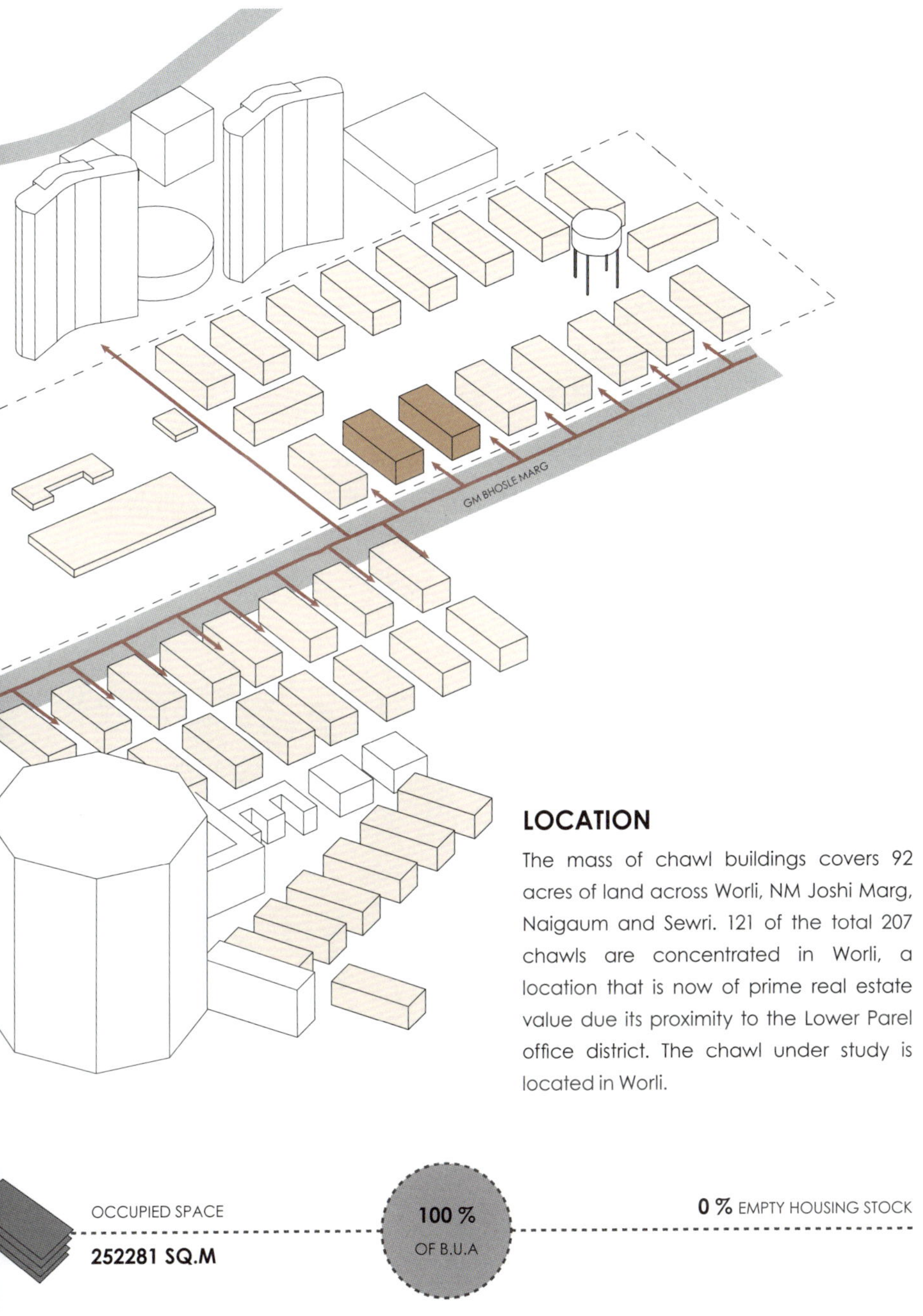

LOCATION

The mass of chawl buildings covers 92 acres of land across Worli, NM Joshi Marg, Naigaum and Sewri. 121 of the total 207 chawls are concentrated in Worli, a location that is now of prime real estate value due its proximity to the Lower Parel office district. The chawl under study is located in Worli.

OCCUPIED SPACE

252281 SQ.M

100 %
OF B.U.A

0 % EMPTY HOUSING STOCK

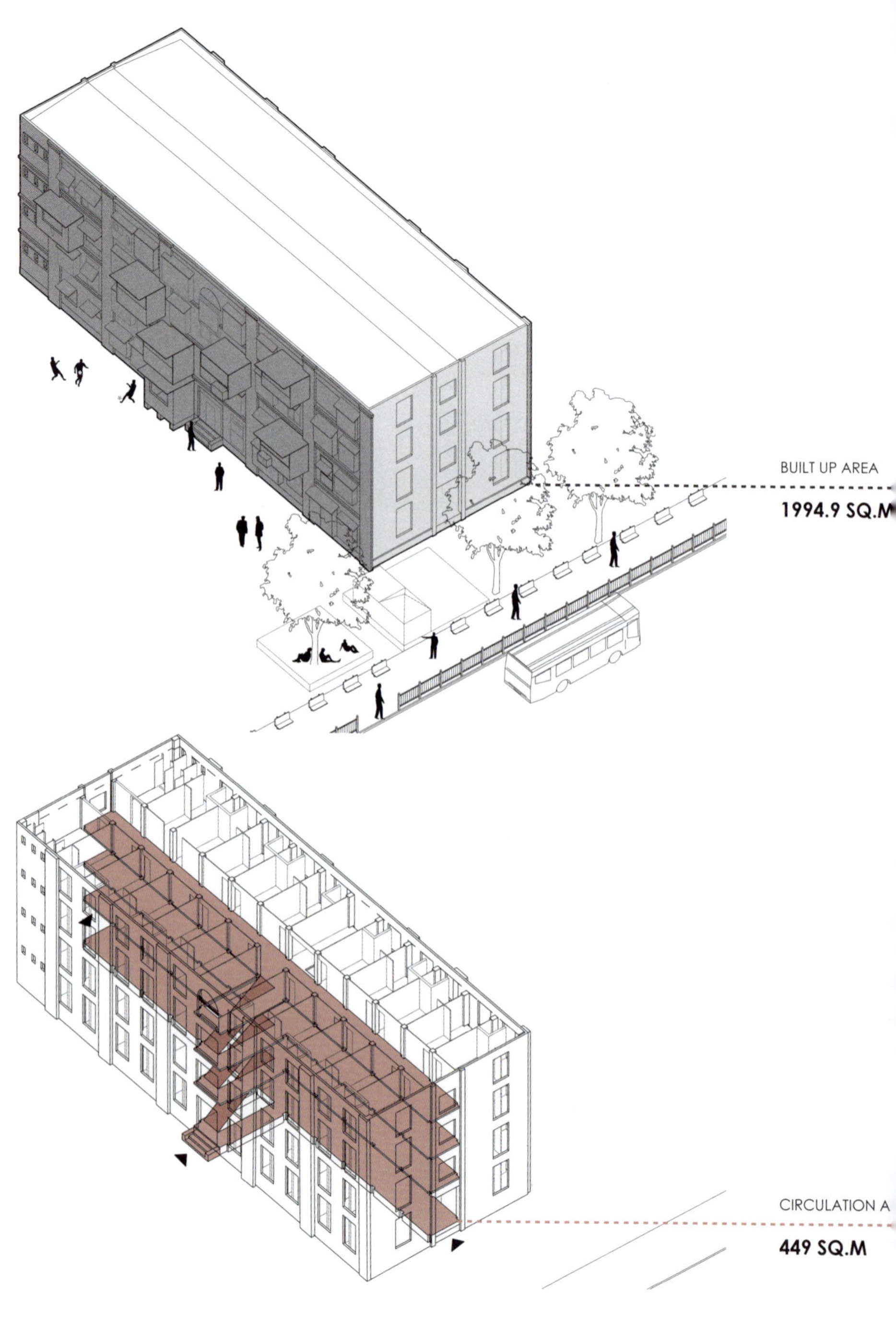
BUILT UP AREA
1994.9 SQ.M
CIRCULATION A
449 SQ.M

BUILDING FORM

Often compared to army barracks, each chawl building is a rectangular block split down its length by a spacious corridor and with a toilet block at its far end. The buildings in Worli are spread over 59 acres, parallel to each other and identical in form. They were constructed out of precast RCC (Reinforced Cement Concrete) blocks in the interest of mechanisation and standardisation, and as a result, speedier work that did not involve skilled labour.

BUILT UP AREA PER PERSON

4.99 SQ.M
CONSIDERING 5 PEOPLE PER UNIT

CIRCULATION

The area was originally low-lying and undeveloped and the BDD had provided only two roads along the west and through the site. The original estimate did not provide for adequate utilities, and later in order to make the chawls habitable, the government was forced to upgrade transportation infrastructure and other amenities.

The current site plan consists of a network of roads within which the buildings are situated. In the building under study – like the others in the project – units are organised around a 2.66 m wide corridor that forms the central circulation spine. It is accessed on the ground floor at three points – the two ends and at the centre where there is also a staircase for vertical circulation.

22.5 %
OF B.U.A

CIRCULATION AREA PER PERSON

1.12 SQ.M
CONSIDERING 5 PEOPLE PER UNIT

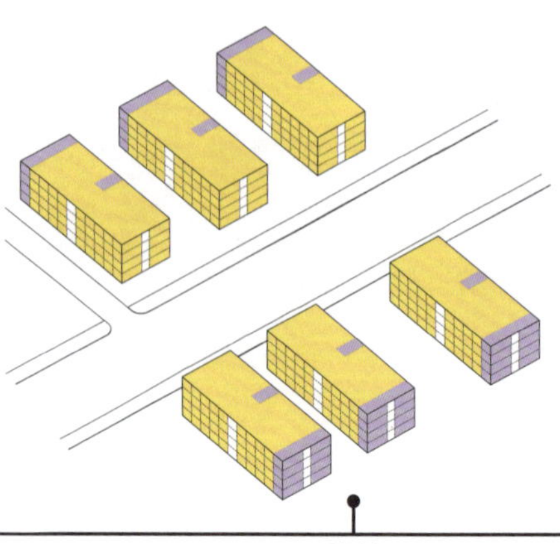

Massive housing scheme designed in Worli to decongest southern Bombay, financed through development loans and tax on cotton bales entering the city

1920
Governor, Sir George Lloyd sets up the Bombay Development Department (BDD)

1924-1925
BDD Chawls in Worli are constructed
Housing stock remains unoccupied

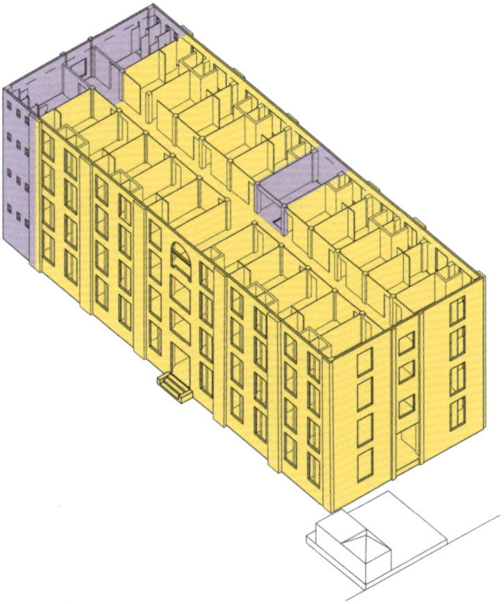

PROGRAMME

95% of all units across the BDD Chawls are residential, the remaining used for public amenities like hospitals and school rooms. Of the 121 buildings in Worli, six are religious and one is a hospital.

The chawl under study is entirely residential, every floor having services units at its end. There are six toilets on every floor – three each for men and women.

RESIDENTIAL

AMENITIES

COMMERCIAL

INSTITUTIONAL

SHARED SERVICES

JAILS

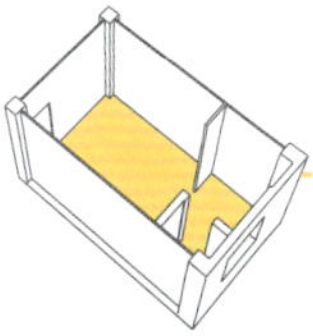

TOTAL RESIDENTIAL AREA

1328 SQ.M

16.6 SQ.M

X 80 NOS = 1328 SQ.M

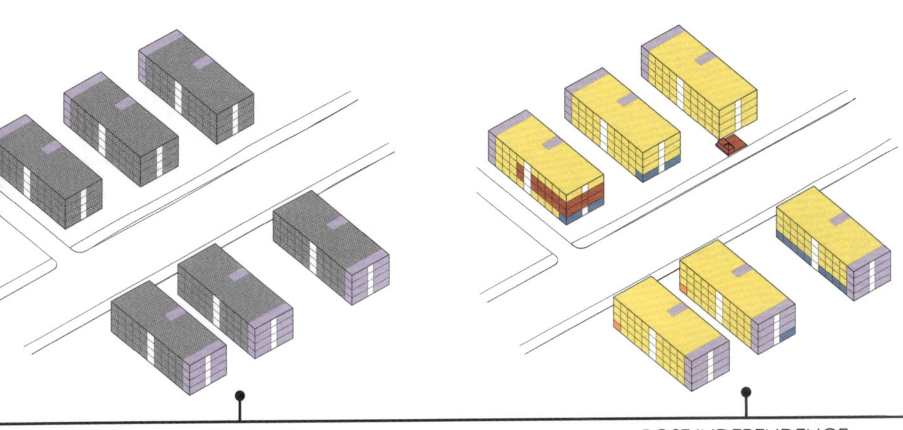

1935-1947

Empty housing stock used as jails by British Government for Indian freedom fighters

POST INDEPENDENCE

Ownership transferred to Bombay PWD. Housing stock rented to mill workers for the most part and also to other migrant workers

OPEN SPACE	90.95 % OF B.U.A	OPEN SPACE PER PERSON
229445 SQ.M		4.54 SQ.M CONSIDERING 5 PEOPLE PER UNIT

SHARED SERVICES AREA	10.65 % OF B.U.A
212.4 SQ.M	

FLOOR PLANS

All buildings are four storey structures and each floor has 20 rooms – ten on either side of the corridor. All units are of standard size – 16.6 sq.m in area – and each is provided with a *mori*, an element that was absent in one of the original test designs, so as to reduce plumbing and construction costs.

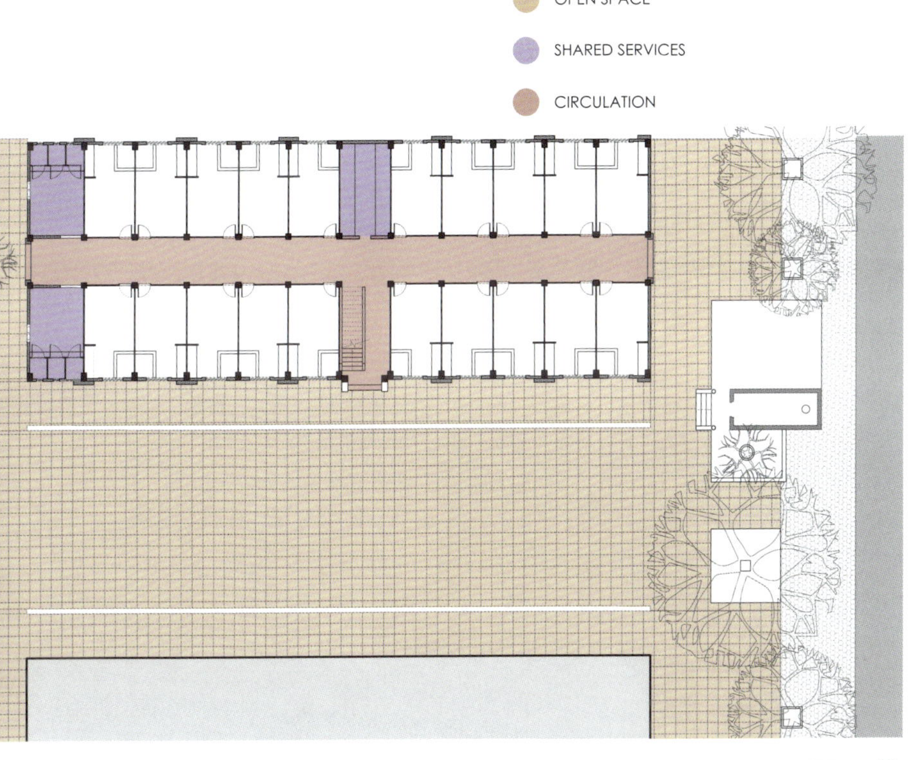

CAL FLOOR PLAN

0 1 2 5 10M

RED SERVICES AREA PER PERSON

3 SQ.M

NSIDERING 5 PEOPLE PER UNIT

CIRCULATION AREA

449.8 SQ.M

22.5 %

OF B.U.A

CIRCULATION AREA PER PERSON

1.12 SQ.M

CONSIDERING 5 PEOPLE PER UNIT

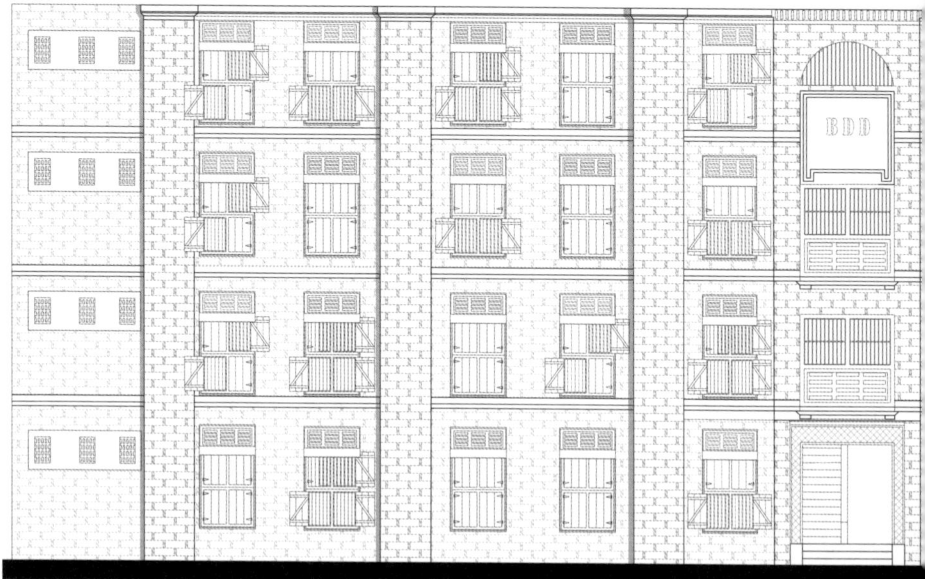

TYPICAL LONGITUDINAL ELEVATION (1925)

TYPICAL LONGITUDINAL ELEVATION (2016)

ENVELOPE

As a result of the modifications at the unit level, the façade of the building is vastly different from the original design. Considerable projections – in some cases up to 2.2 m deep – from the external faces where windows once were, have been added over time and are used as kitchens, sleep spaces and services areas. The extensions are not unique to any particular building, but a pattern visible across the entire precinct. In some places they manifest as porous balcony enclosures, while in others they are opaque containers of interior programmes.

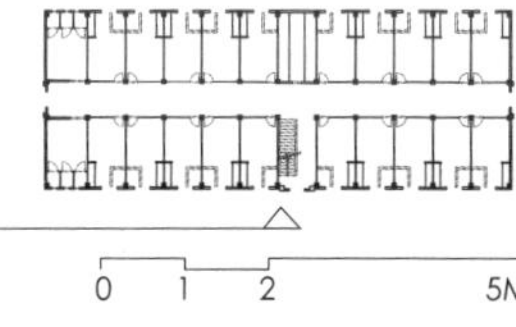

LG

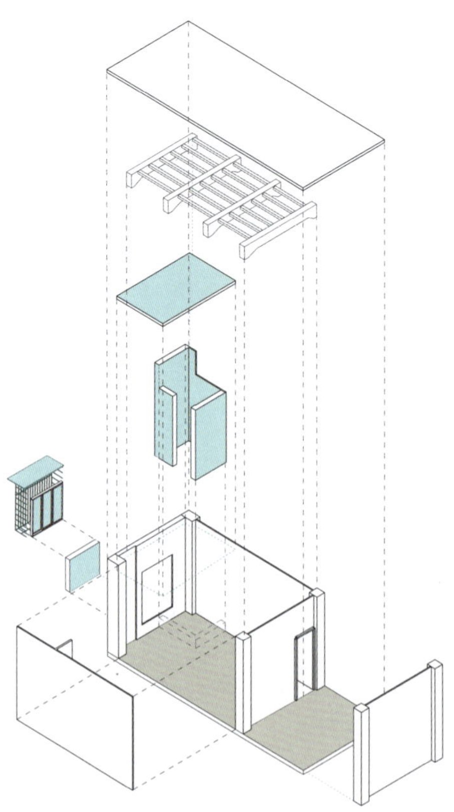

UNIT TYPE 1

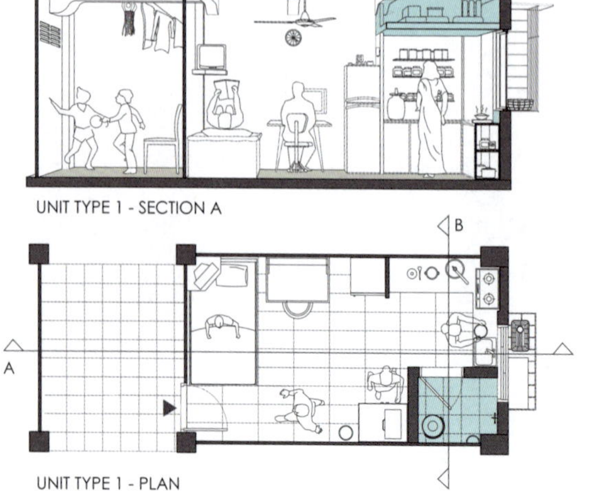

UNIT TYPE 1 - SECTION A

UNIT TYPE 1 - PLAN

UNIT TYPE 1 - SECTION B

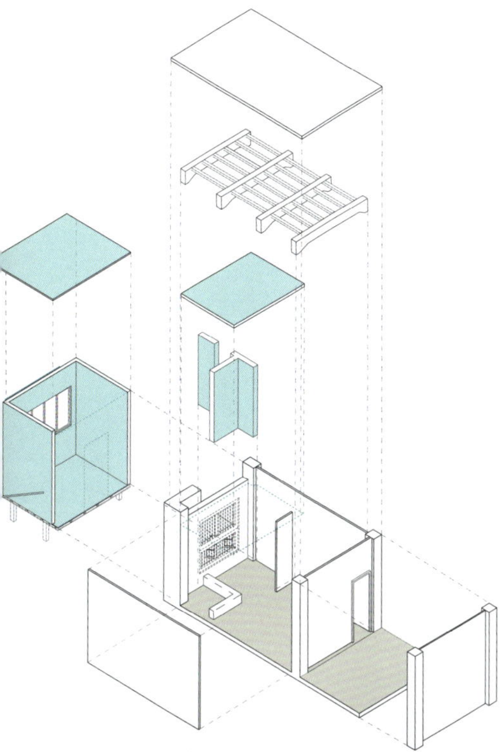

UNIT TYPE 2

UNITS

The appropriations in the cases of Units 1 and 2 are restricted to the interior and the single external face of each of these units. As a result, modifications are minor in comparison with other units in the chawl block that have a greater range of extensions incorporating multiple functions.

In these two units, residents have converted their *moris* into closed bathrooms and added lofts, as is usually the case. Additionally, Unit 2 has expanded to about one and a half times its original area. This has allowed for the creation of a multipurpose space that is used both for sleeping and as storage.

This kind of augmentation of interior space is an example of the transformation of several houses in the BDD Chawls, where entire programmes cantilever out into the common open space between buildings, as structural plug-ins to existing building frameworks.

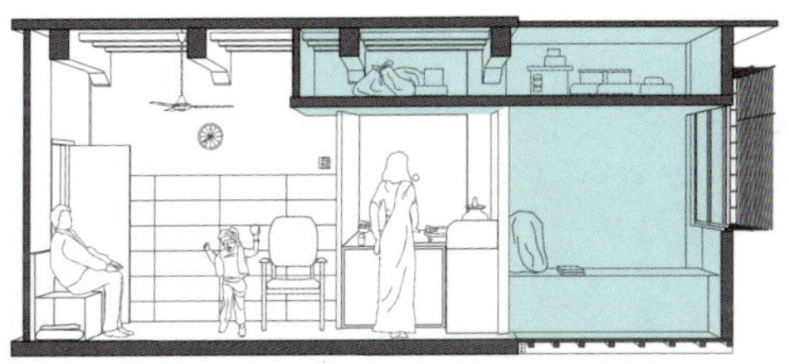

UNIT TYPE 2 - SECTION A

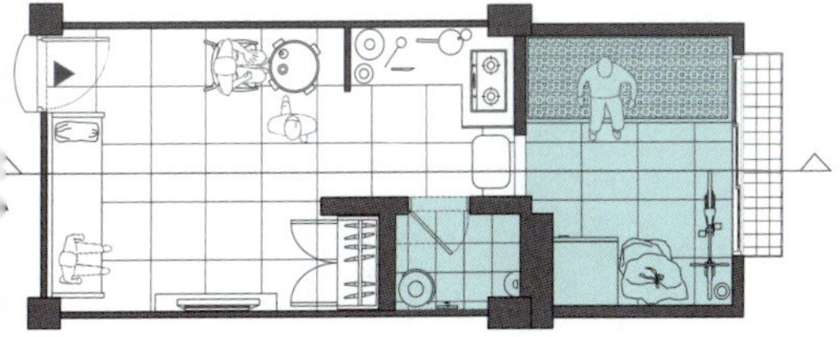

UNIT TYPE 2 - PLAN

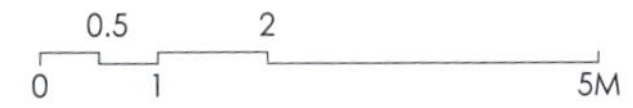

॥श्रीशिव - समर्थ॥

UNITS

Unlike units that are flanked by houses on both sides, those at the ends of the corridors have two external faces and protrusions from both. In Unit 3, a 1.4 m deep projection becomes a utility space, while a similarly large projection on the perpendicular face creates an extended living room. In the corner unit on the other side of the corridor, a kitchen – nearly half the size of the original unit – has been added.

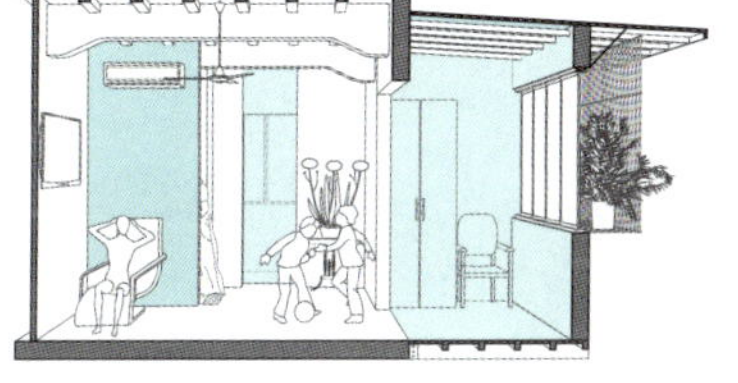

UNIT TYPE 3 - SECTION B

The floor plate extensions are the result of the construction of cantilevers as I-beams laid on existing slabs, and embedded within stone and cement infill. This raises the floor and can also be a means to distinguish one programme from another.

APPROPRIATIONS

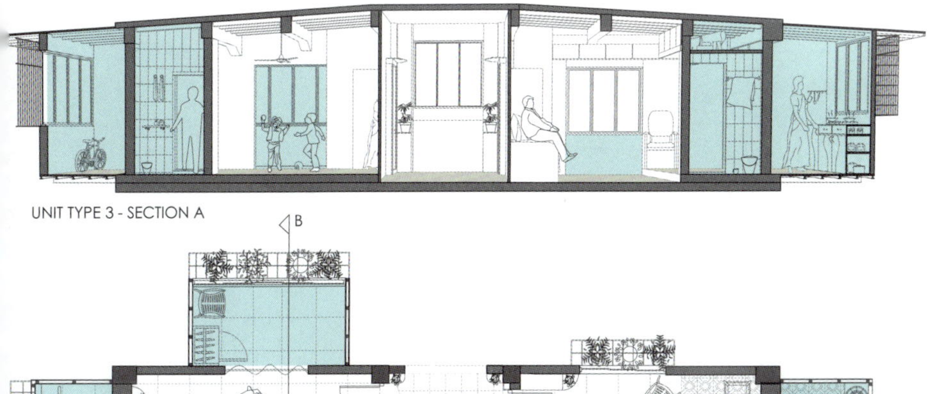

UNIT TYPE 3 - SECTION A

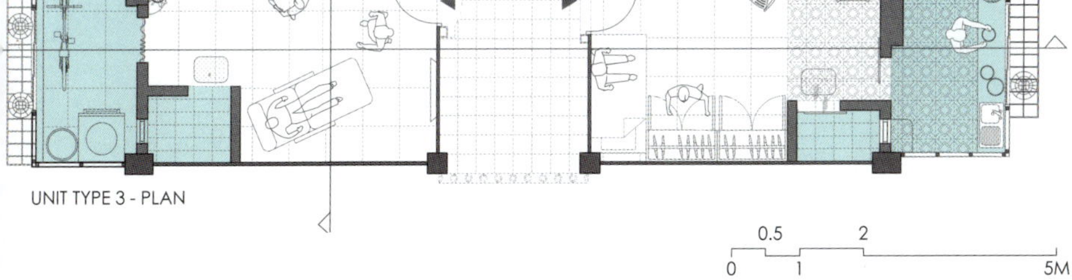

UNIT TYPE 3 - PLAN

0 0.5 1 2 5M

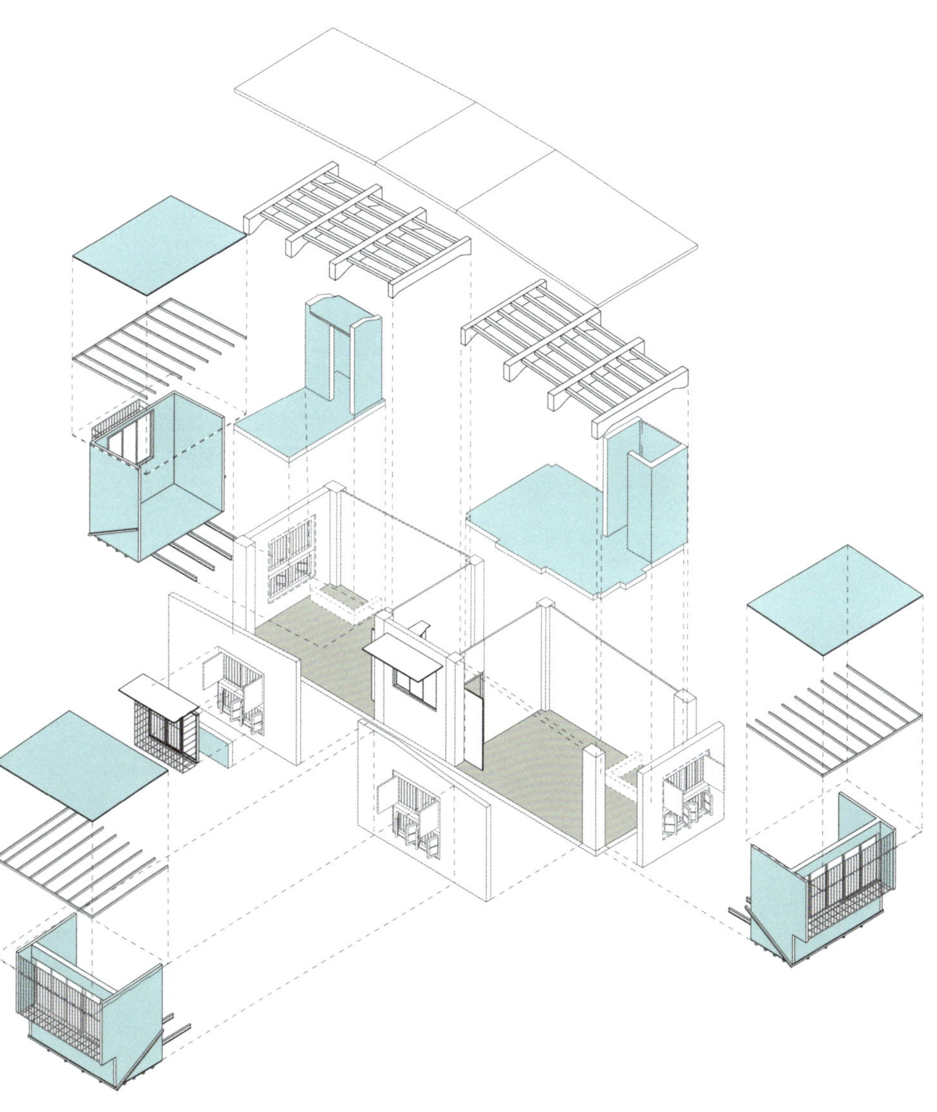

UNIT TYPE 3

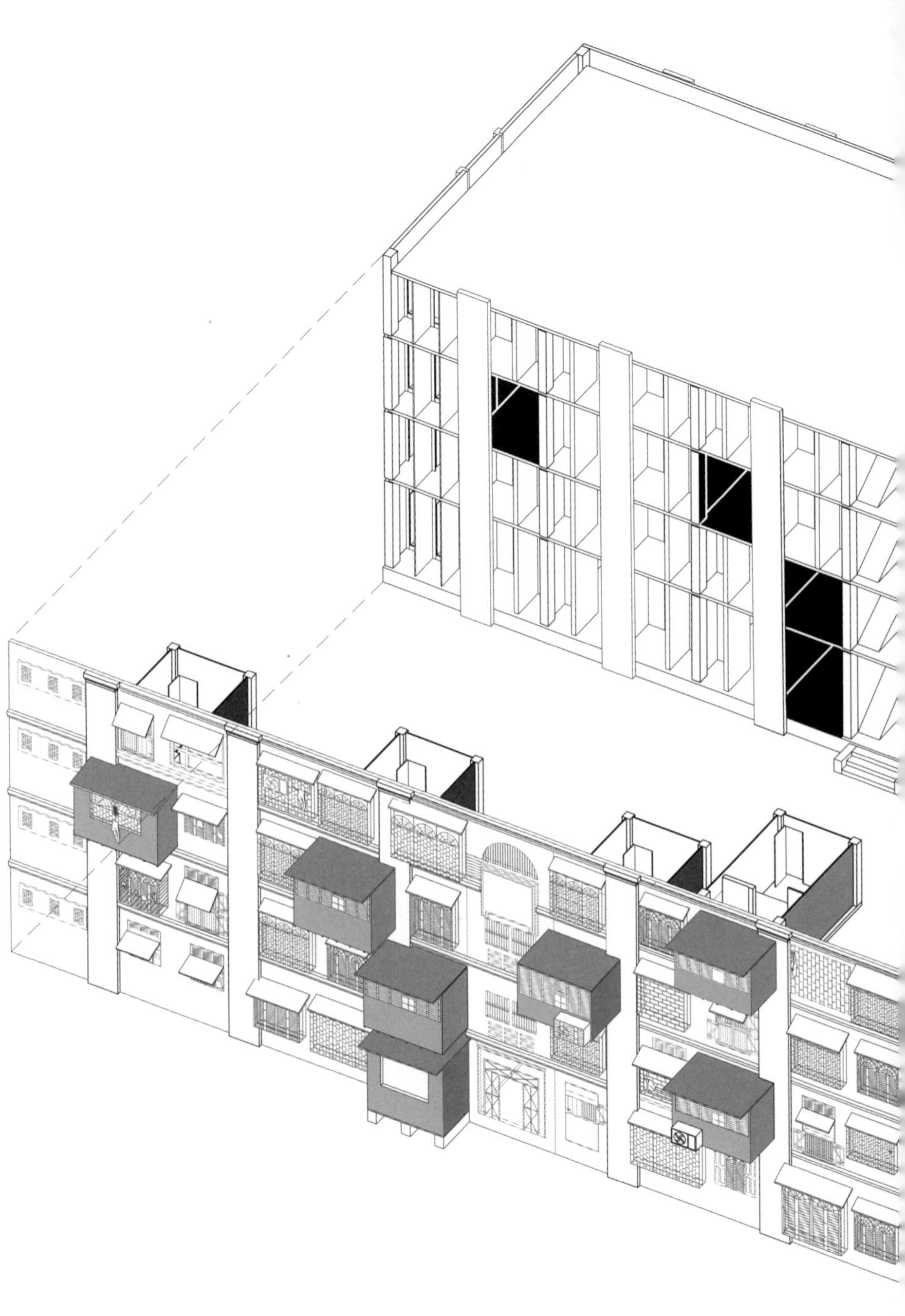

ANALYSIS

The vitality of the BDD Chawls lies in the nature of their appropriations. While originally these chawls were symbols of a colonial vision of social housing, over time they have evolved into a unique and specific construct. Contrary to what has been merely notional appropriation of common space or internal conversions in most chawls where single communities reside, here the corridors and common spaces stay uncluttered, with appropriations manifesting on the façade as bulging cantilevered extensions. The burgeoning building forms a direct commentary on the need for habitable space as demographics of families change.

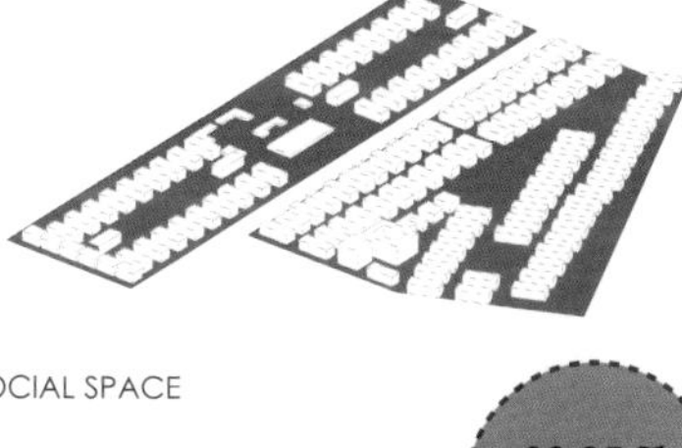

SOCIAL SPACE

90.95 %
OF B.U.A

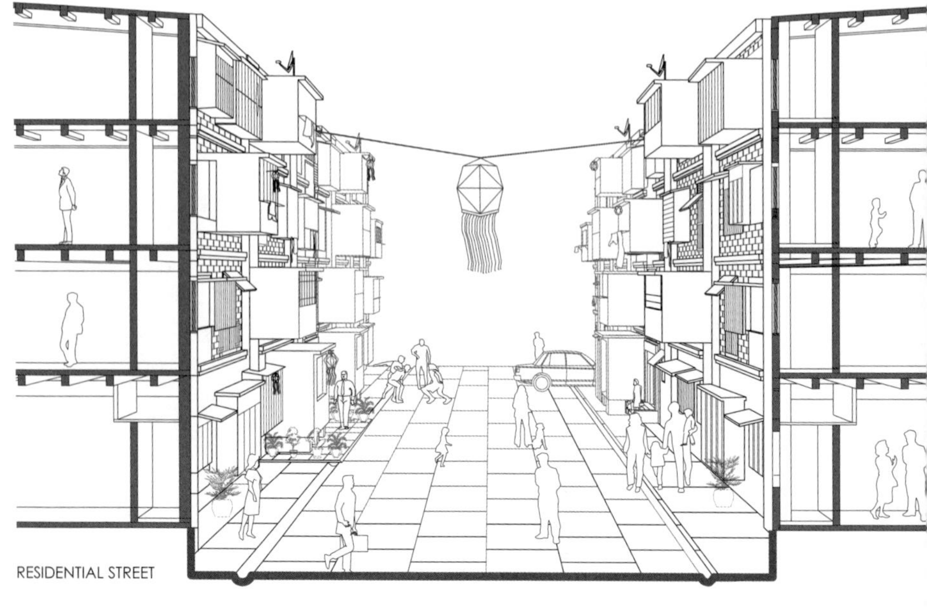

RESIDENTIAL STREET

ANALYSIS

The BDD Chawls, constructed by the government differ from private chawls in terms of built form. Unlike mill owner-built chawls that had internally incorporated courtyards, BDD has open space between regularly spaced individual structures. The open spaces were non-hierarchical, but today show a distinct change of use from public pop-up markets along arterial roads to more private social spaces as one moves inward from the main street. These spaces also function as celebratory spaces during festive occasions.

The protrusion of individual units and the appropriation of common space are testimony to the fact that the BDD Chawls, far from being outdated, are relevant models with a rich socio-cultural fabric expanding through their design framework.

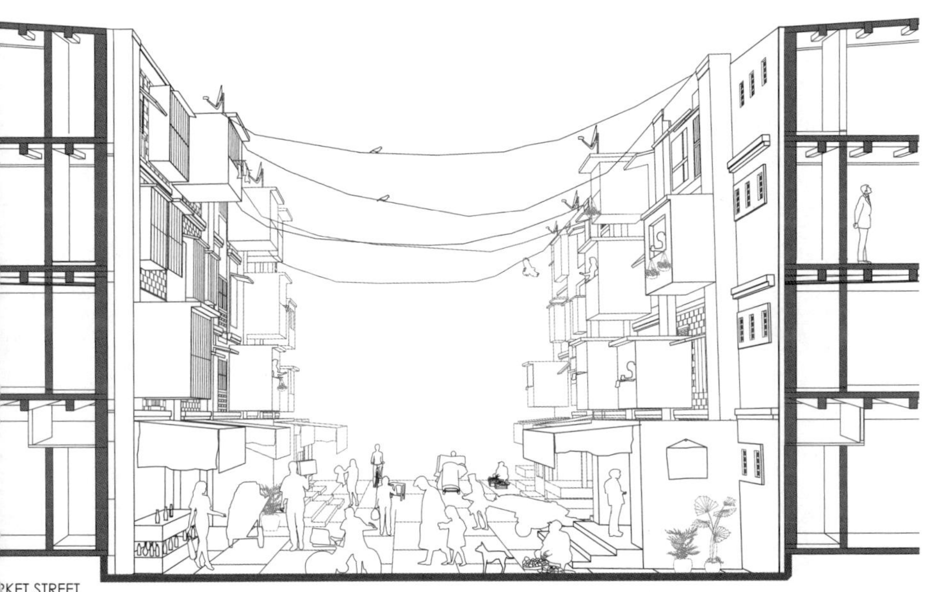

ꞦKET STREET

05
BHATIA CHAWL

05| BHATIA CHAWL

VOID AS CONNECTOR

1930

BHULESHWAR

Built in 1930 by a private trust, Bhatia Chawl was intended as accommodation for a group of Kutchis, recently migrated to the city for mercantile purposes. Being devotees of Shiva, the community built a temple housing a *linga*, adjoining the entrance to the chawl.

In 1975 the tenants bought the chawl over from the trust and formed a co-operative housing society. As some of the original inhabitants moved away, they sold their tenements in the free market and this has resulted in the community patchwork now prevalent.

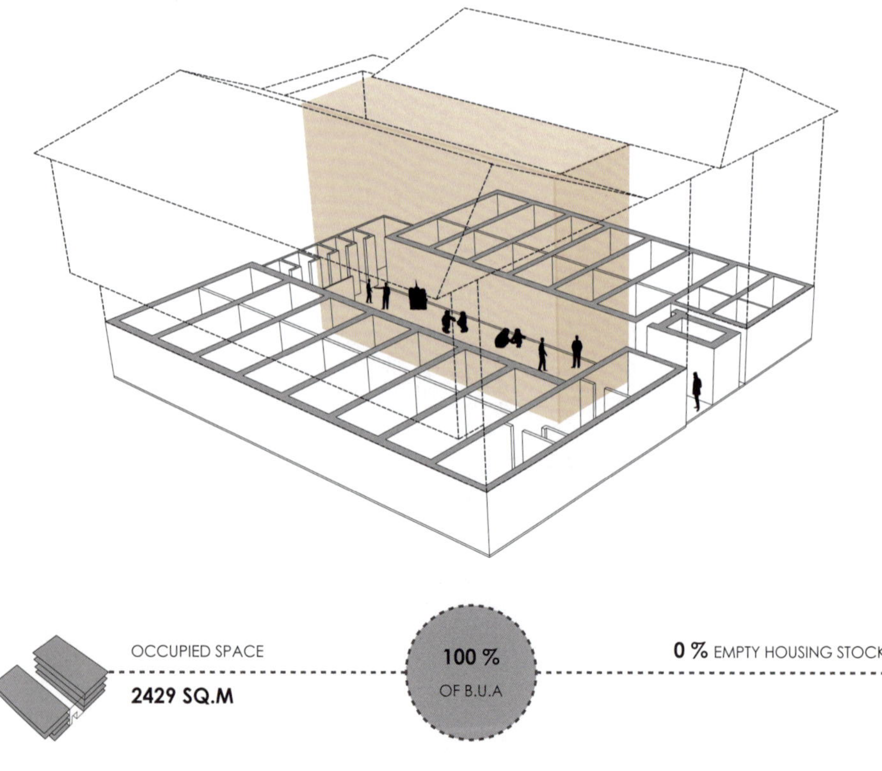

LOCATION

The chawl is located on Jagannath Shankar Seth Road in the heart of the populous inner city of Bhuleshwar. The area is occupied by several mercantile communities and is a thriving commercial district.

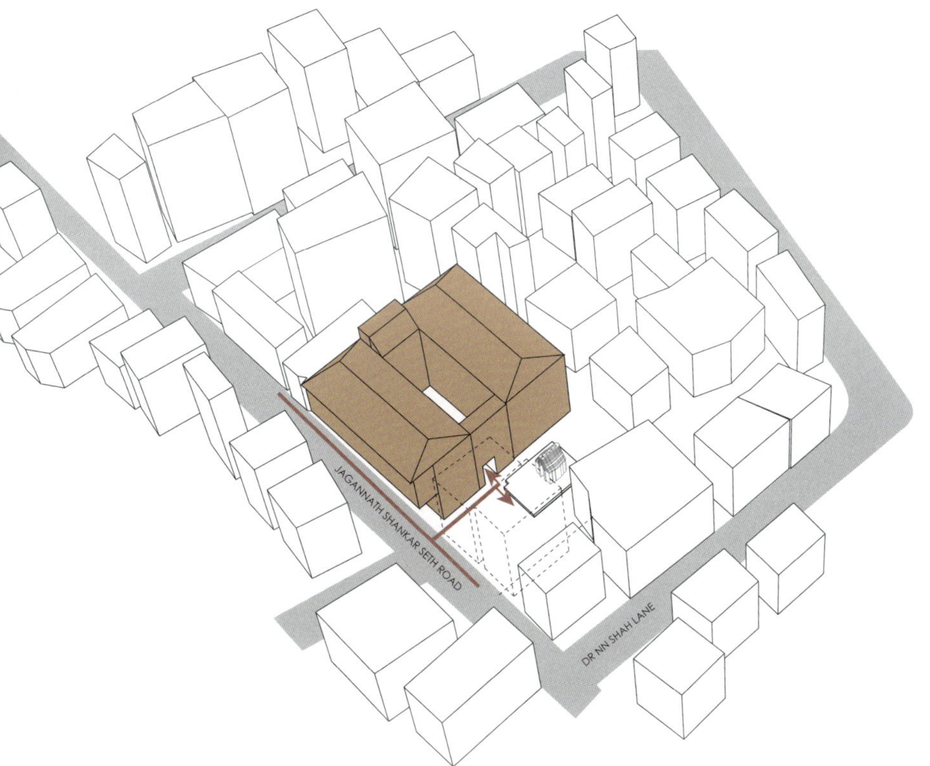

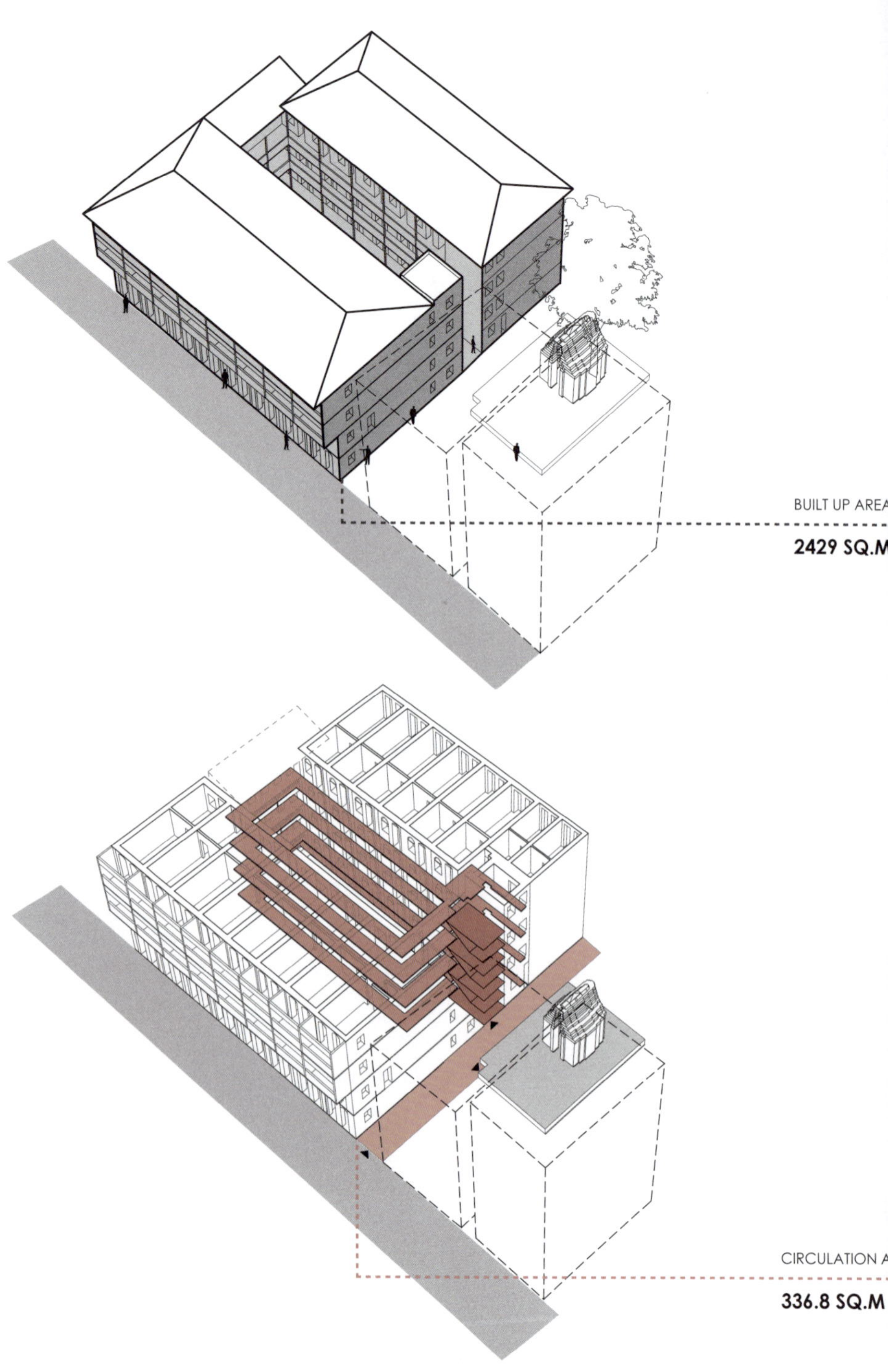
BUILT UP AREA
2429 SQ.M
CIRCULATION A
336.8 SQ.M

BUILDING FORM

Bhatia Chawl panders to the most typical image of a chawl – two parallel housing blocks looking into a central courtyard space, which forms the focus of activity within the building. The courtyard in Bhatia Chawl is completely shielded, visually and spatially, from the road and accessed from the northeast by means of a pathway.

The two blocks are connected at their ends by a strip of toilets in the southeast and a staircase in the northwest. Outside this enclosure of structures, at a distance of about 4 m to the northwest lies the temple. The plot boundary angles around it, including it within its fold. The temple, while being set slightly apart from the formal geometry of the plot, has its own circumambulatory space.

BUILT UP AREA PER PERSON

10.38 SQ.M
CONSIDERING 4 PEOPLE PER UNIT

CIRCULATION

A 2 m wide pathway from the road connects to the plot through an arched doorway and leads to a stair, set up against the backdrop of the courtyard. The pathway is partly covered by a slab, compressing visitors through a narrow access and eventually releasing them into the vertical space of the central court.

At the upper levels, the corridor wraps around the courtyard and is lined with houses, also providing access to the services block and the main stair.

13.86 %
OF B.U.A

CIRCULATION AREA PER PERSON

1.4 SQ.M
CONSIDERING 4 PEOPLE PER UNIT

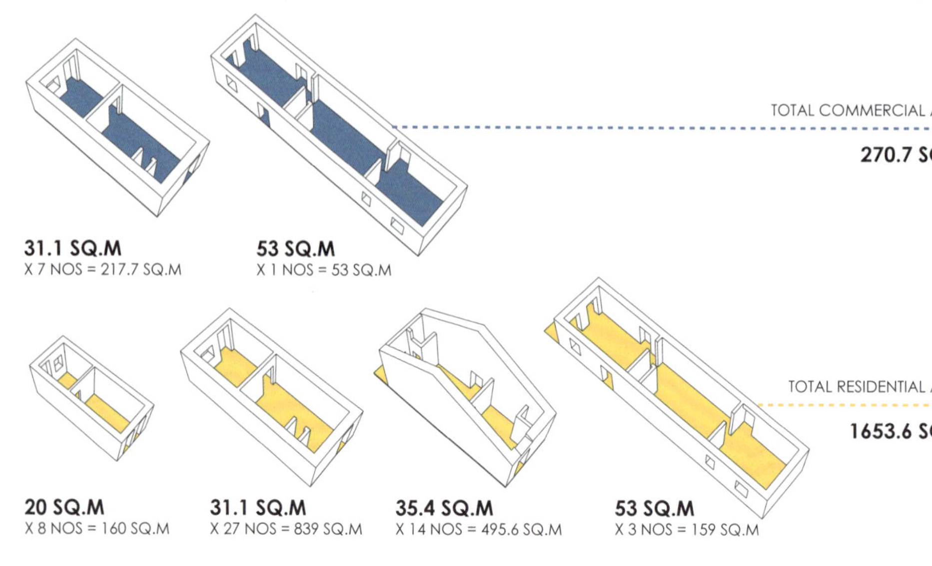
TOTAL COMMERCIAL A
270.7 SQ
31.1 SQ.M
X 7 NOS = 217.7 SQ.M
53 SQ.M
X 1 NOS = 53 SQ.M
TOTAL RESIDENTIAL A
1653.6 SQ
20 SQ.M
X 8 NOS = 160 SQ.M
31.1 SQ.M
X 27 NOS = 839 SQ.M
35.4 SQ.M
X 14 NOS = 495.6 SQ.M
53 SQ.M
X 3 NOS = 159 SQ.M

PROGRAMME

The road facing units on the ground floor are dedicated to commercial purposes, their store windows fronting the road. The rest of the units are residential.

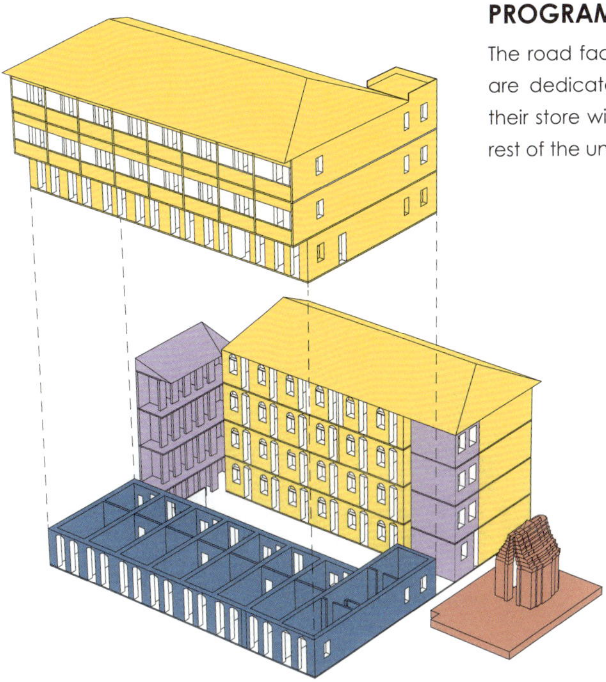

RESIDENTIAL

COMMERCIAL

SHARED SERVICES

INSTITUTIONAL

COMMUNITY

Apart from the original Kutchi Bhatias, inhabitants include Marwaris, Gujaratis and Maharashtrians.

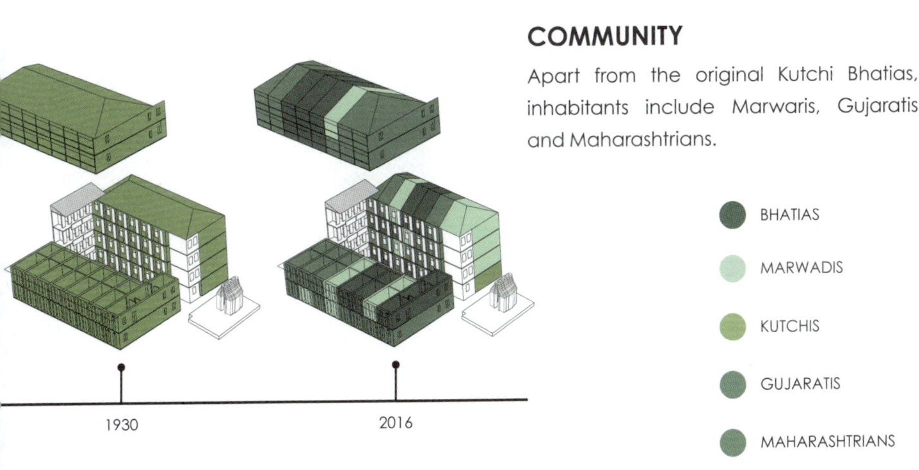

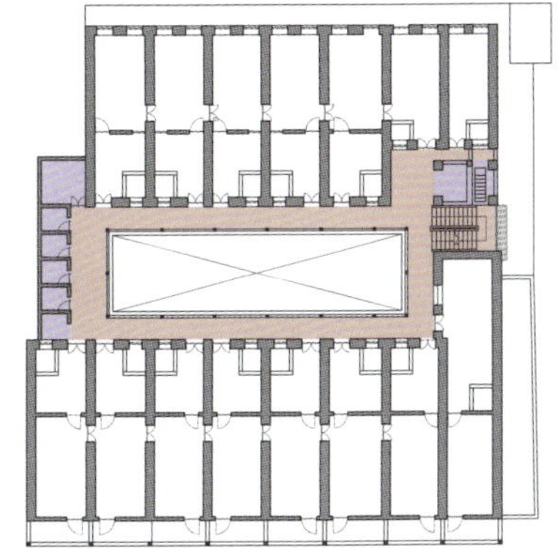

SECOND/THIRD FLOOR PLAN

FLOOR PLANS

Four storeys tall, the building contains housing units, the majority of which measure 31.1 sq.m each. The road facing façade is staggered such that the ground storey abuts the pavement with the first floor stacked above it, while the second and third floors, with projecting balconies, cantilever over the pavement below. The road facing housing units are large and medium sized while the rear block consists of medium and small units.

The interior space of each house is split by a partition wall. Originally, the entrance portion was taken up by a *mori* and kitchen, while the rear portion was used as a multipurpose space. Now however, many inhabitants have refurbished the interior, designing the front as a multipurpose space and relegating utility areas to the back of the house.

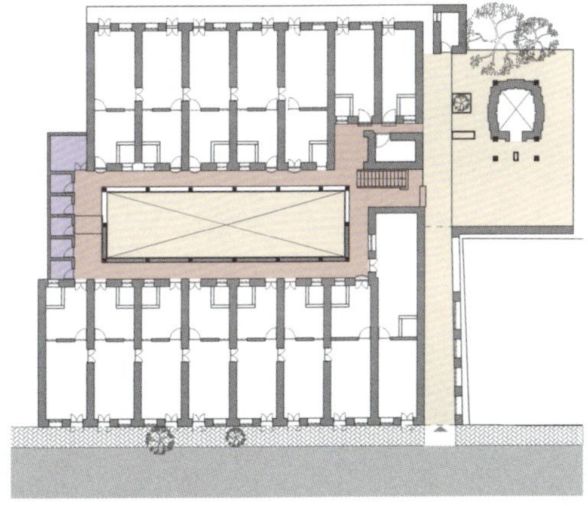

GROUND/FIRST FLOOR PLAN 0 1 2 5 10M

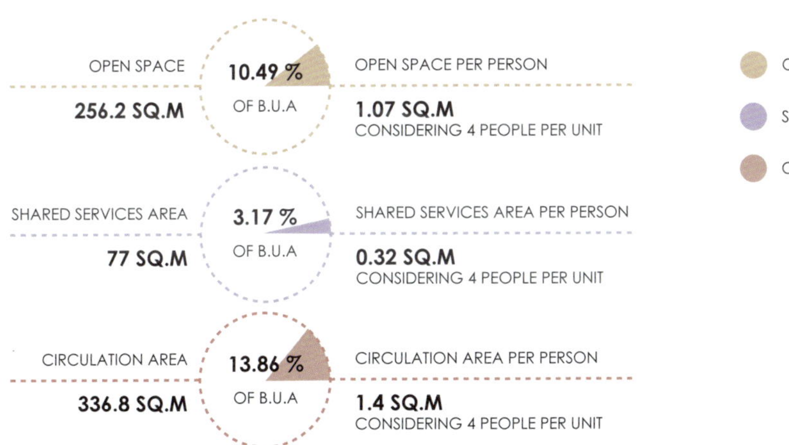

OPEN SPACE

SHARED SERVICES

CIRCULATION

NORTHEAST SIDE ELEVATION

ENTRANCE GATE

0 1 2 5M

ENVELOPE

The chawl is built out of stone masonry with posts, floors and railings out of timber. Identical in design, these railings line the external balconies of the second and third floors lending a uniformity to the upper levels that lies in sharp contrast with the commercial clutter of the ground floor.

The houses facing the street on the first floor are homogeneous with tripartite windows positioned within arched openings. The ventilators allow for hot air to move out of the interior space, while also letting in diffused light during the day, and the bottom two shutters ensure the passage of cool air at the body level while sitting and sleeping on the floor. The middle portion – used for viewing and communication – allows residents the flexibility of having a private space when desired.

The balconies of the residences on the top two storeys manifest on the façade as individual frames, each consisting of a band of pivoted ventilators supported by wooden brackets at the top and hand-crafted wooden railings at the bottom.

The arched entrance to Bhatia Chawl exhibits the original decorative grill and below it, a more recently added sliding grill door.

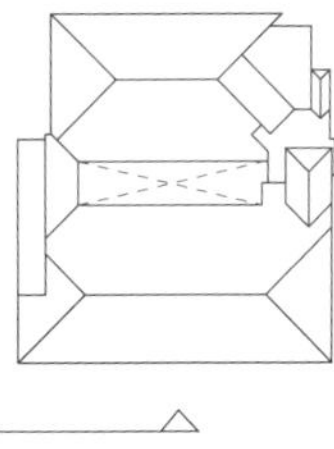

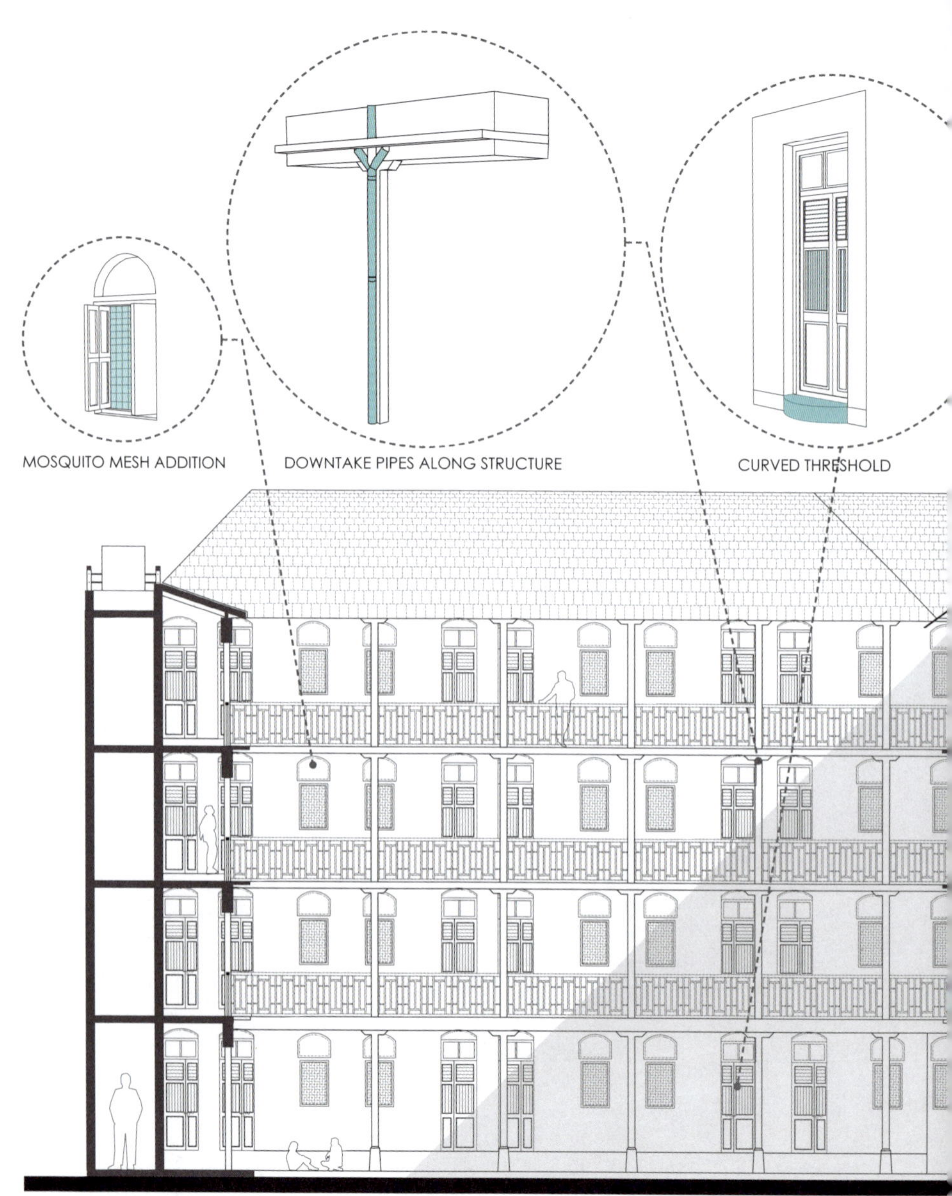

LONGITUDINAL SECTION

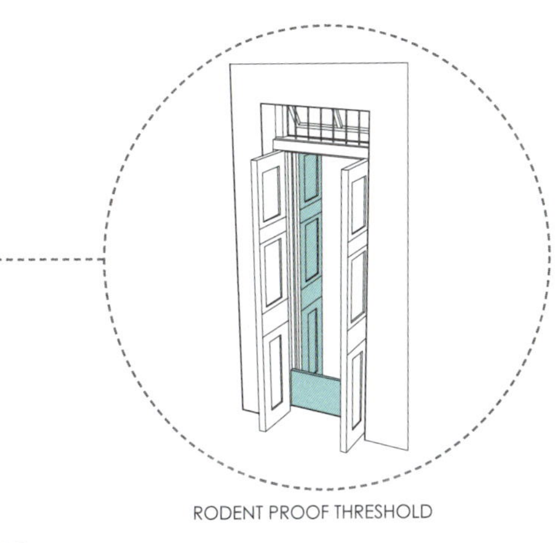

RODENT PROOF THRESHOLD

ENVELOPE

The façade overlooking the courtyard has undergone modifications that reflect the changing times and a revision in the needs of the community. Residents have fixed mosquito meshes within window openings and with the advent of more advanced sanitation systems, downtake pipes have been drawn from bathrooms. These drainage lines run along the structural grid not completely violating the system of the façade.

In some houses, the treatment of the entrance to the house is different from what it formerly was – some residents have added a curved threshold and additional grills within door panels, while others have added whole door shutters and wooden boards at the bottom of door openings. These act as a deterrent to rodents.

House owners have also treated their front walls as per their individual tastes, some using tiling as cladding and others, wooden panelling.

APPROPRIATIONS

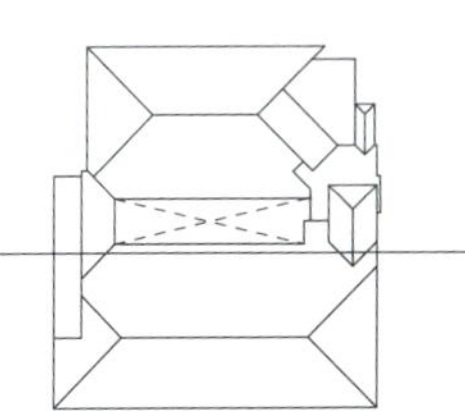

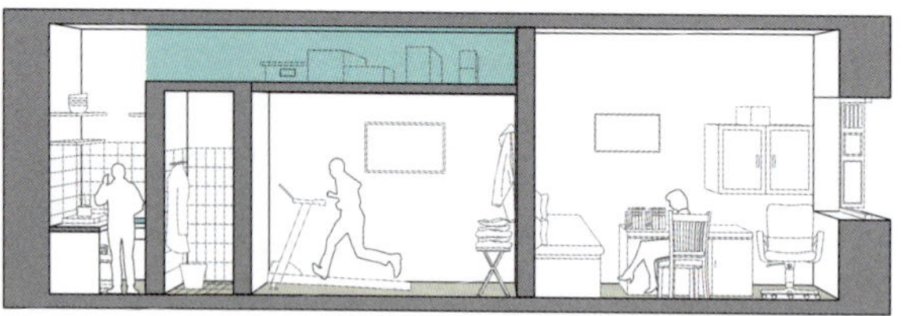

UNIT TYPE 1 - SECTION A

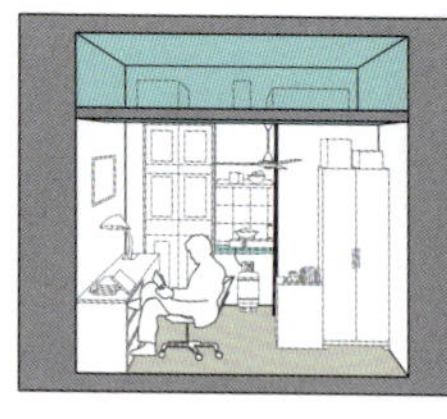

UNIT TYPE 1 - SECTION B

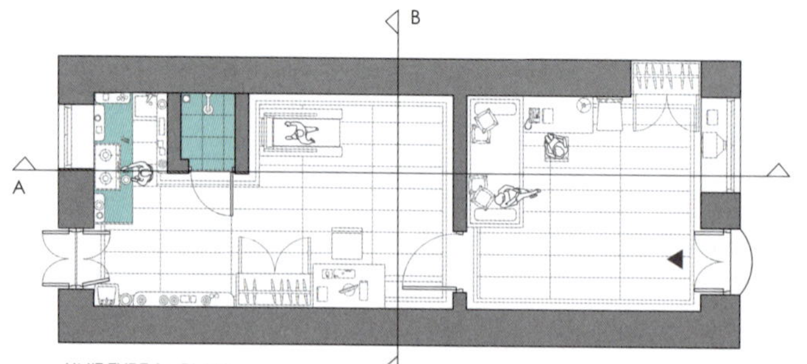

UNIT TYPE 1 - PLAN

UNIT TYPE 2 - SECTION A

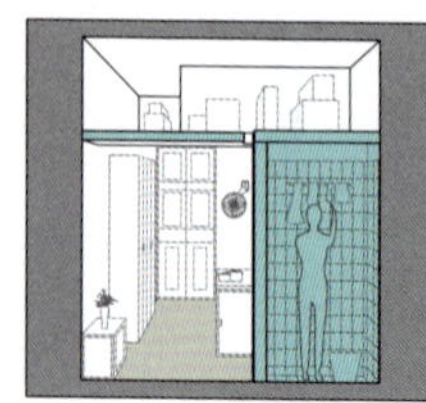

UNIT TYPE 2 - SECTION B

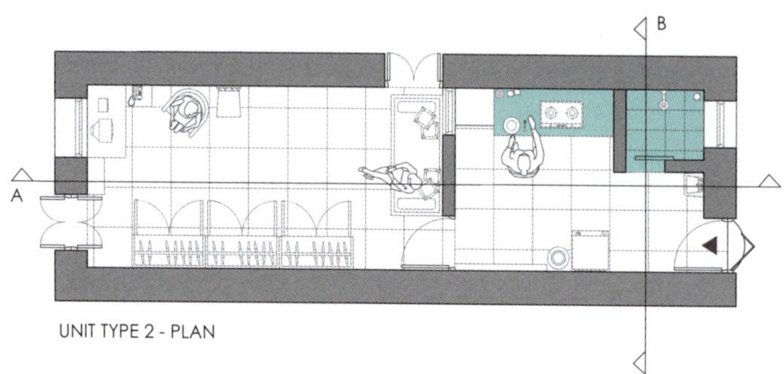

UNIT TYPE 2 - PLAN

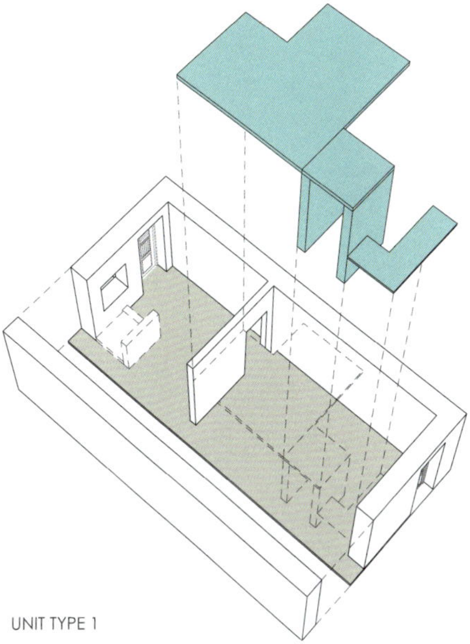

UNITS

Most appropriations are the same across the board. In Unit types 1 and 2 – both 31.1 sq.m in area – *moris* have been built up to form full-fledged bathrooms, and loft slabs and kitchen counters have been incorporated.

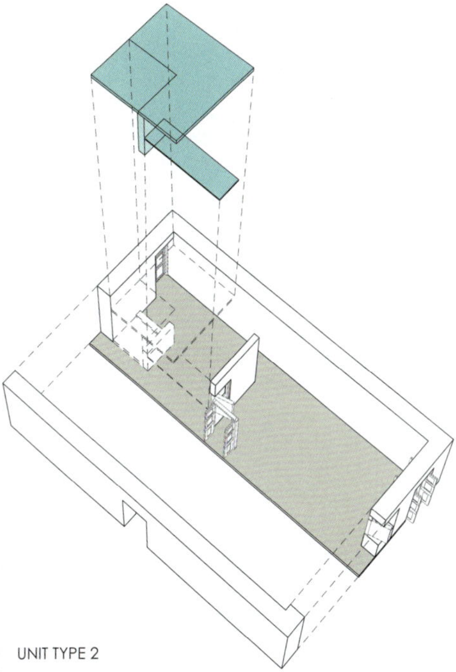

Unit 1 is a ground floor house accessed from the verandah, its original plan in two parts – the front used as a living space and the far end, for storage and services. The *mori* has been moved from its original position near the entrance to the far end.

Unit 2 lies adjacent to Unit 1. Here services and storage are on entry, and a multipurpose space at the rear. In this case the kitchen counter and bathroom are distributed along the length of the front portion.

In both units, the height above the loft is insufficient for habitation and is used as an additional storage area.

APPROPRIATIONS

UNIT TYPE 1

UNIT TYPE 2

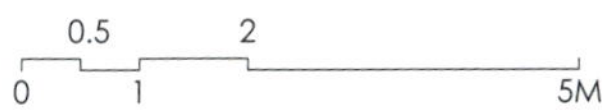

UNITS

35.4 sq.m Unit 3 is at the topmost level of the road facing block. Its pitched roof accommodates a loft that is used as an additional sleep space. This level is accessed by means of a unique collapsible ladder, in which individual rungs are hinged on a frame, which in turn is hinged on the wall. As a result – in an ingenious use of space – when the ladder is not in use, it is folded on itself and fastened to the wall.

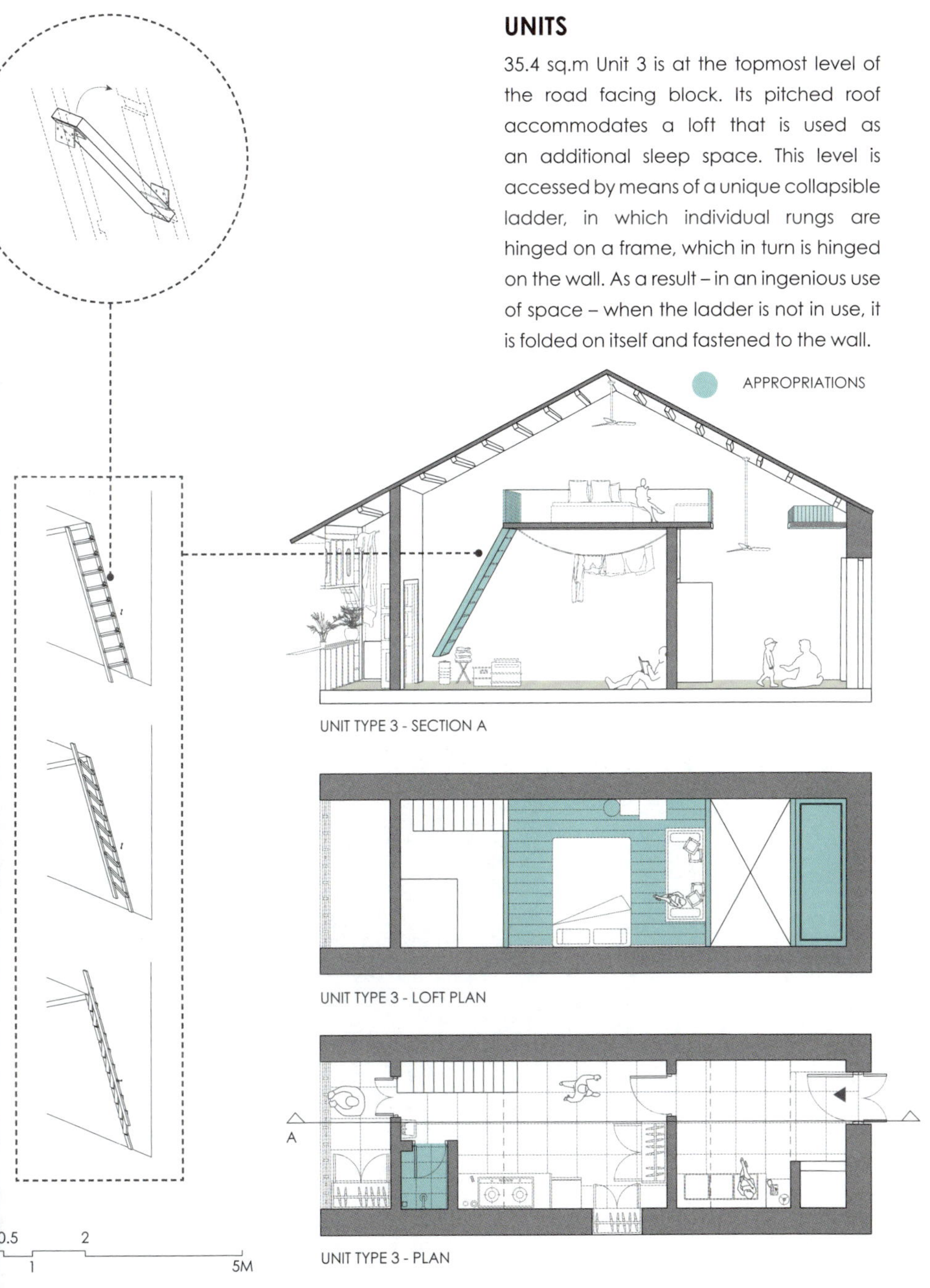

UNIT TYPE 3 - SECTION A

UNIT TYPE 3 - LOFT PLAN

UNIT TYPE 3 - PLAN

UNITS

Measuring 53 sq.m in area, Unit 4 owes its elongated form and sizeable area to its position within the plan. Located on the first floor in the road facing block where the building form modulates to provide privacy to the courtyard, this unit is duplicated from ground to third floor level – in the same position on every floor. There are separate spaces for sleep and common activities, and a balcony that overlooks the road. Alterations and additions include a kitchen counter and built up *mori*.

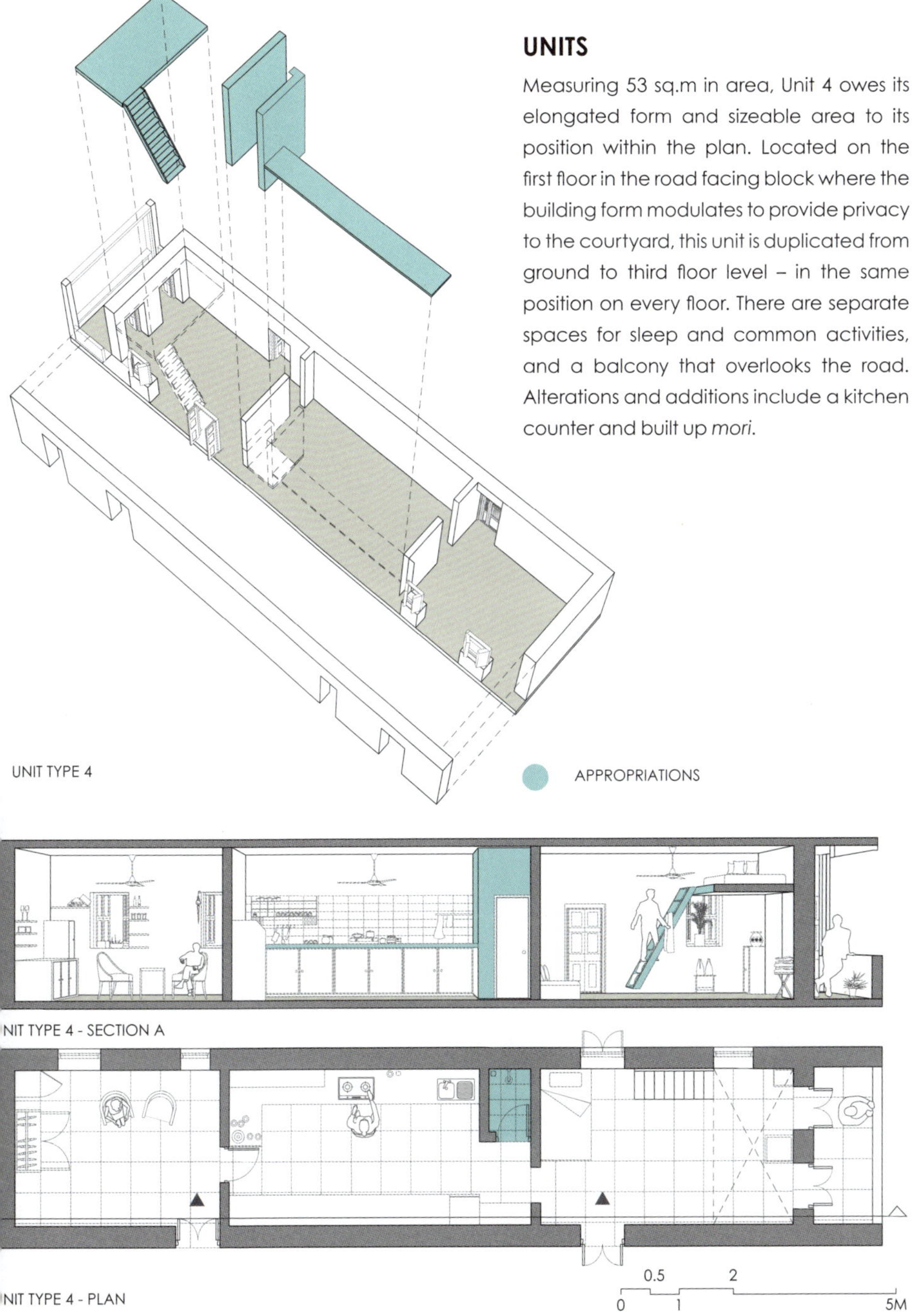

ANALYSIS

Bhatia Chawl's programmatic division defines the way its inhabitants interact with the public, as well as with one another within the chawl. The commercial façade engages with the street through the shop front, while the proportions of the open courtyard create the possibility of interaction across its volume.

Insular and inward looking, the housing units collectively focus on the courtyard at their centre, the volume of which rises uninterrupted through the height of the chawl. At the scale of the individual units the level of interaction is through the verandah and corridors. The sectional proximity of these corridors across the courtyard creates an intimacy between occupants, influencing the nature of the social fabric. Defined by the structural system of the wooden posts and beams, they frame an embedded social space.

The temple has been positioned such that the entrance to the chawl faces it. This, while indicative of the temple being an extension of the chawl, marks it out as separate, further reinforcing the notion of the chawl's insular nature. Thus from its built form – corridors, courtyard, intimacy of scale and siting in the larger scheme – there emerges a distinct community fabric that is a function of its architecture.

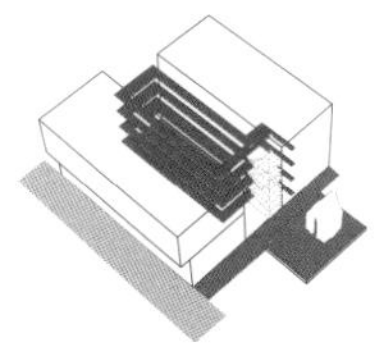

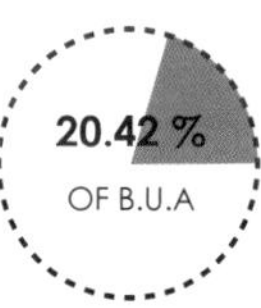

SOCIAL SPACE

DORAEMON

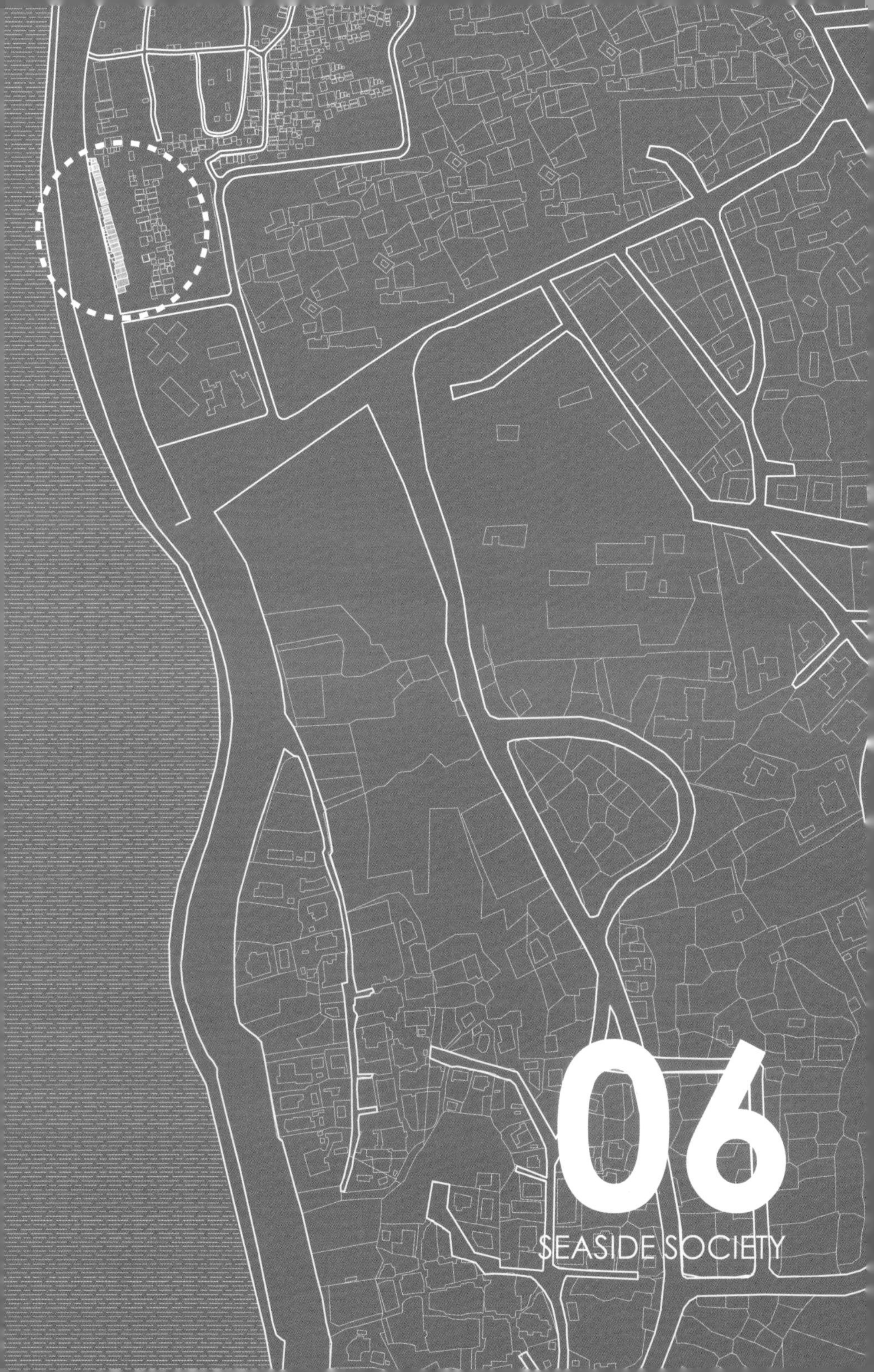

06

SEASIDE SOCIETY

06 | SEASIDE SOCIETY

SLIM CITY
1970
BANDRA

Seaside Society sprung up as an informal pavement settlement around 1970. It is populated by over 30 families from Maharashtra, Gujarat, Delhi and Uttar Pradesh. These families work in blue collar jobs, in most cases within walking and cycling distance of the settlement.

The settlement originally consisted of only a few houses, but with time has grown – more families have moved in and existing ones have added upper levels. In many cases, one of the levels has been given out on rent, with the owners staying on either the first or ground floor, and renting out the other for commercial or residential purposes.

Each house has a tap so the residents no longer depend on the common tap in the cemetery behind the settlement. Many owners have also built toilets outside their houses.

Being an informal homegrown settlement, there is no legal mechanism of lease, tenure and ownership. The inhabitants are occupiers of the land but do not own it.

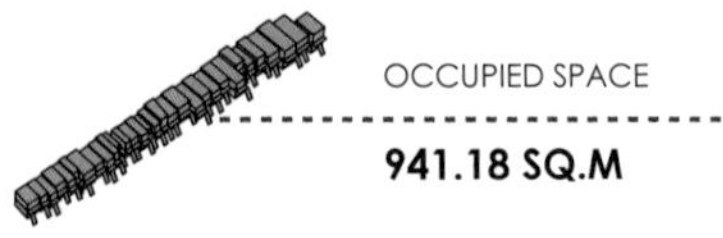

OCCUPIED SPACE

941.18 SQ.M

100 %
OF B.U.A

0 % EMPTY HOUSING STOCK

LOCATION

Seaside Society is laid out in the north-south direction and fronts Carter Road in Bandra, with Khar Danda to its north. The length of the settlement abuts a Buddhist burial ground along its rear.

Seaside Society is contiguous with another slum, Seaface Society at its south end.

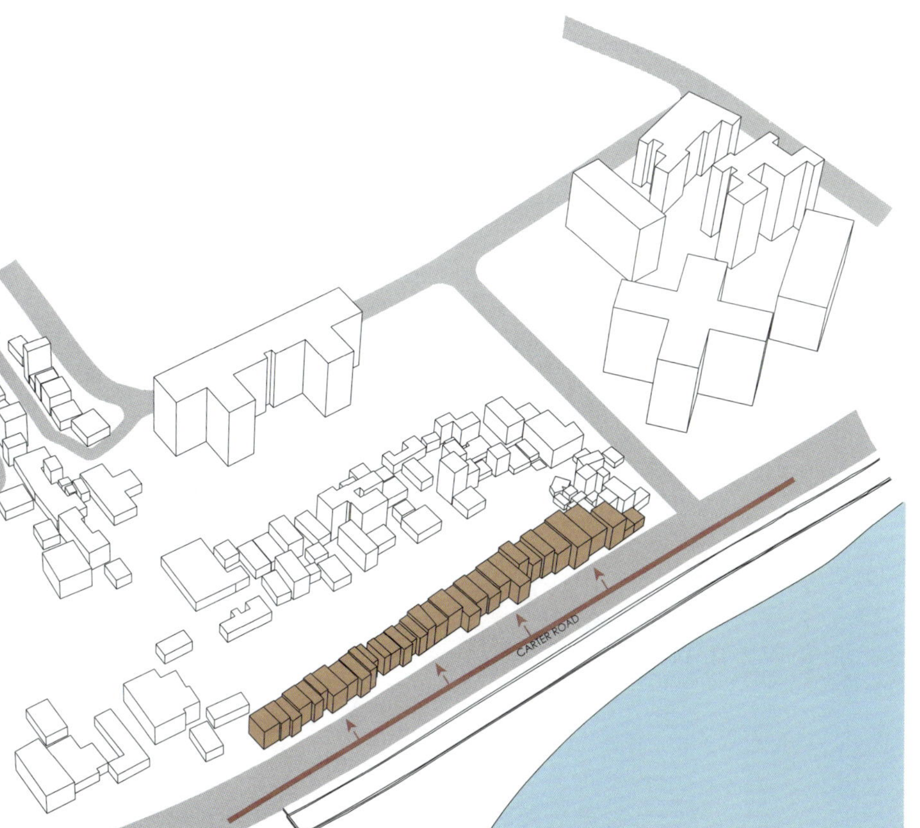

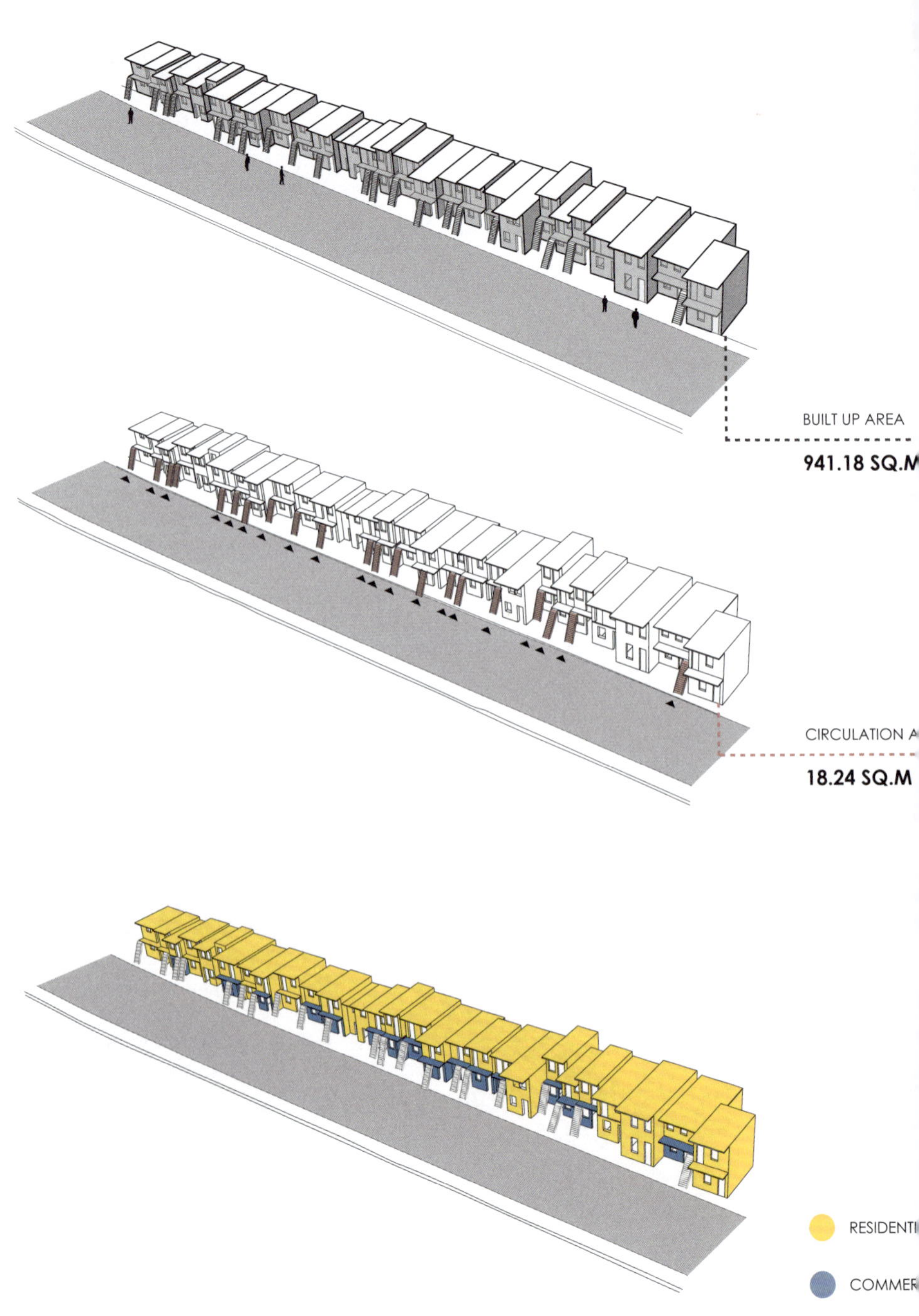

BUILT UP AREA
941.18 SQ.M
CIRCULATION A
18.24 SQ.M
RESIDENTI
COMMER

BUILDING FORM

The settlement – formally a thin sliver clinging to the road edge – is a tightly knit set of live-and-work spaces arranged in a row with first floor units in most cases residential, stacked above ground floor commercial programmes. Every unit has access to light and ventilation along its width and the settlement has developed as a row of staggered units, so that the quality and quantity of open space in front of each one varies. In the case of commercial units, the stepping back in plan creates space for allied activities, be it cycle repair or customer benches for a tea stall.

CIRCULATION

The entire settlement sets back from the road with offsets ranging from 1 m to 2.5 m. The setback is used as storage space for water tanks and in commercial units, as an extension of the internal transaction space. In most cases, different families reside on each of the floors, access to the upper levels enabled by means of individual external ladders.

PROGRAMME

Most ground floor units are used for commercial purposes, and the units above them are used as residences. Many owners have built adjoining toilets accessed from outside their houses.

BUILT UP AREA PER PERSON

2.41 SQ.M
CONSIDERING 5 PEOPLE PER UNIT

1.94 %
OF B.U.A

CIRCULATION AREA PER PERSON

0.05 SQ.M
CONSIDERING 5 PEOPLE PER UNIT

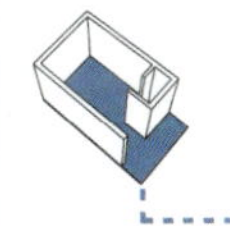

TOTAL COMMERCIAL AREA

183.26 SQ.M

78 SQ.M
NOS = 183.26 SQ.M

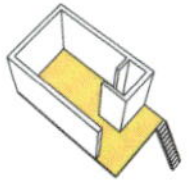

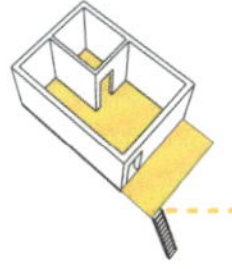

78 SQ.M
NOS = 150.92 SQ.M

12.8 SQ.M
X 9 NOS = 115.2 SQ.M

11.8 SQ.M
X 31 NOS = 365.8 SQ.M

14 SQ.M
X 9 NOS = 126 SQ.M

TOTAL RESIDENTIAL AREA

757.92 SQ.M

J.S AIR COOL
श्री साई बाबा
ऑटो पार्ट्स

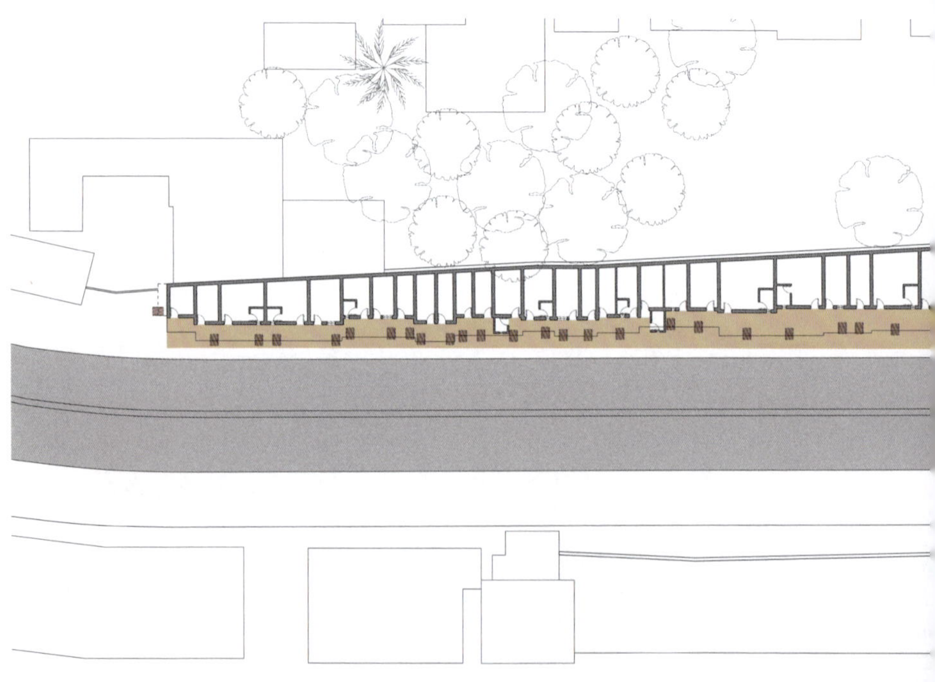

GROUND FLOOR PLAN

OPEN SPACE

198.95 SQ.M

21.14 %

OF B.U.A

OPEN SPACE PER PERSON

0.5 SQ.M

CONSIDERING 5 PEOPLE PER UNIT

SHARED SERVICES AREA

0 SQ.M

0 %

OF B.U.A

FLOOR PLAN

On the ground floor, commercial units have an open face fronting the road, and residential units are larger and multipurpose in nature – a single room devoid of partitions. The same plan is repeated on the level above, and accessed in all cases by an external ladder.

Outside the constructed space of their homes, inhabitants have personalised their porches by laying potted plants or incorporating various forms of signage for their commercial activities.

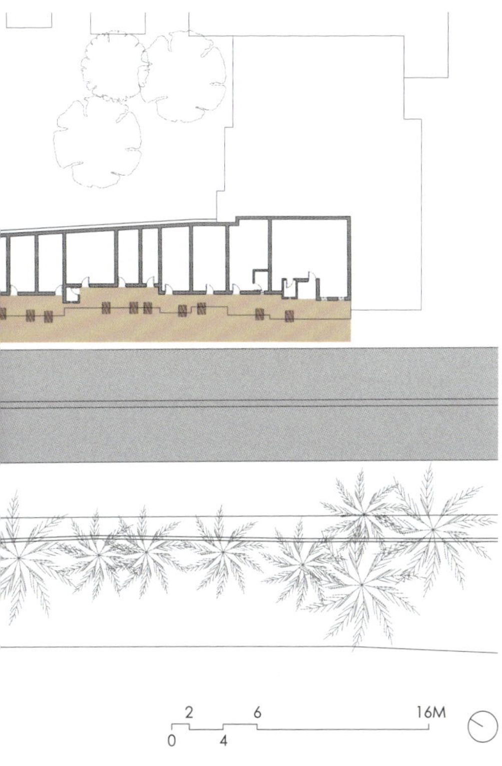

OPEN SPACE

CIRCULATION

RED SERVICES AREA PER PERSON

Q.M

NSIDERING 5 PEOPLE PER UNIT

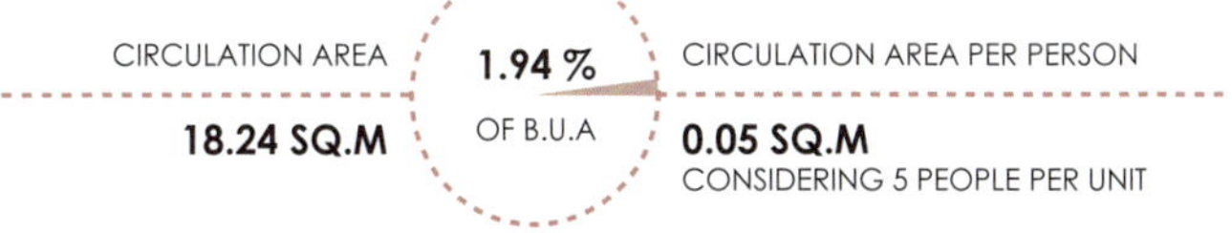

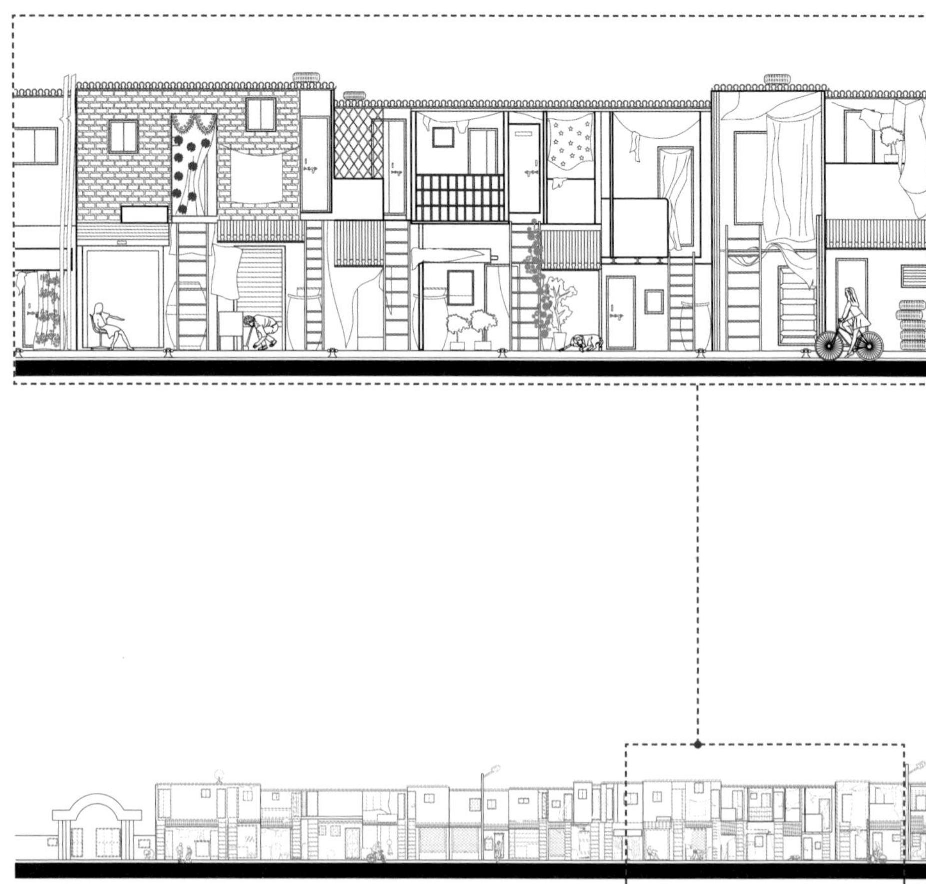

WEST SIDE ELEVATION

ENVELOPE

Seaside Society is characterised by a multitude of units arranged shoulder-to-shoulder with their neighbours; each house set apart from the others by virtue of its personalised façade and customisation. Details like artwork on the façade, banners and colourful curtains are markers of variety. Owners have painted their external walls in colours different from their neighbours' with the intention of demarcating personal space. Attempts such as these give a sense of ownership that state-provided formal housing leaves little room for.

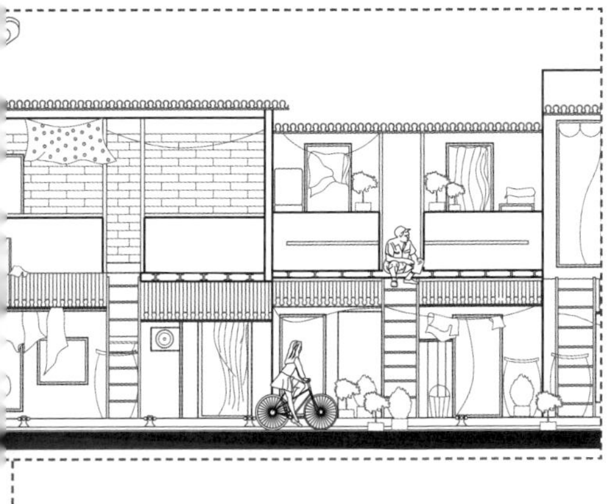

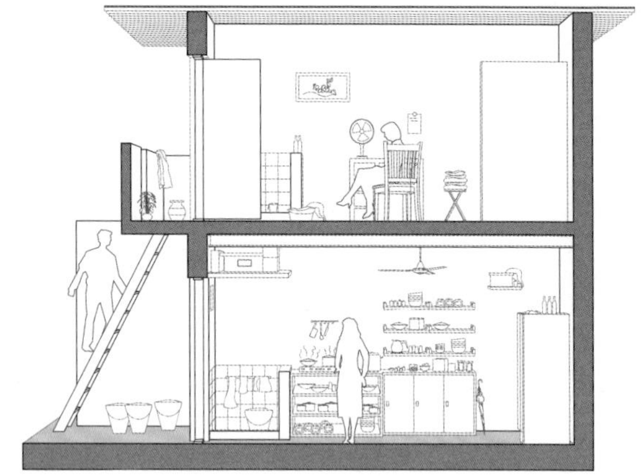

SECTION A

UNIT TYPES 1 AND 2 - FIRST FLOOR PLAN

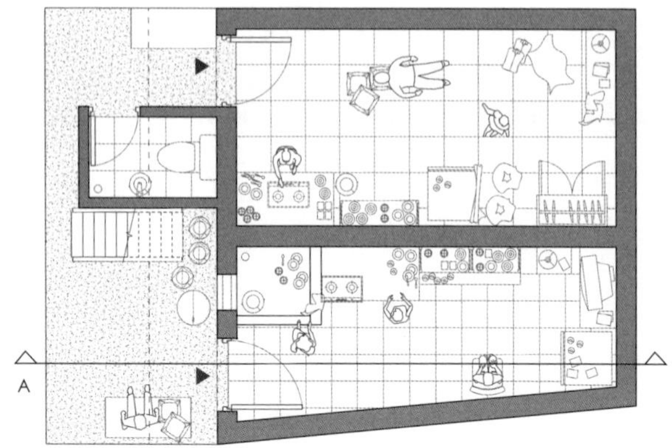

UNIT TYPES 1 AND 2 - GROUND FLOOR PLAN

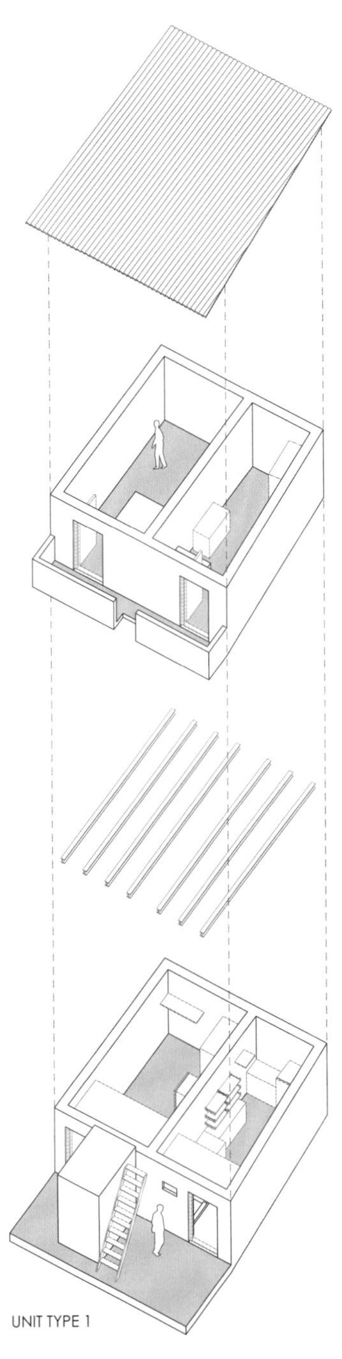

UNIT TYPE 1

UNITS

Being homegrown and designed by the owners themselves, the entire built fabric is incremental with constant modifications and appropriations. Inhabitants fashion their space as per their individual needs at a given time.

The units studied are four distinct living spaces, two on the ground floor and two above, one of which is rented out. Much of the household activity – like washing clothes and utensils and chopping vegetables – takes place in the setback from the street or on the street itself, and the interior of each of the four houses is a multipurpose room – utilised mainly as a sleep-cum-kitchen space with cupboards backed up against the walls.

The external toilet on the ground floor is an example of bathrooms that are proliferating the elevation of Seaside Society. In many houses, *moris* were incorporated in the original designs, and – as seen in the case of the rental unit – some of these have now been converted into internal toilets.

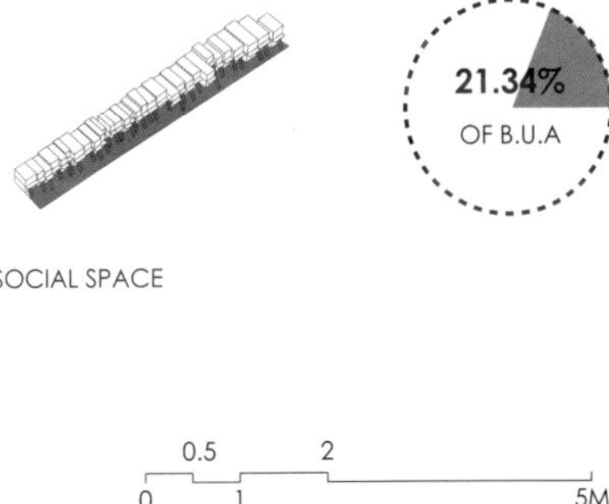

SOCIAL SPACE

0.5 2
0 1 5M

श्री साई बाबा

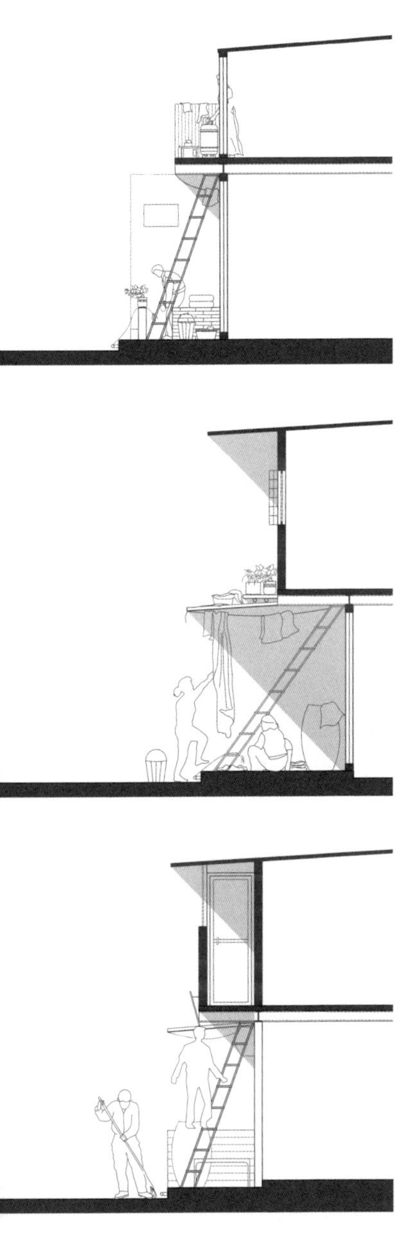

ANALYSIS

Seaside Society is an example of an informal settlement that has grown in the form of hybrid row houses with extreme customisation. Thus, the character of living space differs from house to house, in terms of articles on the façade and adornments, leading to a rich and personalised built form. Settlements like this are symptomatic of gaps within the state's planning strategy and also instructive as models of urbanism that need validation as future urban typologies.

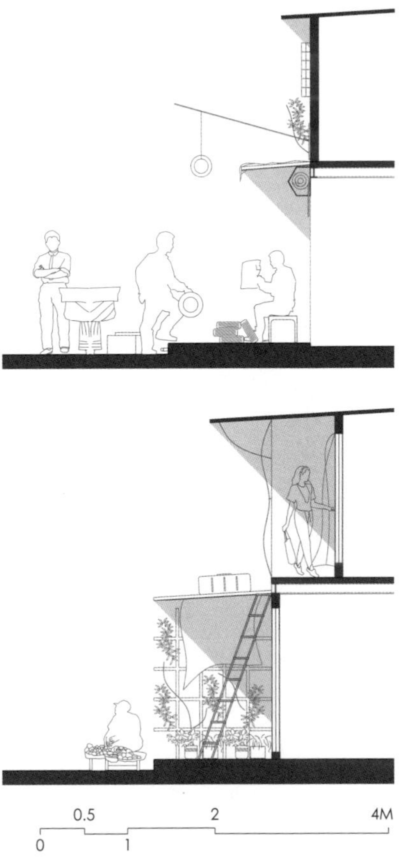

बौध्द स्मशान भूमि ट्रस्ट
यांचे
हार्दिक अभिनंदन
शुभेच्छुक
राहुल विजय असावा
SARDAR

07
RK CHAWL

07 | RK CHAWL

CORRIDOR AS A LIVING ROOM

1980
KHETWADI

Built in 1980, RK Chawl is a comparatively new addition in chawl typology. In keeping with the times, it has been constructed in RCC (Reinforced Cement Concrete) as opposed to materials like timber and stone, that are seen in older chawls.

The construction of RK Chawl at a time when this typology was in sharp decline is a rare occurrence but is indicative of the relevance of this housing type within contemporary contexts.

The original inhabitants and owners of the units were from the Gujarati community, and even today are predominantly so.

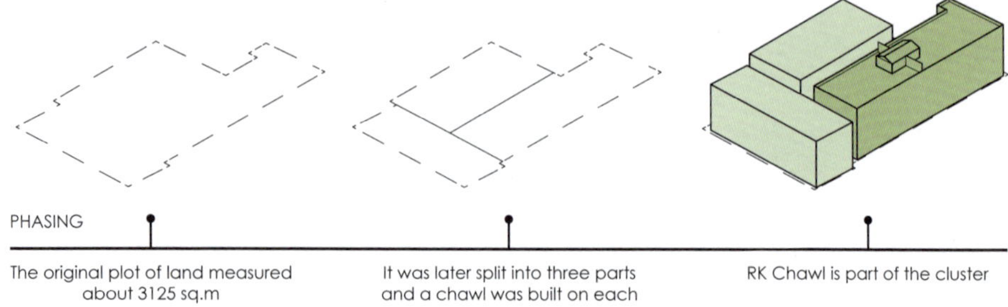

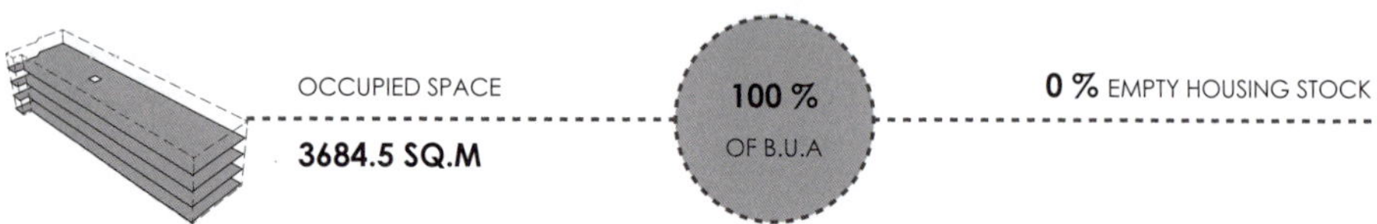

LOCATION

The chawl building is one of three structures built by the same developer, and is located in Khetwadi, a predominantly Gujarati neighbourhood.

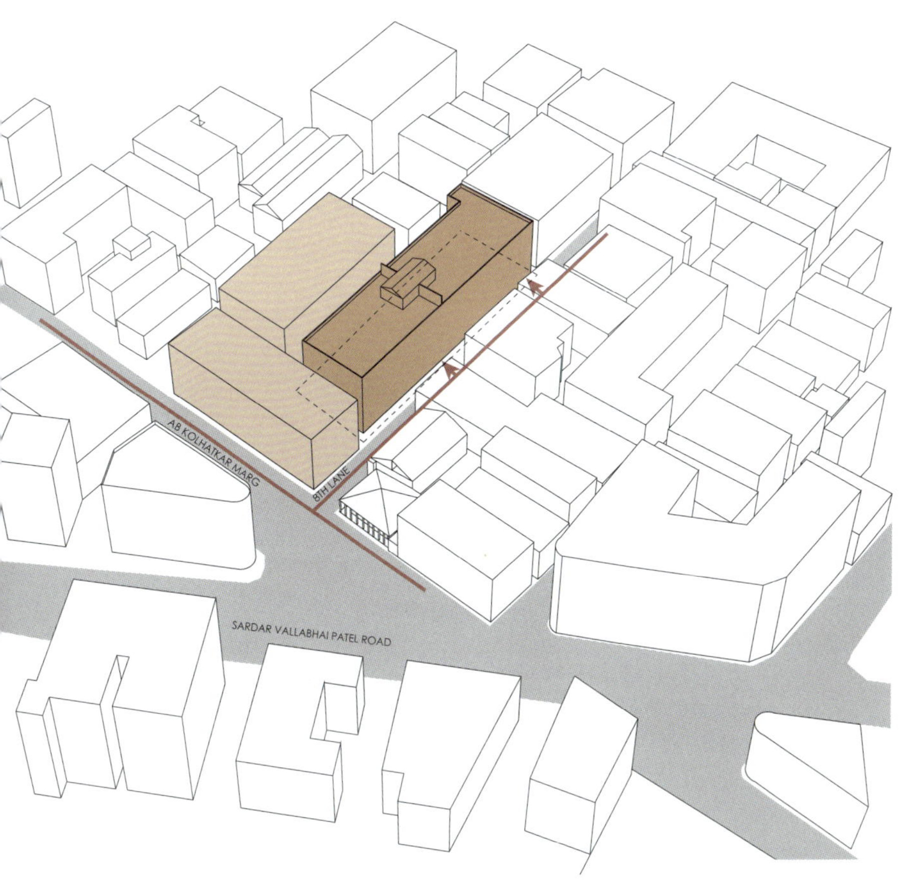

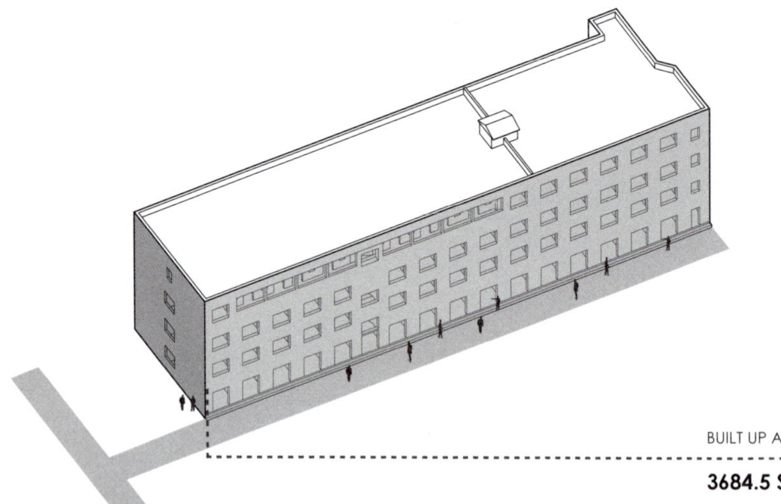

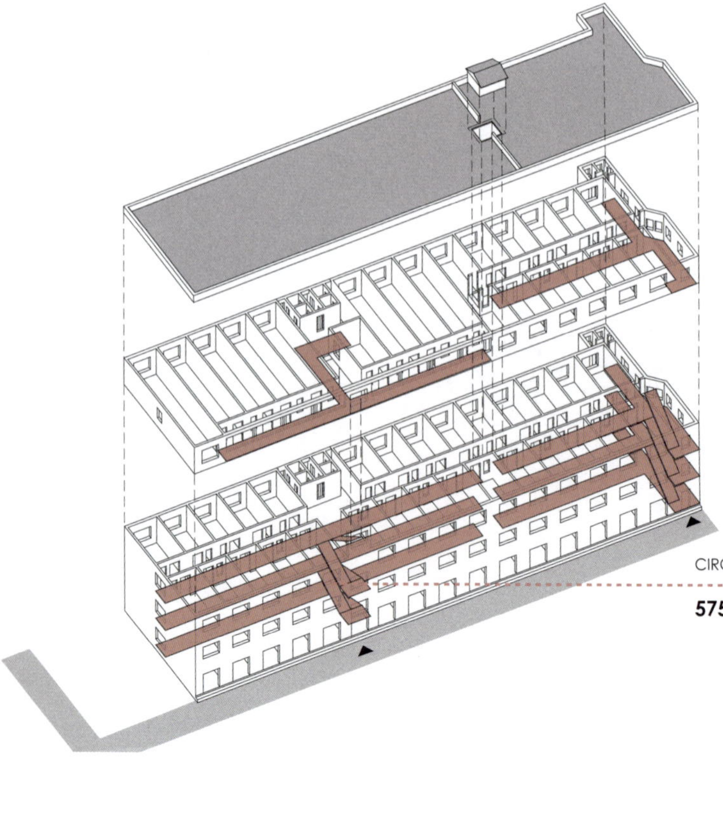

CIRCULATION A

575.6 SQ.M

BUILDING FORM

RK Chawl is a simple four storey rectilinear block with two wings, perfectly aligned but internally separated by a small square of open space that rises through the height of the building and serves as a light well. The wings are further divided into residential and commercial units, the majority of which are of two basic sizes. The building is topped by a slab, except for the structure above the light well, that rises above the terrace slab and terminates in a pitched roof. The four walls of this structure are provided with louvres that allow natural light to illuminate the length of the corridor at every level and also enable ventilation through the Venturi effect.

BUILT UP AREA PER PERSON

6.40 SQ.M
CONSIDERING 6 PEOPLE PER UNIT

CIRCULATION

The chawl is serviced by two separate entrances from the main road that connect to individual staircases at the ends of the building. These main accesses lead to a passage running northeast-southwest, split along its length by the light well that breaks the circulation path.

The corridors on the upper levels service the same portions of the building as below, however on the third floor of the south block, the circulation path shifts from being internal to external. Here the corridor fronts the road on one side and units on the other, creating a variation in section and a larger unit size.

15.62 %
OF B.U.A

CIRCULATION AREA PER PERSON

0.9 SQ.M
CONSIDERING 6 PEOPLE PER UNIT

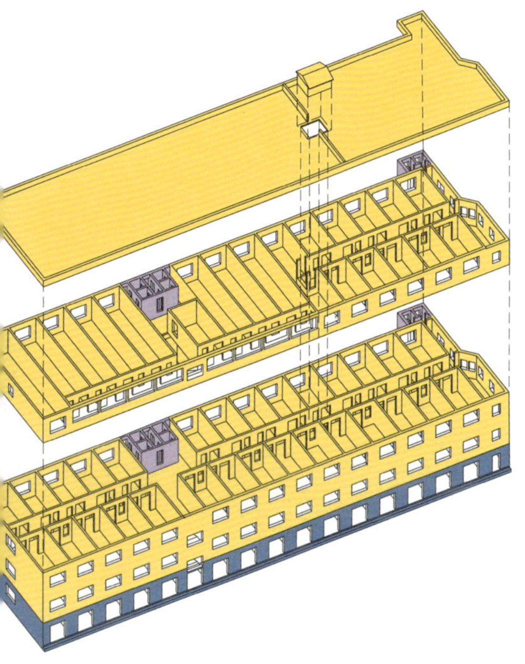

PROGRAMME

The ground floor is purely commercial in function – some shops being for metal works and tailoring – while the floors above are residential. Road facing shops are accessed from the street, while those at the rear are accessed from the corridor. Each wing is serviced by its own set of common toilets.

RESIDENTIAL

COMMERCIAL

SHARED SERVICES

TOTAL COMMERCIAL AREA

687.3 SQ.M

7 SQ.M
NOS = 687.3 SQ.M

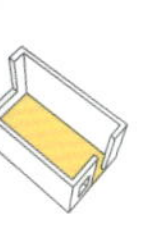

7 SQ.M
NOS = 1611.6 SQ.M

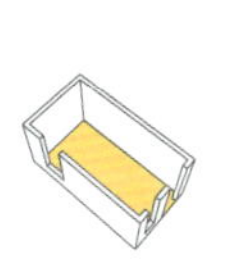

25.5 SQ.M
X 1NO = 25.5 SQ.M

48.4 SQ.M
X 7NOS = 338.8 SQ.M

53.85 SQ.M
X 2NOS = 107.7 SQ.M

TOTAL RESIDENTIAL AREA

2083.6 SQ.M

GROUND FLOOR PLAN

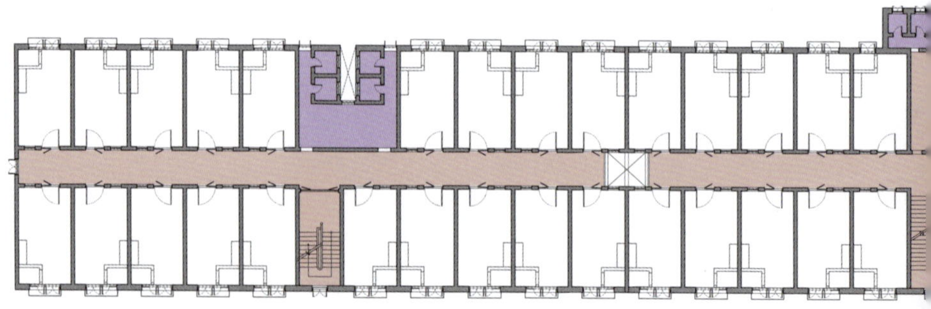

FIRST/SECOND FLOOR PLAN

OPEN SPACE

260.8 SQ.M

7.08 %

OF B.U.A

OPEN SPACE PER PERSON

0.41 SQ.M

CONSIDERING 6 PEOPLE PER UNIT

SHARED SERVICES AREA

160.6 SQ.M

4.36 %

OF B.U.A

FLOOR PLANS

Despite being designed on a repetitive structural grid, the building shows four different unit types, their lengths varying to fit into the constraints of the structural frame. Ground, first and second floor units are of standard size, however on the third floor – excepting one residence – the units in the south wing elongate to more than double this size. One of the longer units embraces the atrium and has three windows looking into it, and at the corridor on the other side.

In the north wing, all units are of standard size and the floor plan repeats – ground to third floor. The segregation between wings extends even to the roof, where a rigid boundary bars access between terraces. The terrace area on both sides is used by residents as exercise space.

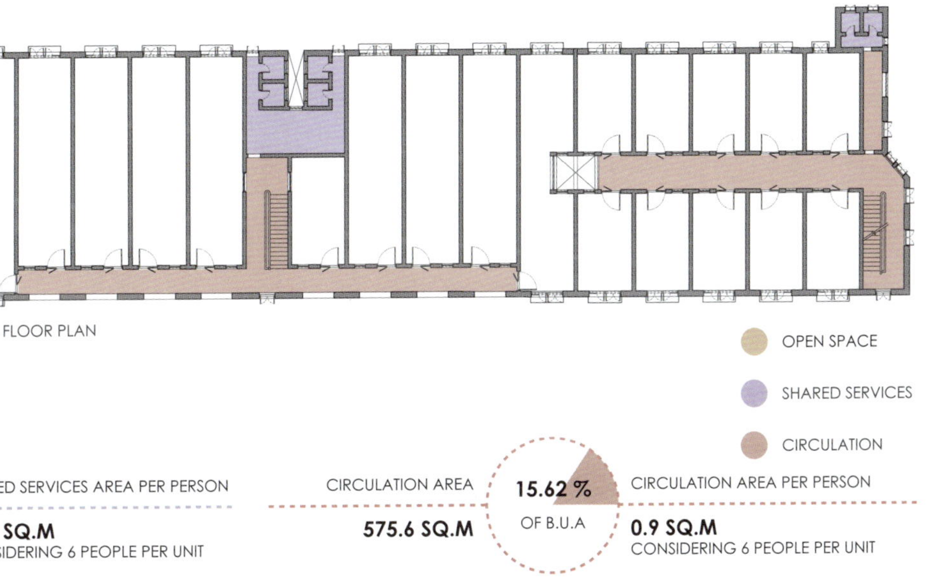

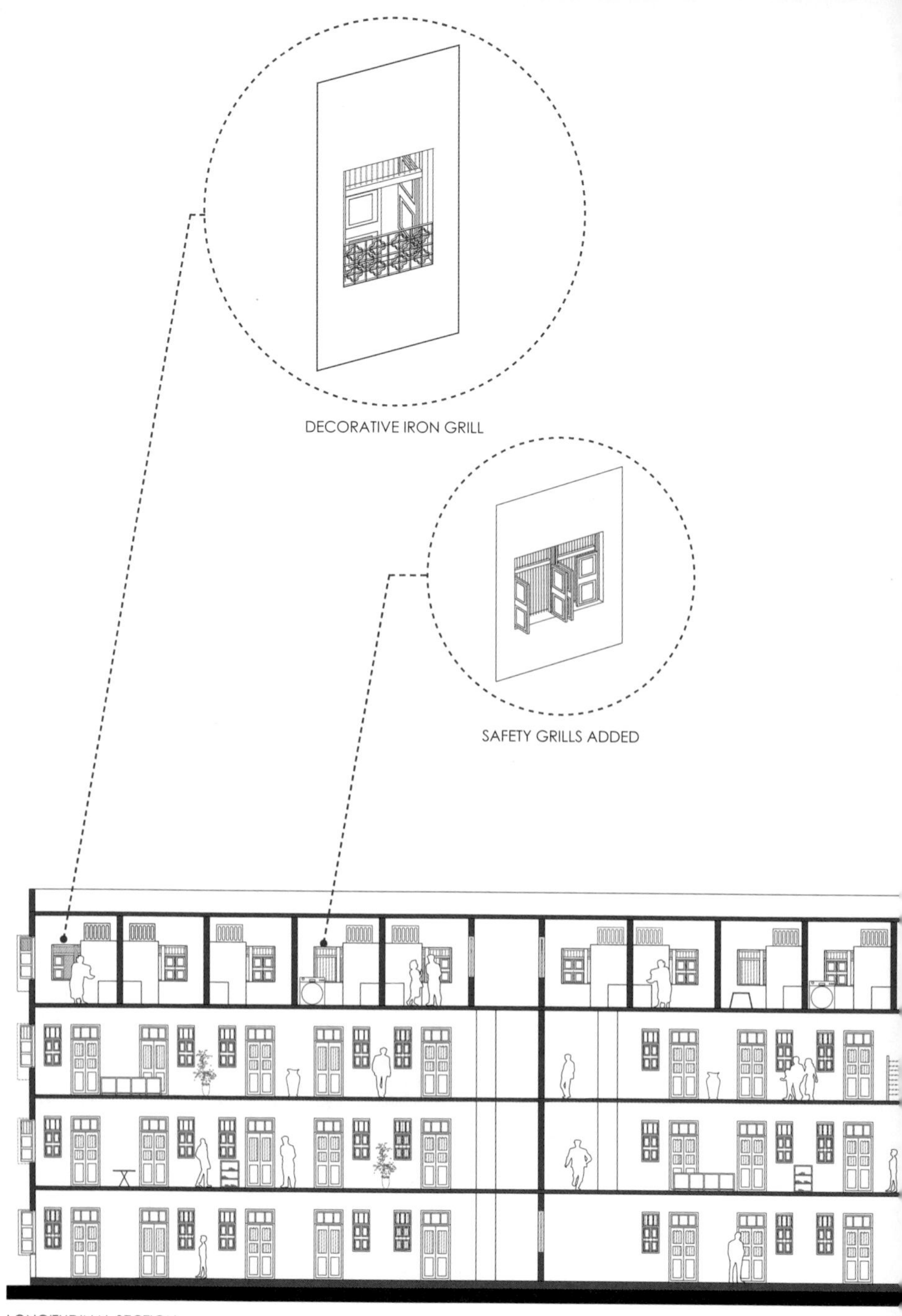

LONGITUDINAL SECTION

ENVELOPE

The modifications made in the building envelope are minor. Residents have installed patterned grills on nearly half the openable area of some external windows. The sill space is used to keep an assortment of items.

Other external windows have been encased in box grills; the bottom surfaces of these form space for the placement of potted plants and their volumes accommodate air conditioner units. Such additions – though minor – show attempts to expand interior living space.

Windows that open into corridors have been grilled with straight bars. With both internal and external window shutters along the northwest-southeast direction left open, air moves freely through the units, keeping the interiors well ventilated.

BOX GRILL

0 1 2 5 10M

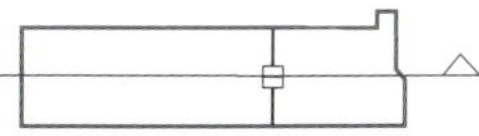

UNIT TYPE 1 - FLOOR PLAN

UNIT TYPE 2 - FLOOR PLAN

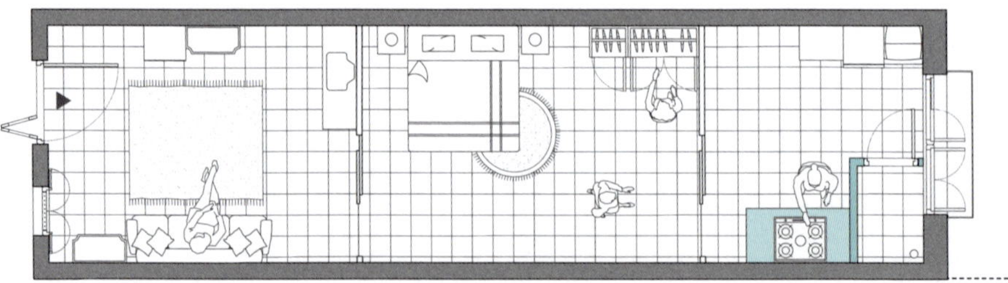

UNIT TYPE 3 - FLOOR PLAN

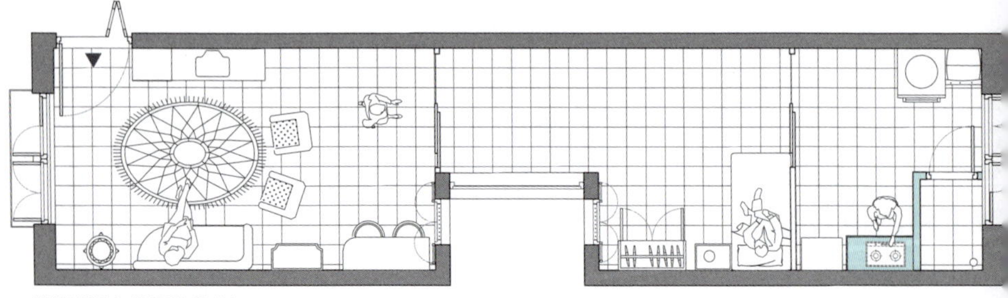

UNIT TYPE 4 - FLOOR PLAN

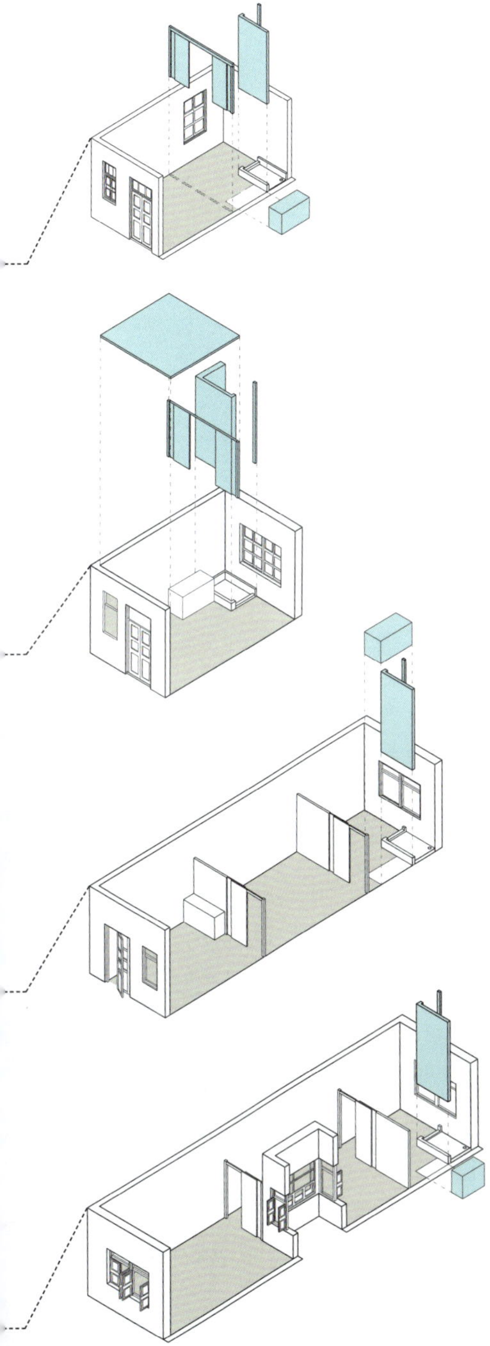

UNITS

Unit level appropriations have been kept to the minimum. The smaller units – Units 1 and 2 – have been divided into two parts by means of partition walls, such that the front portion is used as a living space, and the rear as a utility space. The *moris* in all the units have been converted into bath areas.

Unit 1 at 25.5 sq.m, is the only one of its type. It is located on the third floor of the south wing and has no external windows, so despite the presence of the internal window that opens into the corridor, cross ventilation is rendered impossible. Unit type 2 – measuring 23.7 sq.m in area – represents ground, first and second floor units of both wings, and additionally, residences of the third floor of the north wing.

Both Units 3 and 4 – measuring 48.4 sq.m and 53.85 sq.m respectively – are the elongated houses on the third floor of the south wing that result from the shift of the corridor to the road face. Residents of these unit types have built intermediate partition walls, separating living, sleeping and utility spaces. Unit 4 is representative of both, the house around the light well, as well as the one at the far end of the corridor. The former is amply lit and ventilated by windows on its external faces and also those opening into the shaft. Further, these enable visual connectivity and communication between the residents and those in the corridor at the same and lower levels.

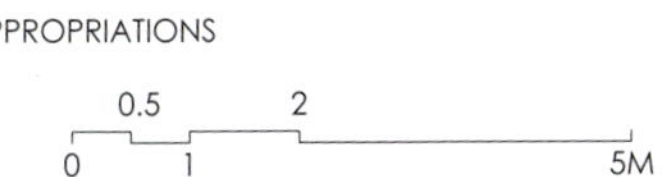

13
033
003
511
513
609
4

30
Y बांद्रा
G

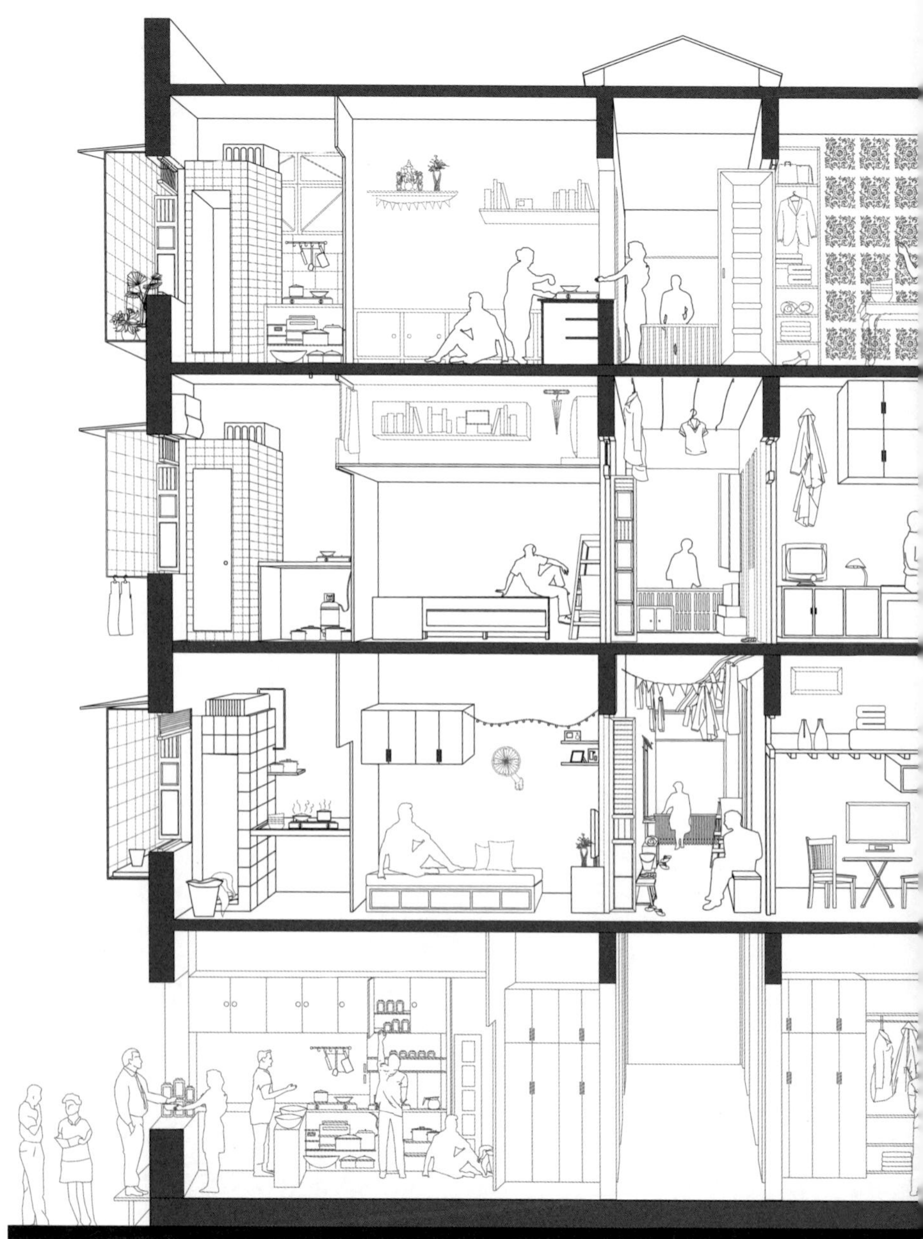

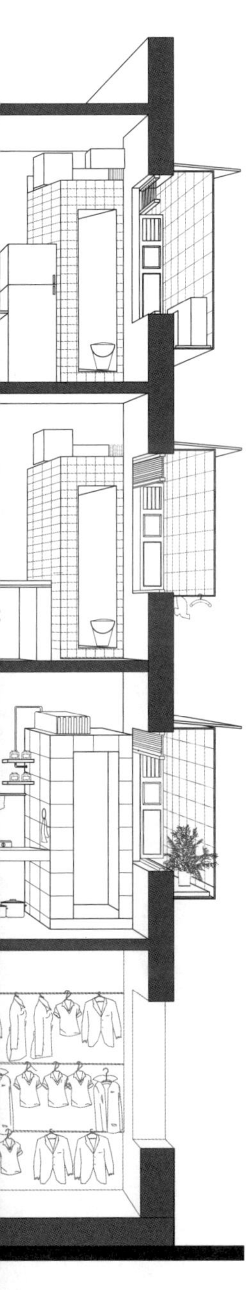

ANALYSIS

The building is outwardly a monolithic uniform structure, while internally is variegated. The central circulation spine that would typically have connected all units, is split midway by a light well, which though constrained in size, does provide relief from what might have been an oppressive corridor length. Despite physically dividing the building, it allows residents the opportunity to interact across its volume.

The 2.1 m wide corridor on each of the first three levels is a vital social binder, as residents, being from the same community end up appropriating it as an extension of their interior spaces, effectively transforming circulation space into a giant linear common living room. Also a facilitator of social interaction is the internal window – between private living space and passage – that creates porosity through the width of the building.

On the third floor of the south wing however, housing units become larger, facilitating a mix of economic classes. On this level, the increase in private space seems to have led to an insularity and diminishing social interaction between the residents.

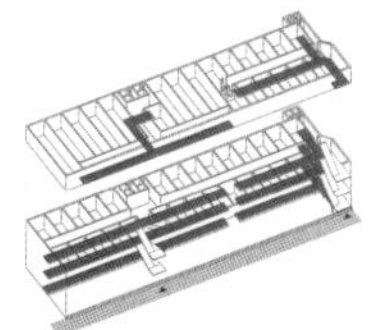

SOCIAL SPACE

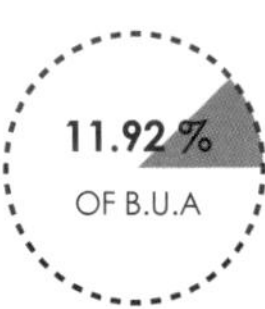

08
SITE AND SERVICES

08 | SITE AND SERVICES

DO IT YOURSELF
1986
CHARKOP

The Site and Services scheme at Charkop was part of the World Bank-instituted Bombay Urban Development Project in 1979 that recognised the need for a programme that considered land, infrastructure and shelter development as severely unaddressed problems. As a result, the Maharashtra government put in place an Affordable Low Income Shelter five-year programme in 1982.

There are over 15,000 individual plots in the scheme and the objective of overall site planning was to ensure that a minimum of 45-55% plots would be occupied by very low income families (Rs. 250-625/month) and 10-20% by low income families (Rs. 625-875/month). Since plots were reserved based on income type, a survey of income groups was carried out and a lottery was held for their sale. While house owners were allowed to pay for their units in instalments, buyers of commercial holdings were required to pay the full price up front. Tenure for residences was in the form of renewable leasehold agreements, applicable for 60 years.

The project came under the Land Infrastructure Servicing Program (LISP) along with similar projects in Airoli and Borivali and was officially launched in 1985. The focus of the study is one cluster within the project. It was built in 1986 and comprises of a series of units grouped around a common courtyard.

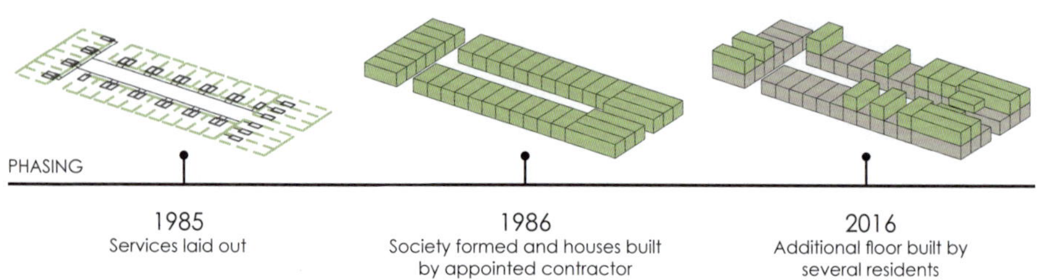

LOCATION

The 90 ha plot is located in Charkop, Kandivali, an area that was originally marsh land. It was drained, filled and prepared in order to accommodate the project. The site at Charkop, like the ones at Airoli and Borivali, was selected based on certain criteria. It was located within 5 km of concentrations of residential, commercial and industrial activities, and connected to the Brihanmumbai Municipal Corporation (BMC) water supply line and Brihanmumbai Electric Supply and Transport (BEST) electrical line. As part of the planning strategy, all houses were to be within 0.5 km of a bus route connected to the city transport network and in terms of local circulation, within 55 m of a road capable of carrying a service vehicle.

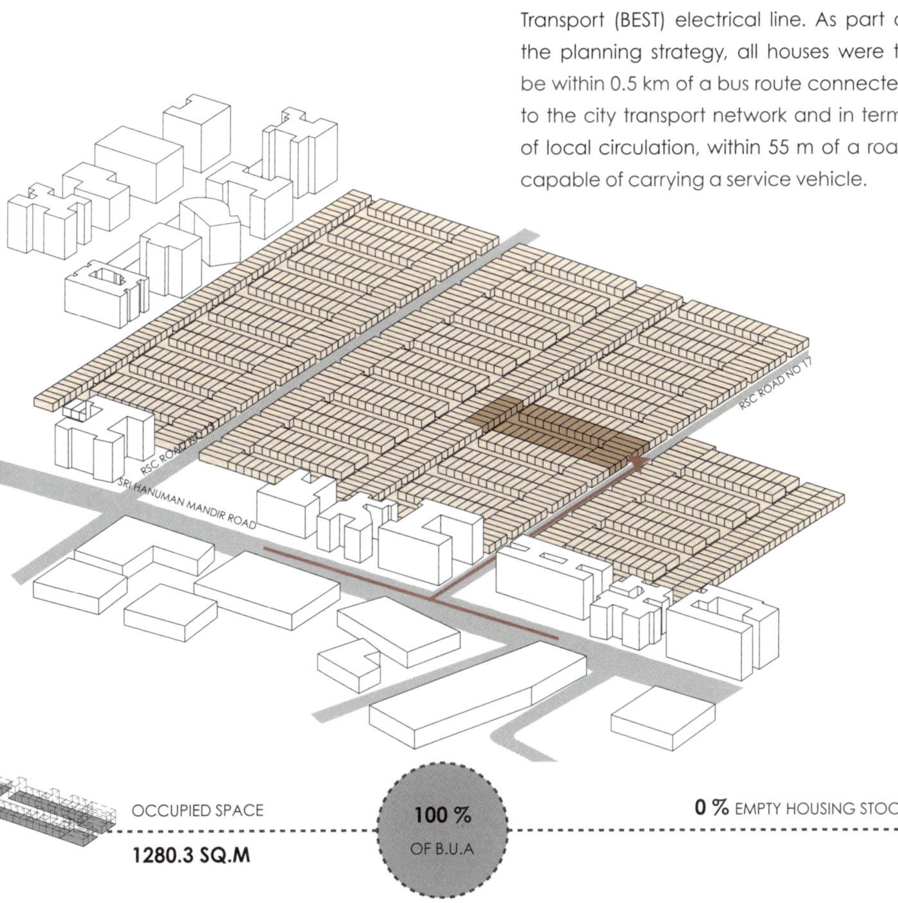

OCCUPIED SPACE
1280.3 SQ.M

100 %
OF B.U.A

0 % EMPTY HOUSING STOCK

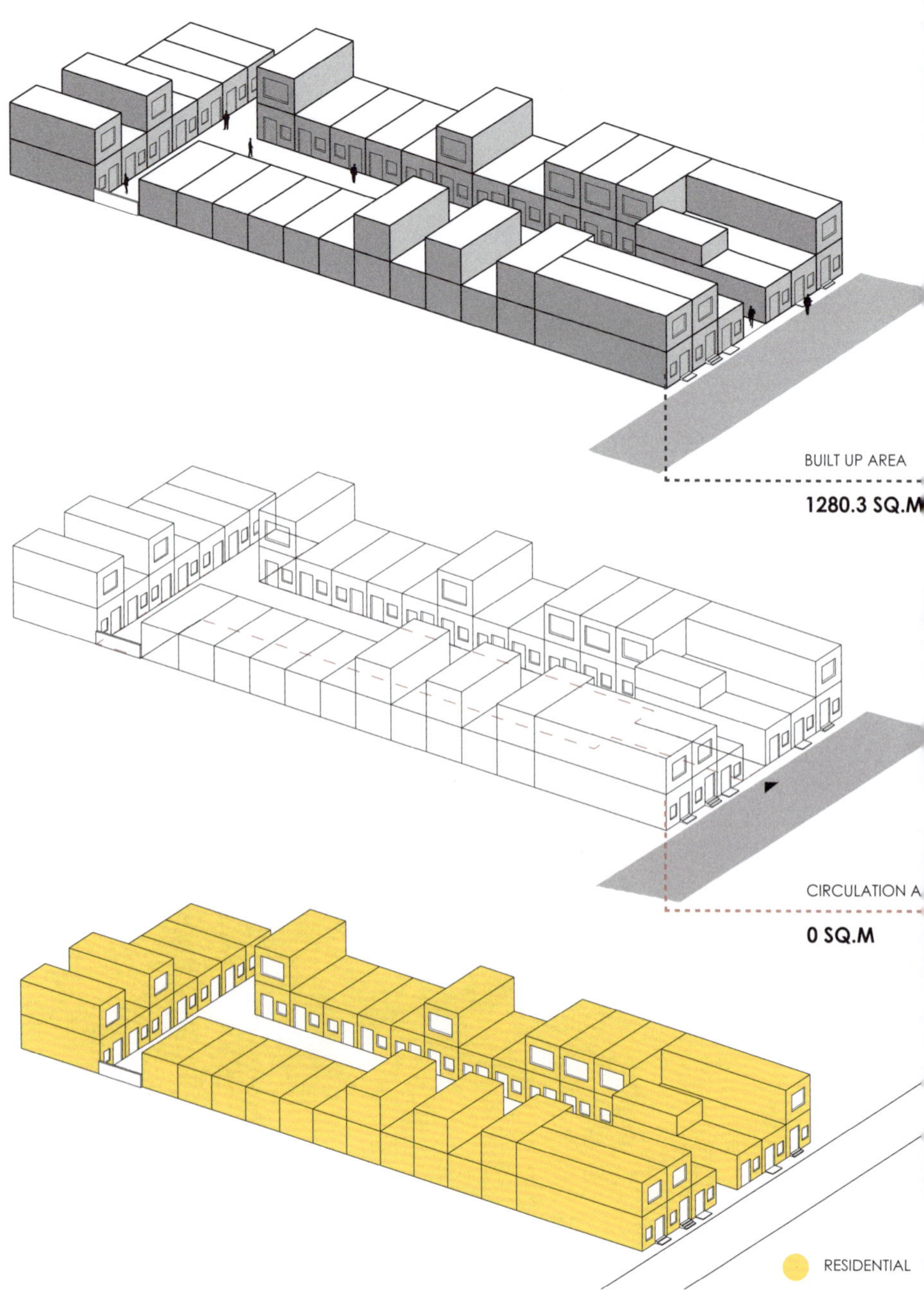
BUILT UP AREA
1280.3 SQ.M
CIRCULATION A
0 SQ.M
RESIDENTIAL

BUILT UP AREA PER PERSON

7.62 SQ.M
CONSIDERING 6 PEOPLE PER UNIT

CIRCULATION AREA PER PERSON

0 SQ.M
CONSIDERING 6 PEOPLE PER UNIT

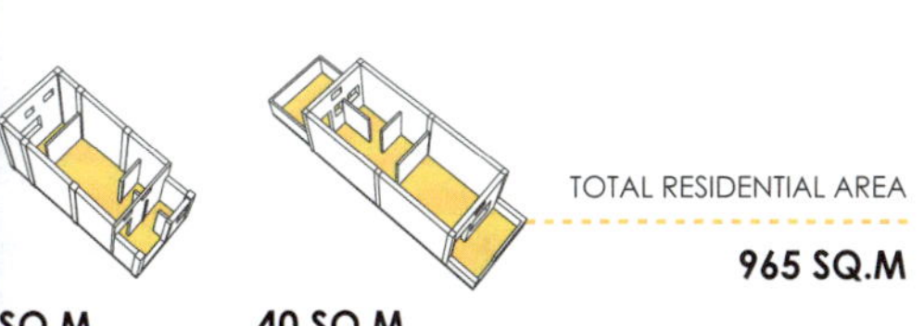

TOTAL RESIDENTIAL AREA

965 SQ.M

SQ.M
NOS = 725 SQ.M

40 SQ.M
X 6NOS = 240 SQ.M

BUILDING FORM

The entire project is laid out in clusters of about 35 plots each and plot sizes were determined by monthly income. In the cluster studied, all the sub-plots are either 25 or 40 sq.m each.

There are six sub-plots of 40 sq.m each – all facing the road – and behind these are the 25 sq.m sub-plots fronting a common courtyard. In the first phase of development, the contractor constructed identical ground storey houses, which resulted in a homogenous sprawl of low rise homes. But with time, the built form has acquired a diverse character, individual owners having made alterations and additions to their houses. Several units have vertically expanded by the addition of a first floor.

CIRCULATION

The cluster under study, like all the others, is directly accessed from the main road. The 3 m wide pathway is flanked by houses on either side, and leads to an extended common courtyard that is lined with independent residences.

PROGRAMME

The scheme was originally intended for housing and small scale commercial enterprises. In the cluster under study, the original buyers of the road facing plots were given the option of developing their land as mixed-use programmes. Currently all the units are used as residences.

KALAPI

सह. गृहनिर्माण
संस्था मर्यादित
कांदिवली (प.) मु ६७.
विश्वास नाजरेकर

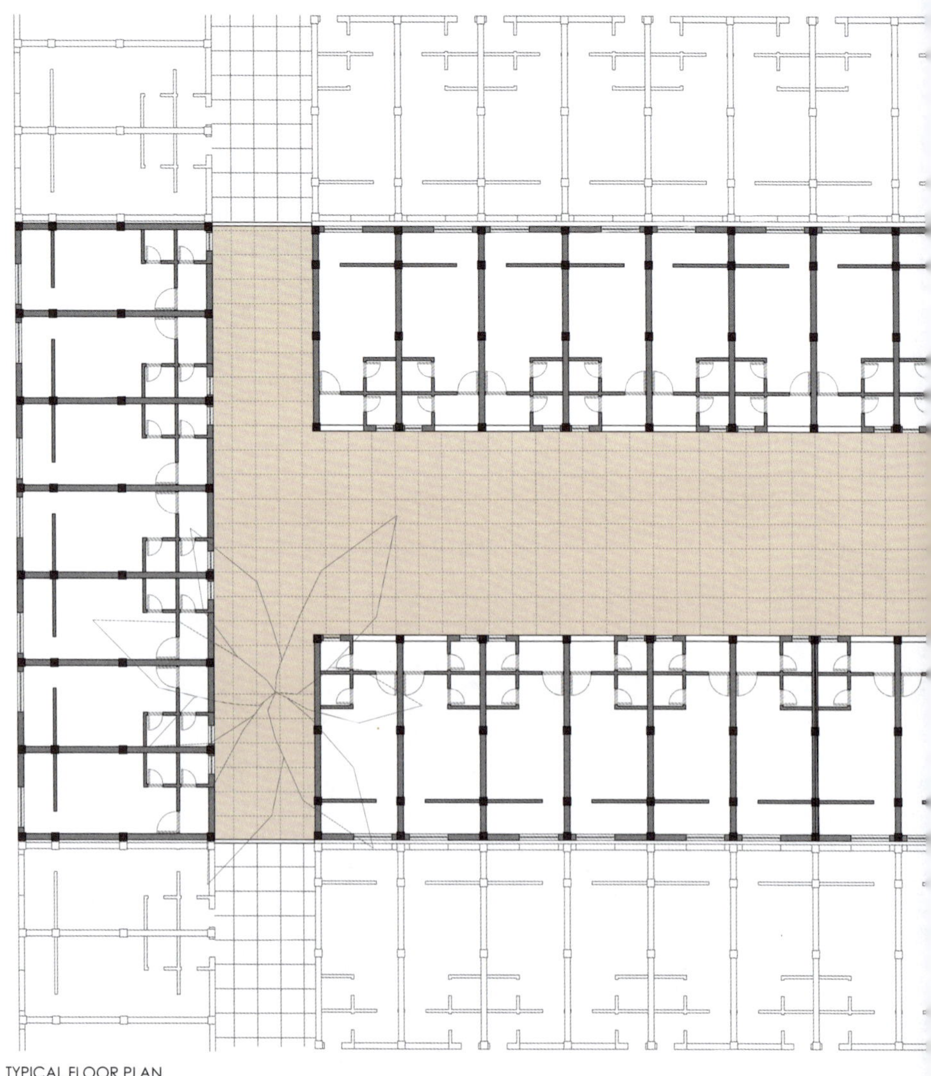

TYPICAL FLOOR PLAN

OPEN SPACE	32.75 %	OPEN SPACE PER PERSON	SHARED SERVICES AREA	0 %
419.3 SQ.M	OF B.U.A	**2.50 SQ.M** CONSIDERING 6 PEOPLE PER UNIT	**0 SQ.M**	OF B.U.A

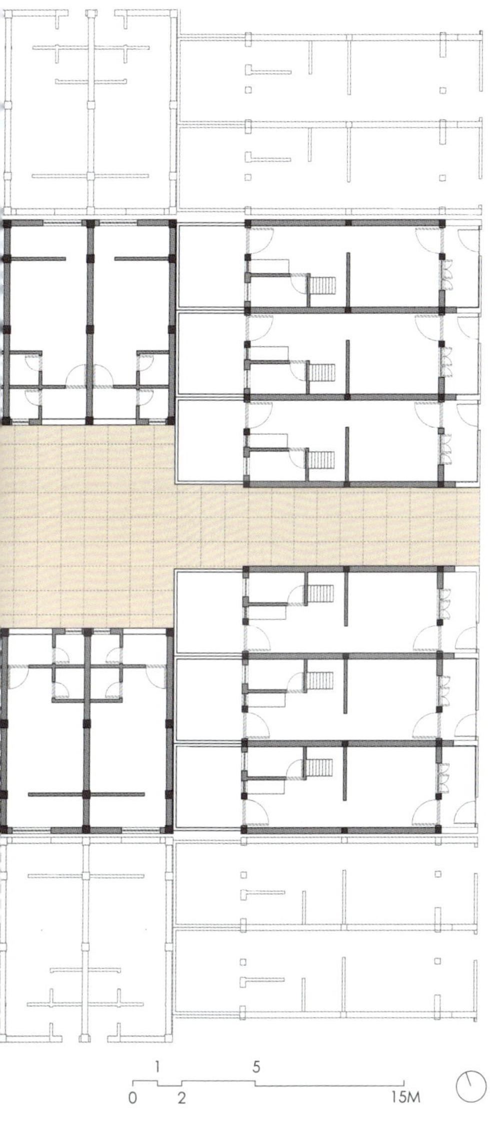

FLOOR PLANS

At the inception of the project, the contractor constructed identical units. Road facing units had open space at the entrance, as well as a backyard space, accommodating a *mori* at the rear. Houses around the courtyard were constructed on 25 sq.m plots and had a small porch between the main living space and common courtyard.

The progression of movement is clear and hierarchical; while road facing plots are accessed directly from the street, houses in the interior of the cluster are accessed from the courtyard that is connected to the road by means of a small pathway. In some cases this pathway has been covered by newly constructed rooms overhead.

OPEN SPACE

ꞮED SERVICES AREA PER PERSON

ʔ.M

ISIDERING 6 PEOPLE PER UNIT

CIRCULATION AREA

0 SQ.M

0 %

OF B.U.A

CIRCULATION AREA PER PERSON

0 SQ.M

CONSIDERING 6 PEOPLE PER UNIT

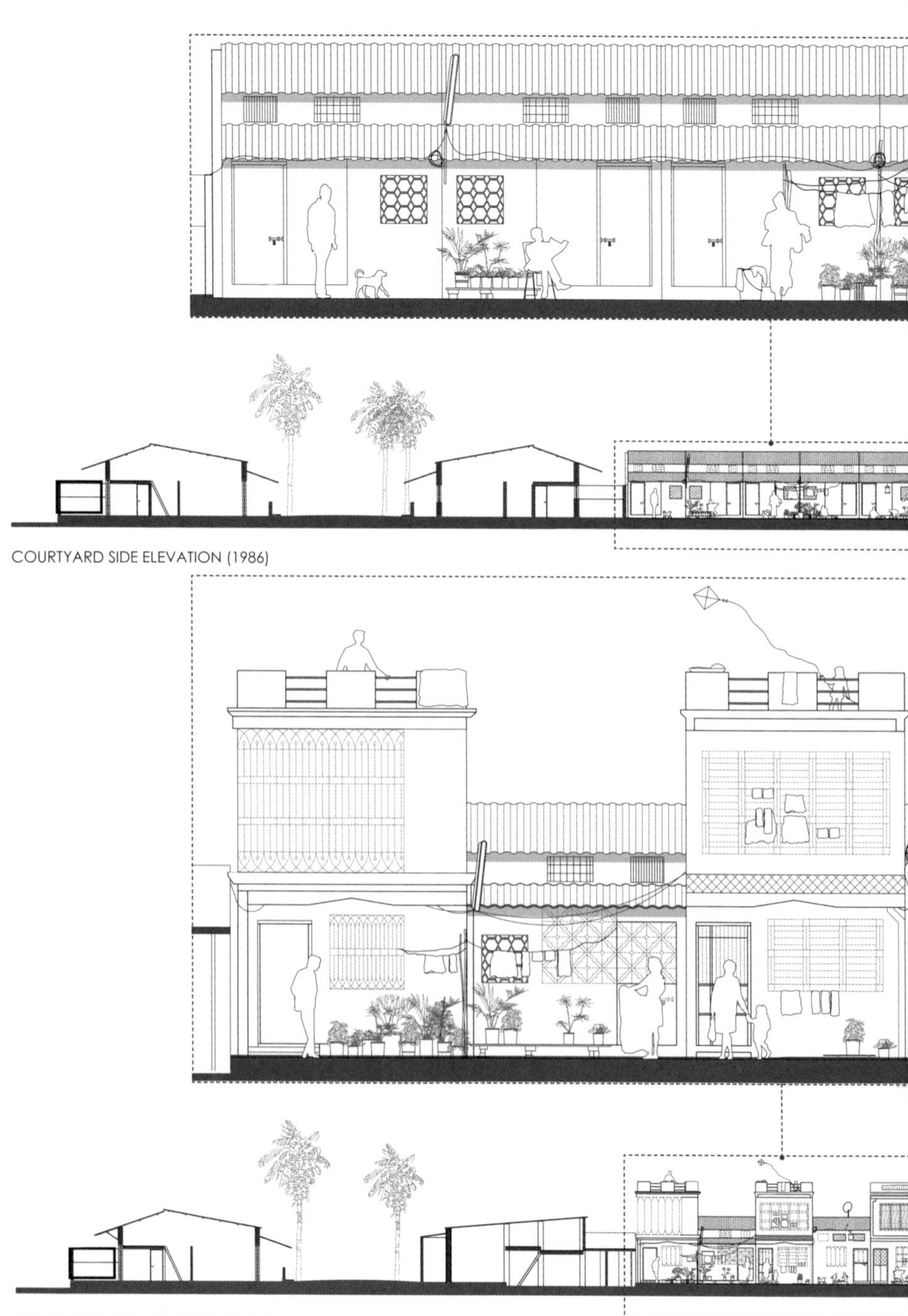
COURTYARD SIDE ELEVATION (1986)
COURTYARD SIDE ELEVATION (2016)

ENVELOPE

The façade of the original row of houses built by the contractor was homogenous, but with time, transforming needs and growing finances, families have developed the interior and exterior of their homes in accordance with their specific requirements. These changing conditions are manifested as additional floors in some cases, and demolition and reconstruction of previously designed structures in others. While some houses have grown rapidly, others remain unaltered.

Owners have also personalised the space in front of their houses by placing potted plants and benches, defining the area as their own.

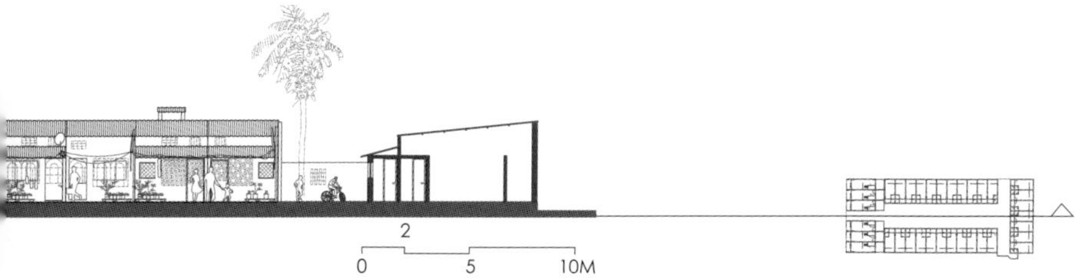

2
0 5 10M

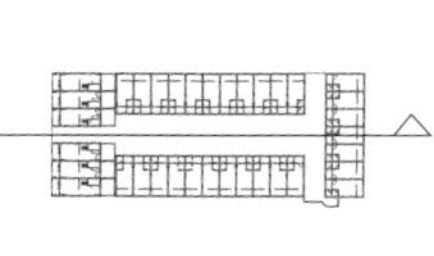

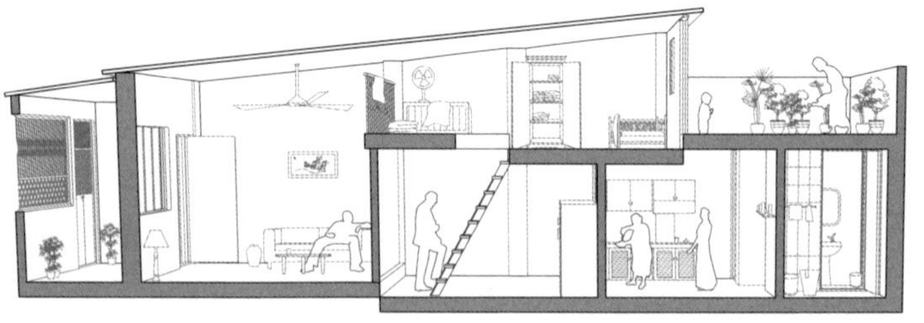

UNIT TYPE 1 - SECTION A

UNIT TYPE 1 - SECTION B

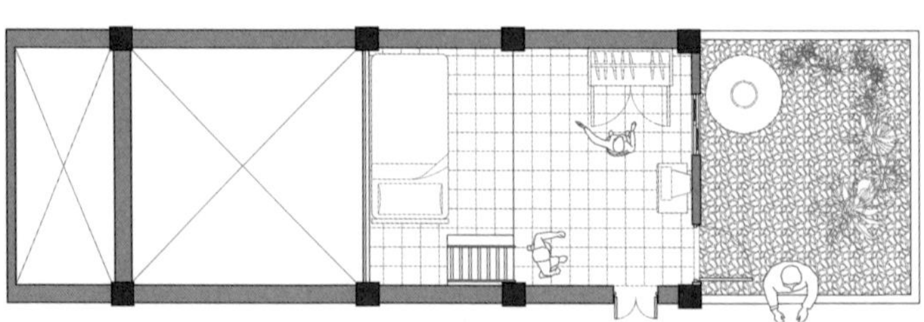

UNIT TYPE 1 - FIRST FLOOR PLAN

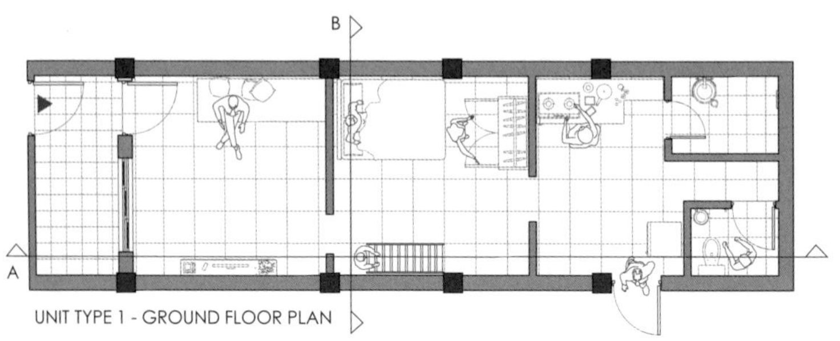

UNIT TYPE 1 - GROUND FLOOR PLAN

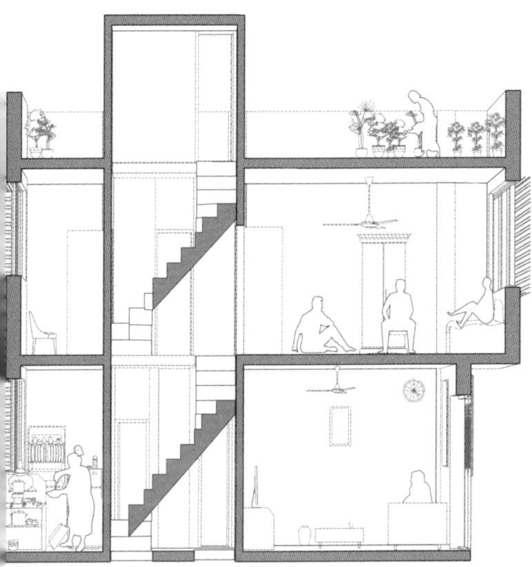

TYPE 2 - SECTION A

UNITS

Modifications to the original design have given the units their own character, lending a richness to the built form.

In the 40 sq.m plots, houses were formerly provided with backyard space at their rear; in Unit 1 this has been built up into a WC, bath area and kitchen, and an internal ladder has been provided for access to the first floor. The sloping roof enables a larger volume above the living space on the ground floor and visual connectivity between the two levels.

In Unit 2 – built on a 25 sq.m plot – what was originally a front porch has been taken over by the interior of the house and is now part of the living room. The WC cubicle that was at the entrance of the house has been demolished and a combined WC-cum-bath unit constructed in a more central location. As per the new configuration, the ground floor is used as a living room, above which is a bedroom with a cantilevering window seat.

In both units, open space at the front has taken the form of an elevated garden at the terrace level.

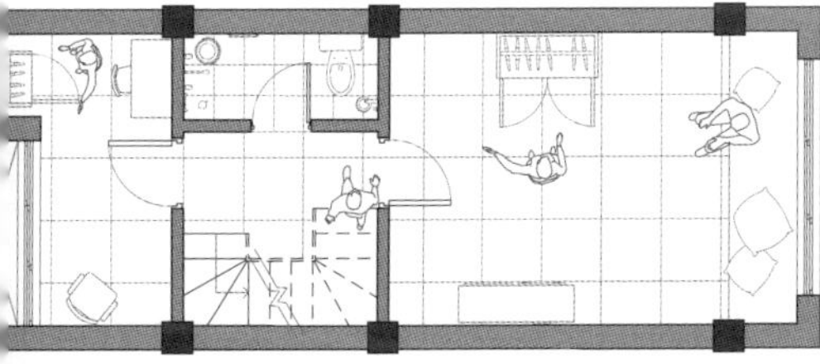

TYPE 2 - FIRST FLOOR PLAN

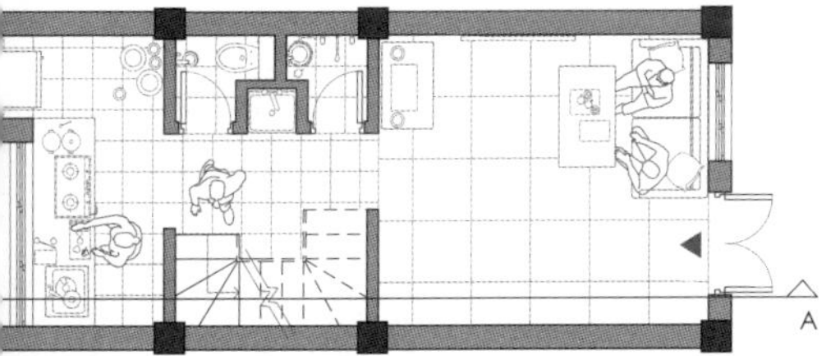

TYPE 2 - GROUND FLOOR PLAN

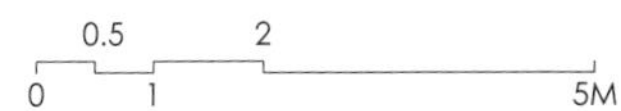

UNITS

Unit 3 – also built on a 40 sq.m plot – has been modified so as to accommodate an additional room on the first floor that the owners rent out. A wall splits the first floor plan, dividing the space into two – the rental unit accessible by means of an external staircase at the front of the house, and an internally accessed additional bedroom for the family at the rear.

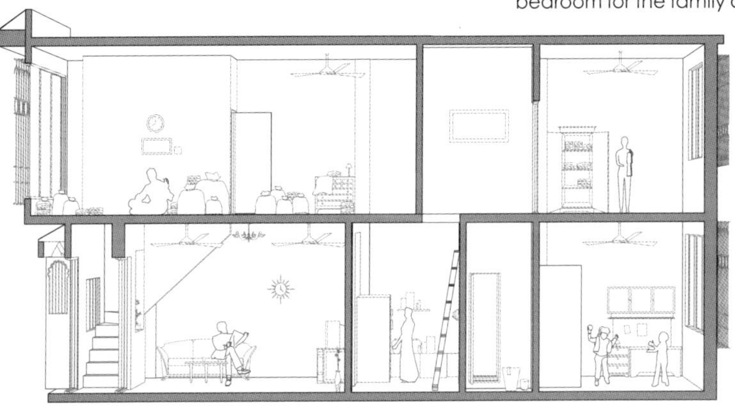

UNIT TYPE 3 - SECTION A

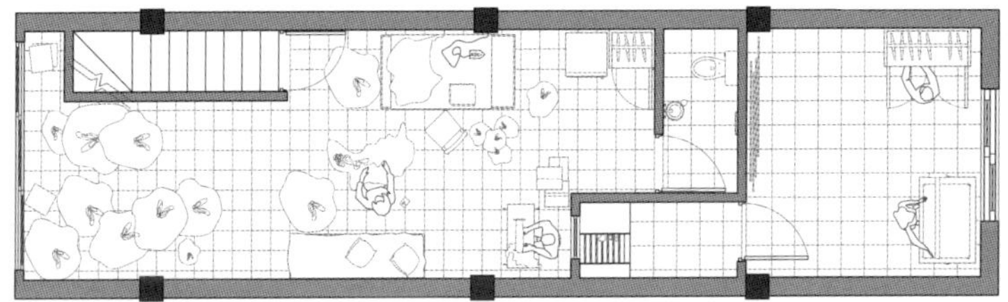

UNIT TYPE 3 - FIRST FLOOR PLAN

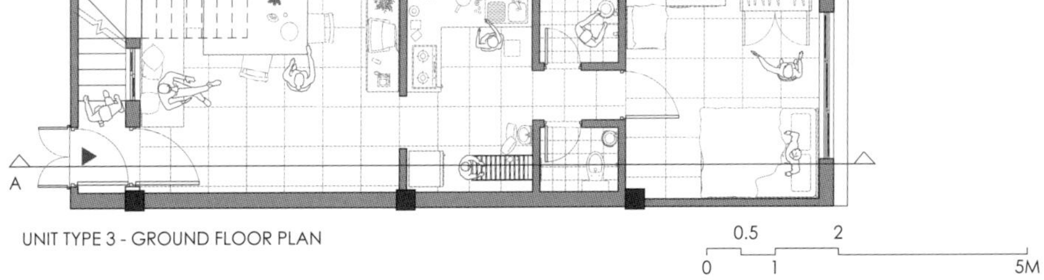

UNIT TYPE 3 - GROUND FLOOR PLAN

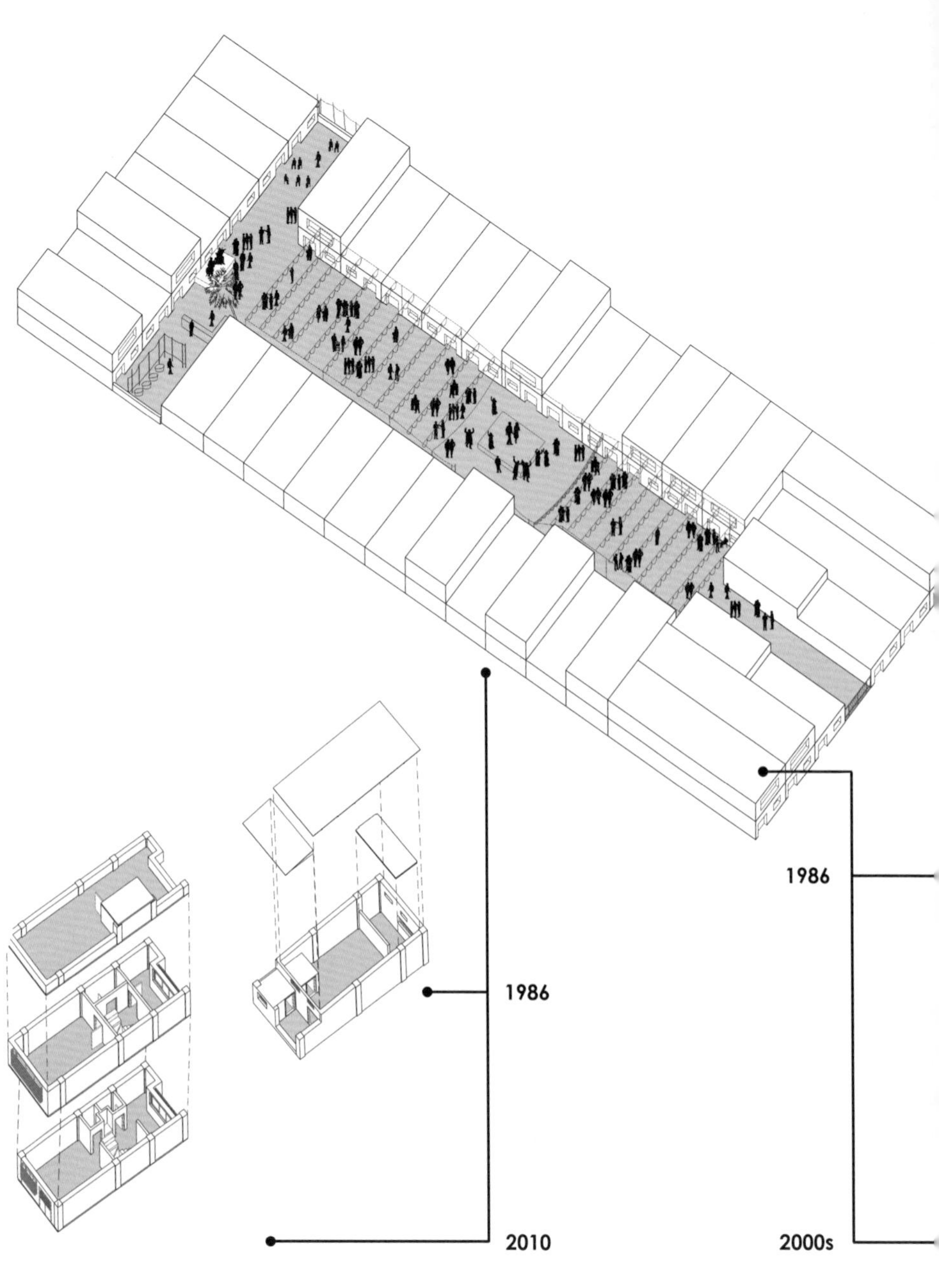
1986
1986
2010
2000s

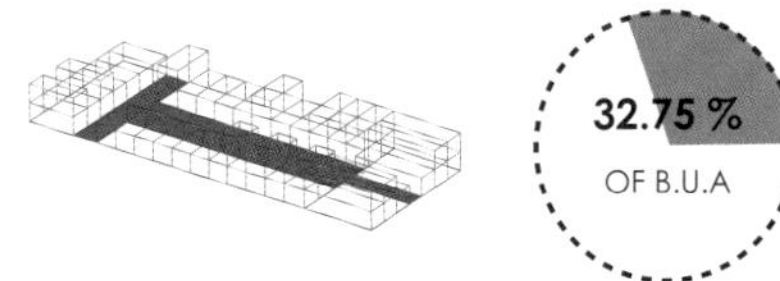

SOCIAL SPACE

ANALYSIS

The families residing in the scheme use the centrally located courtyard as a vital community space. During festivals and social events, the space is transformed into a hub of activity, and during quieter times, children play here. In many cases families are from the same community, having purchased plots accordingly – as a group – and therefore the sense of community is further reinforced.

Ground floor access for every unit is a core element in this project. Not only is it a gathering space, but also enables adults inside the house to watch over their children as they play outside. That this space stands free from encroachment even 30 years on, is testimony to the fact that the community sees open space as a vital common resource, and therefore seeks to preserve it. This condition challenges the assumption of state policy where regulatory frameworks are designed to subvert common space from being encroached on by residents.

The project can be considered a success as it provided a large number of units in a shorter time than most of its predecessors, and has been informative in less quantifiable but equally relevant ways with regard to a rarely seen social vitality in today's state-built housing.

09
SAMBHAJI NAGAR SRA

09 | SAMBHAJI NAGAR SRA

ONE SIZE FITS ALL

2008

ANDHERI EAST

This structure stands on a plot of land that was once an informal homegrown settlement. In 1996 a proposal for rehabilitation was floated, following which the builder, RT Constructions cleared the slum in a phased manner. In 2002, the HDIL Kaledonia commercial tower was constructed and from 2004 through to 2008, the housing blocks came up, replacing the squatter settlement.

1996
Site occupied by homegrown settlement, proposal for rehabilitation floated

2002
Phase 1 of slum cleared and HDIL building construction commenced

LOCATION

The colony is located in Andheri East between Sahar Road on the east and the Western Railway tracks on the west. The plot is bounded by slums in the north and south directions.

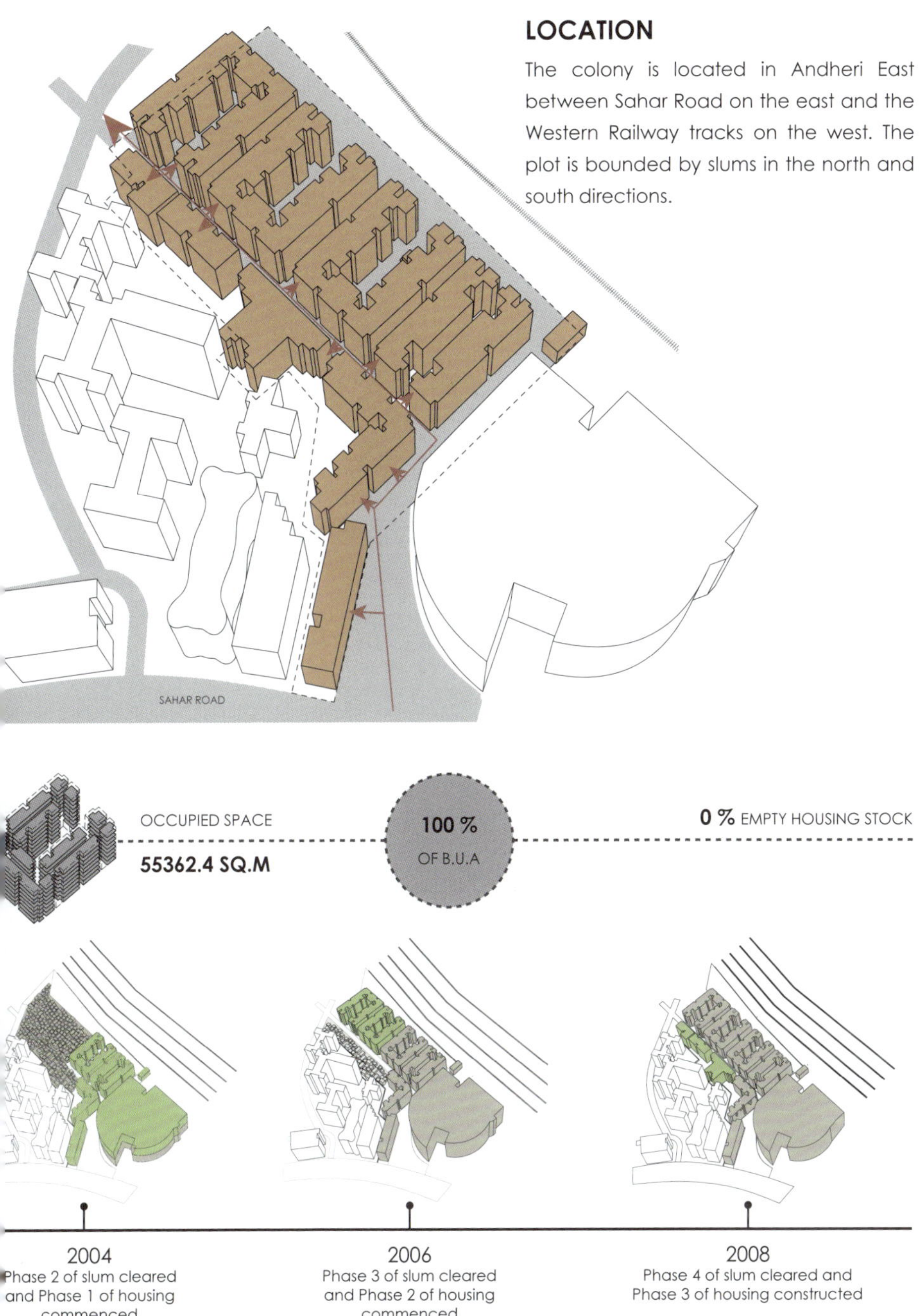

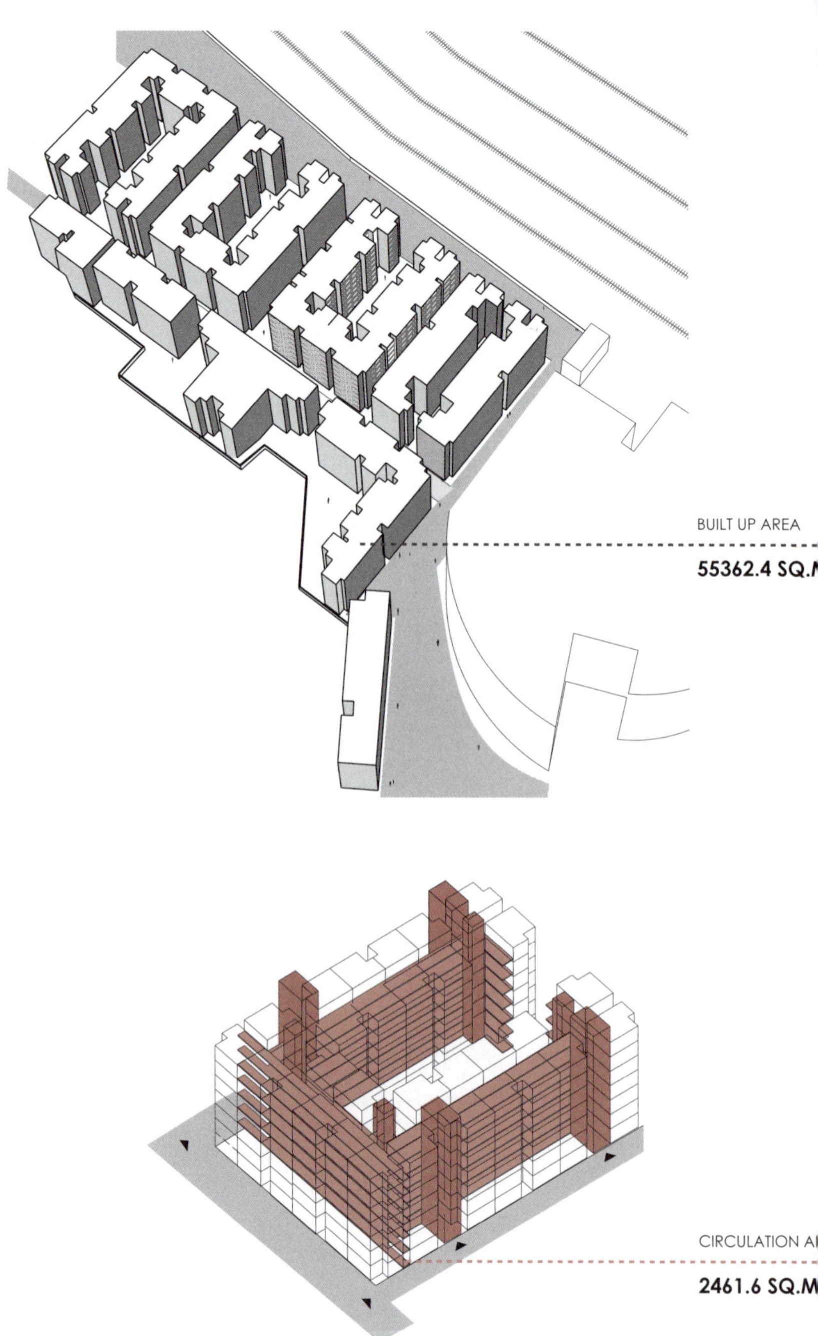
BUILT UP AREA
55362.4 SQ.M
CIRCULATION A
2461.6 SQ.M

BUILDING FORM

The entire project is comprised of a number of independent 8 storey structures, the form of each determined by the aggregation of the individual standard house units in plan. The organisation results in large communal open spaces in some places and residual unusable spaces in others.

The building under study is a C-shaped structure, which though planned cheek-by-jowl with its neighbours contains within its form a large open ground. The houses on the outer periphery of the 'C' however, do not enjoy such open space on account of the close proximity between buildings.

BUILT UP AREA PER PERSON

6.46 SQ.M
CONSIDERING 6 PEOPLE PER UNIT

CIRCULATION

Corridors take the profile of the built form and are double-loaded, ill-lit and poorly ventilated. The only intersection of the circulation path with natural light is through the staircases and windows at the corners.

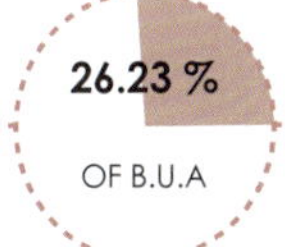

CIRCULATION AREA PER PERSON

1.68 SQ.M
CONSIDERING 6 PEOPLE PER UNIT

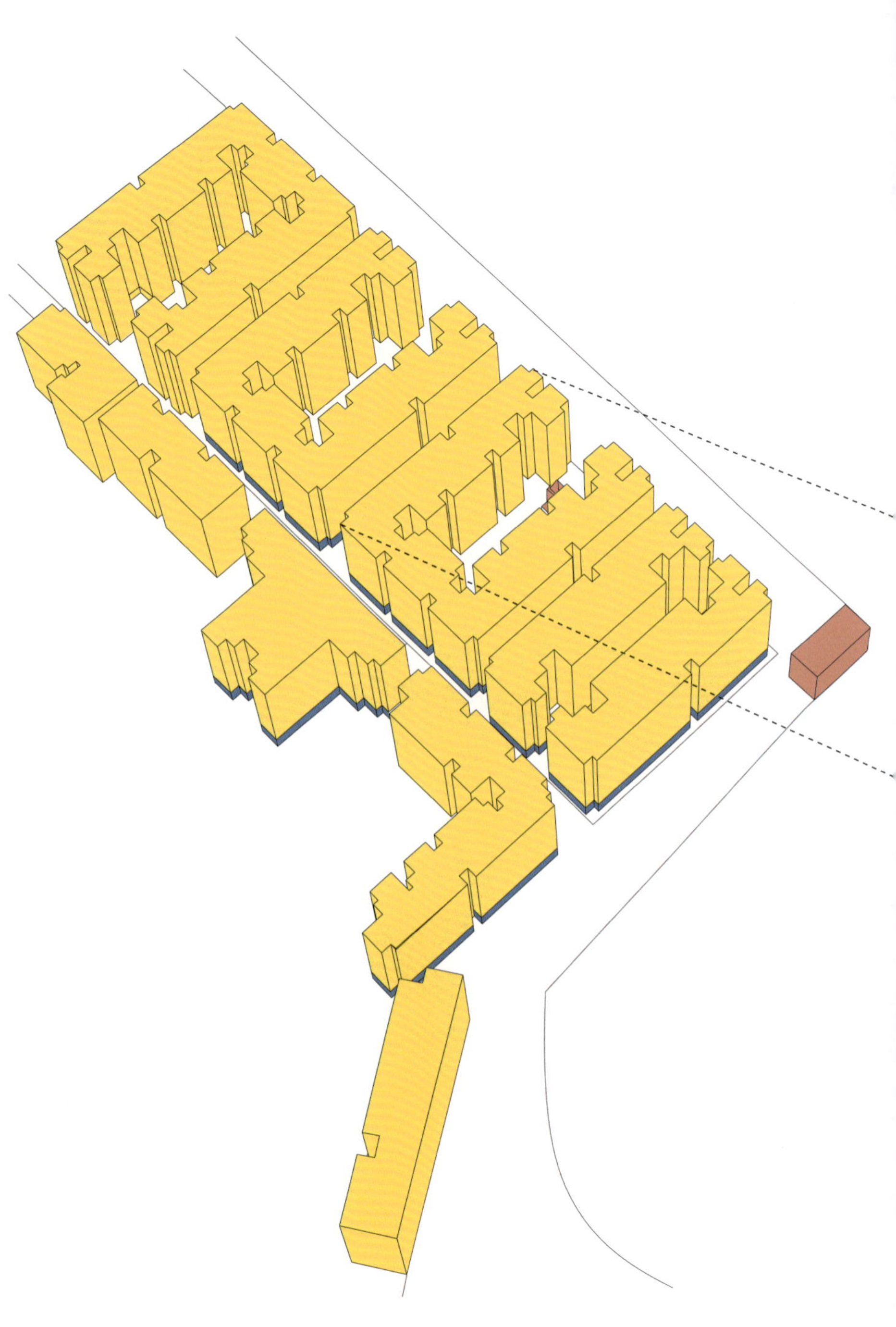

PROGRAMME

The six units fronting the internal road are commercial while the rest of the units in the building are residential. Formally, both unit types are identical.

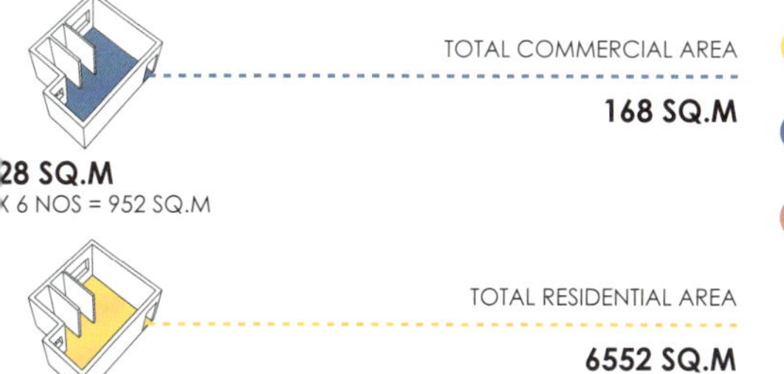

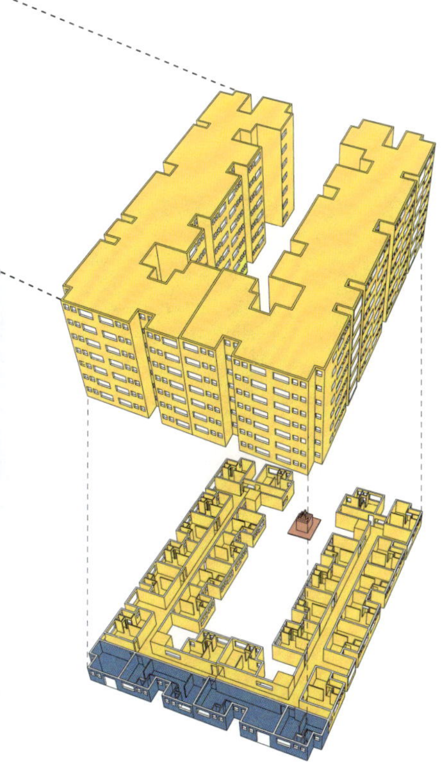

OPEN SPACE	13.87 %	OPEN SPACE PER PERSON
7681 SQ.M	OF B.U.A	0.81 SQ.M CONSIDERING 6 PEOPLE PER UNIT

SHARED SERVICES AREA	0 %
0 SQ.M	OF B.U.A

FLOOR PLANS

In the building studied, every floor has 30 units of 28 sq.m each, arranged in a C-shape – 12 of these front the courtyard, while the rest bear no connection to it at all. At each level the central double-loaded corridor is the circulation path, so that even at the ground floor, houses are not accessed from the open space, the connection to it being only visual through individual units.

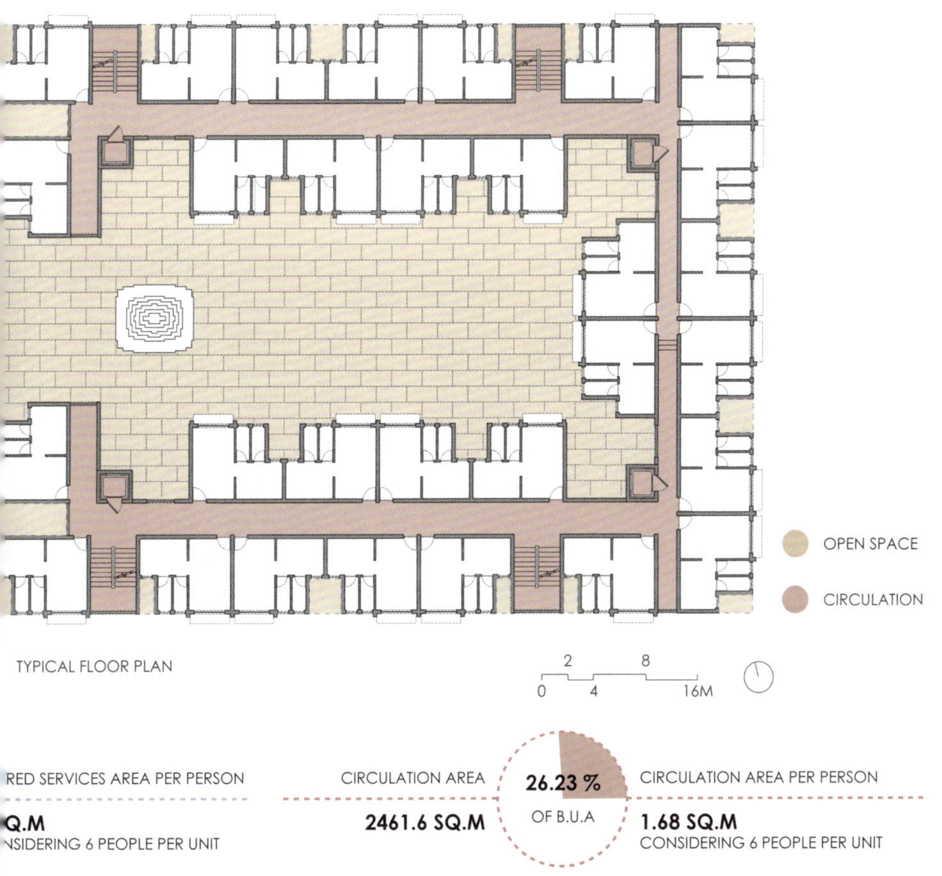

TYPICAL FLOOR PLAN

EAST SIDE ELEVATION

ENVELOPE

The façade of the building is an outward marker of what is internally a monotonous space. The living room of every unit has a single large window that is highlighted on the façade by means of boxed projections that vertically order the windows on every level.

Appropriations have been restricted to the reorganisation of interior space, thereby resulting in an unvarying façade, the homogeneity sporadically broken only by the odd window air conditioner, potted plant or row of hanging clothes fastened to window grills.

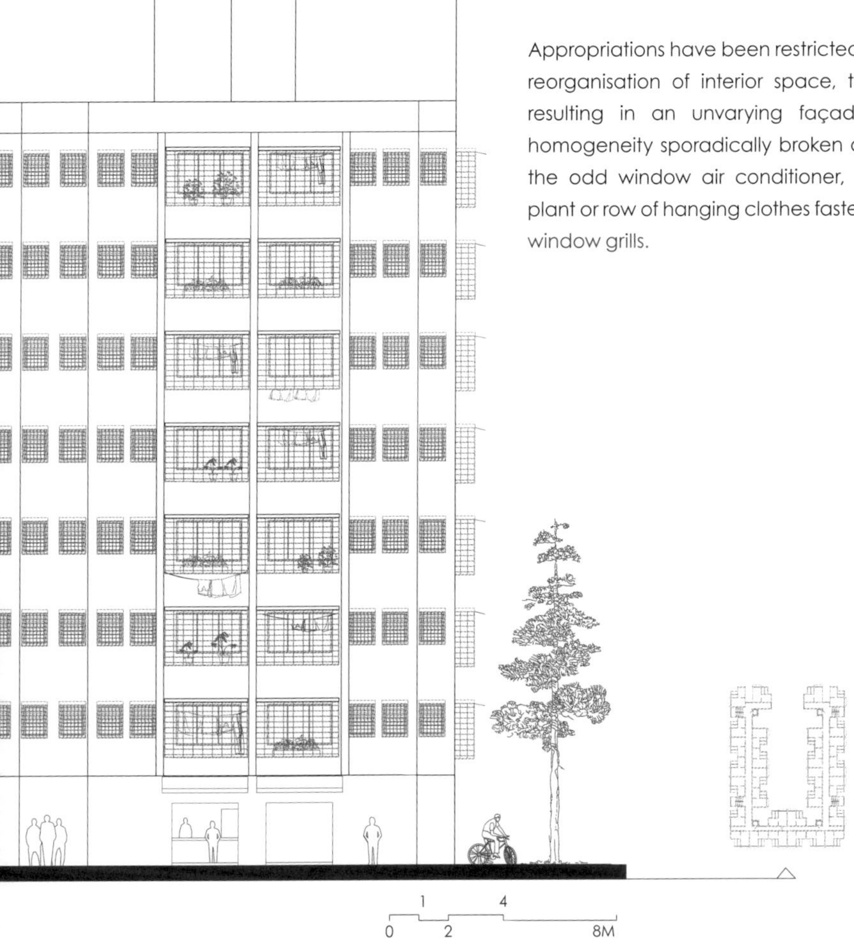

DIAGNOSTIC CENTER

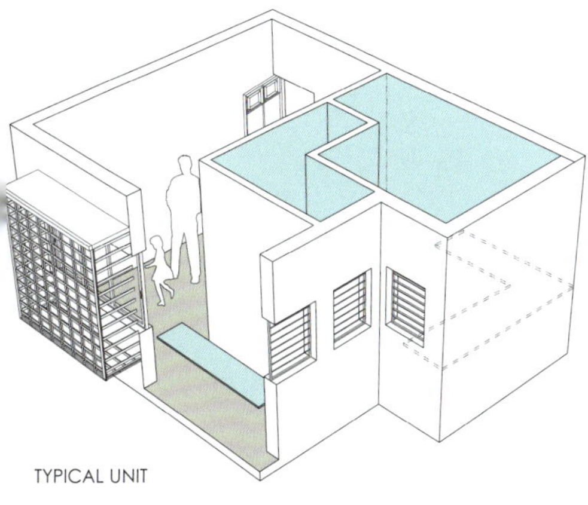

TYPICAL UNIT

UNIT

Residents have reconfigured the interior of their houses so as to maximise living space. WC and bathroom walls have been demolished and the two amalgamated, thus accommodating a slim kitchen where the cubicles originally were. This layout makes space for a second small bedroom in the area formerly designed to be a relatively large kitchen, indicating a prioritisation of additional sleeping spaces over services areas.

APPROPRIATIONS

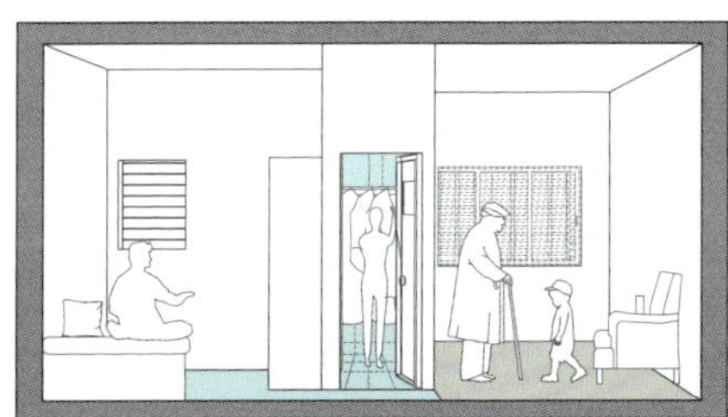

TYPICAL UNIT - SECTION A

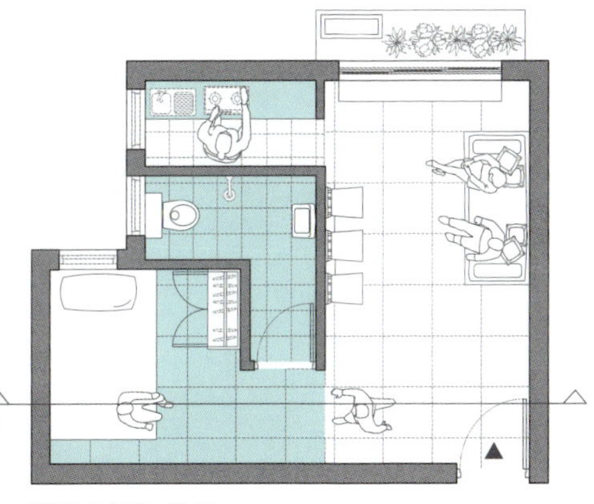

TYPICAL UNIT - PLAN

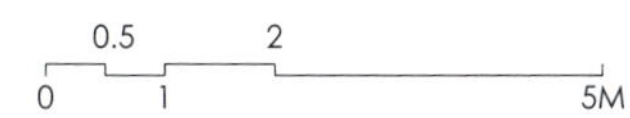

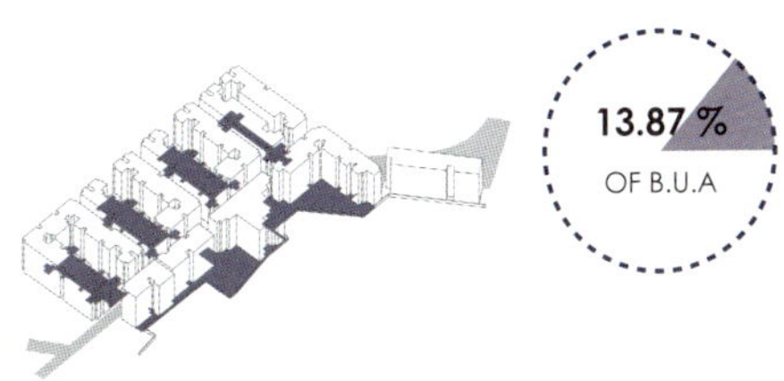

SOCIAL SPACE

ANALYSIS

Despite the lack of variation of the complex and the absence of direct physical access from the units to the courtyard, the project indicates personalisation in the common open space. In one of the clusters, a tree in this space becomes the focal point of activity around which children run and play, and adults interact. In another, it is a centrally located temple that forms an important node of socialisation, binding the community on festive and religious occasions.

This open space however, benefits only a portion of the residents, leaving the units on the periphery of the 'C' little relief by way of space. Adjacent buildings are separated by just a few metres resulting in an acute shortage of light and ventilation in most of the residences.

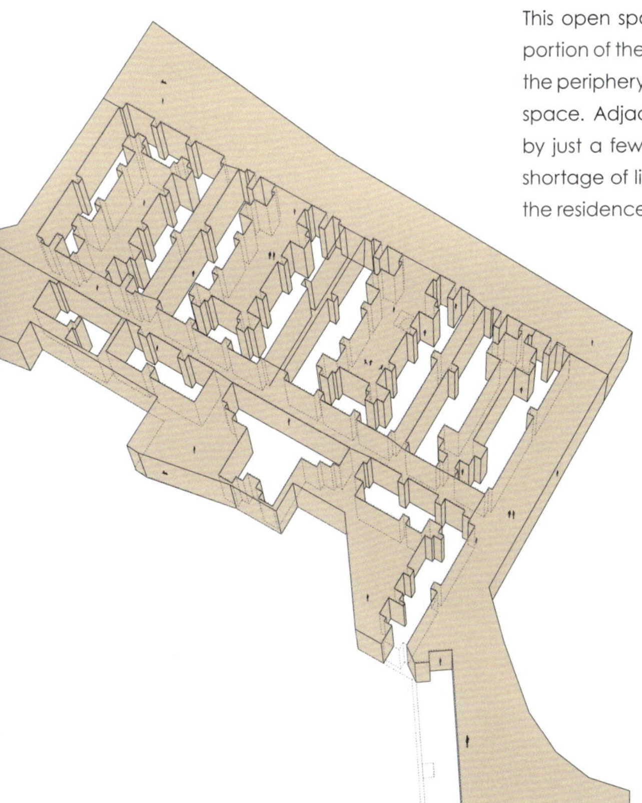

10

PRATIKSHA NAGAR MHADA

10| PRATIKSHA NAGAR MHADA

A KIT OF PARTS

2009
SION

The sprawling Maharashtra Housing and Area Development Authority (MHADA) complex in Sion lies on land that originally housed an informal settlement. This was cleared and the land started being developed by the BG Shirke developer group, a company that has executed many MHADA projects in the past. The earliest structures came up in 2009.

There is a variety of housing for different income groups and carpet area defines socio-economic status. The original inhabitants were accommodated in transit flats which are to be later developed into multistorey apartments. Income brackets include Low, Middle and High Income Groups. There are 616 Low Income Group (LIG) housing flats and the building under study falls in this category. The flats were purchased by people who won the lottery held by MHADA.

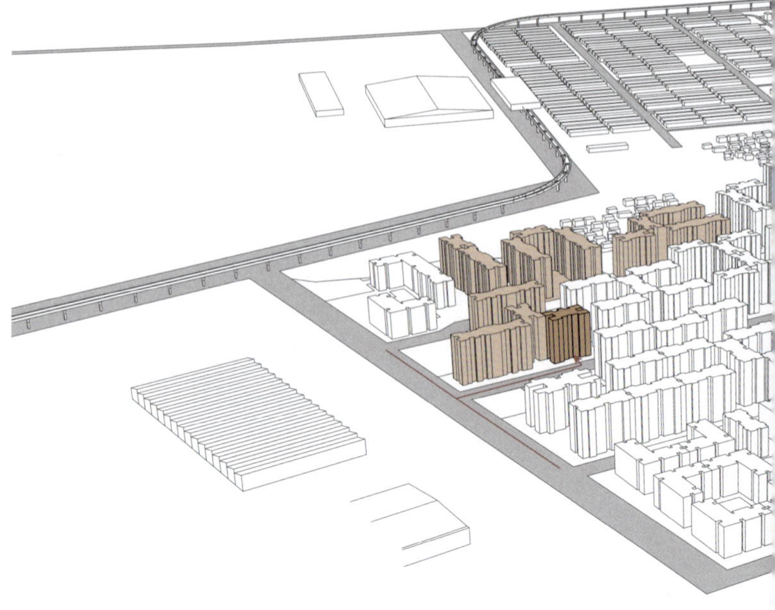

LOCATION

This structure is part of a complex laid out over a large expanse of land in Sion. It is well serviced by buses, close to the Harbour Line railway and also in proximity to the upcoming monorail depot.

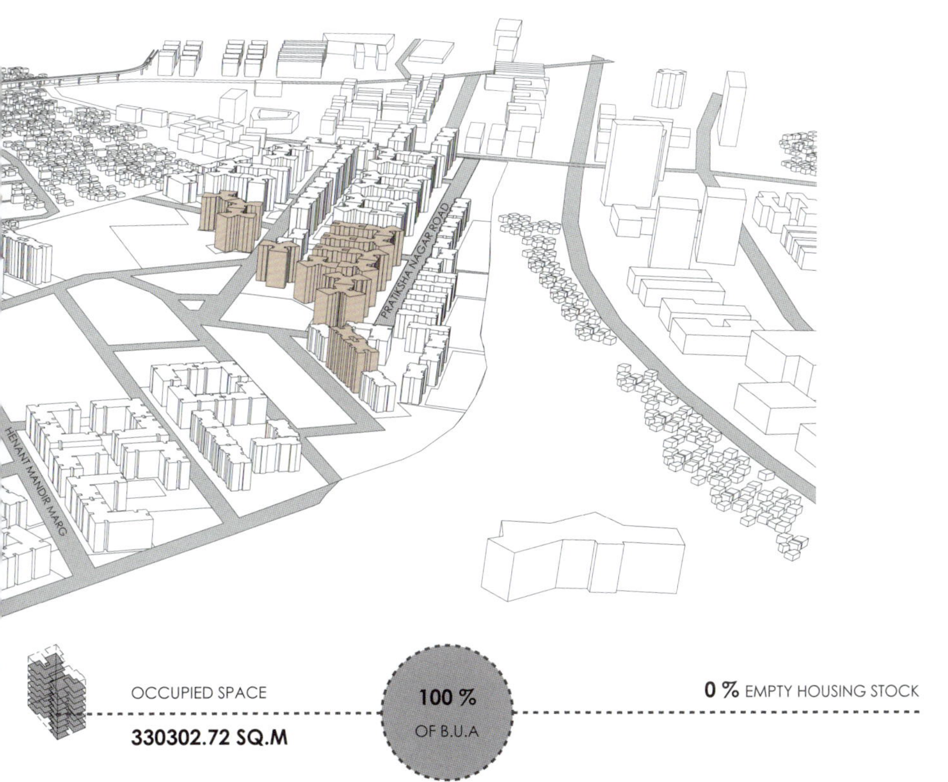

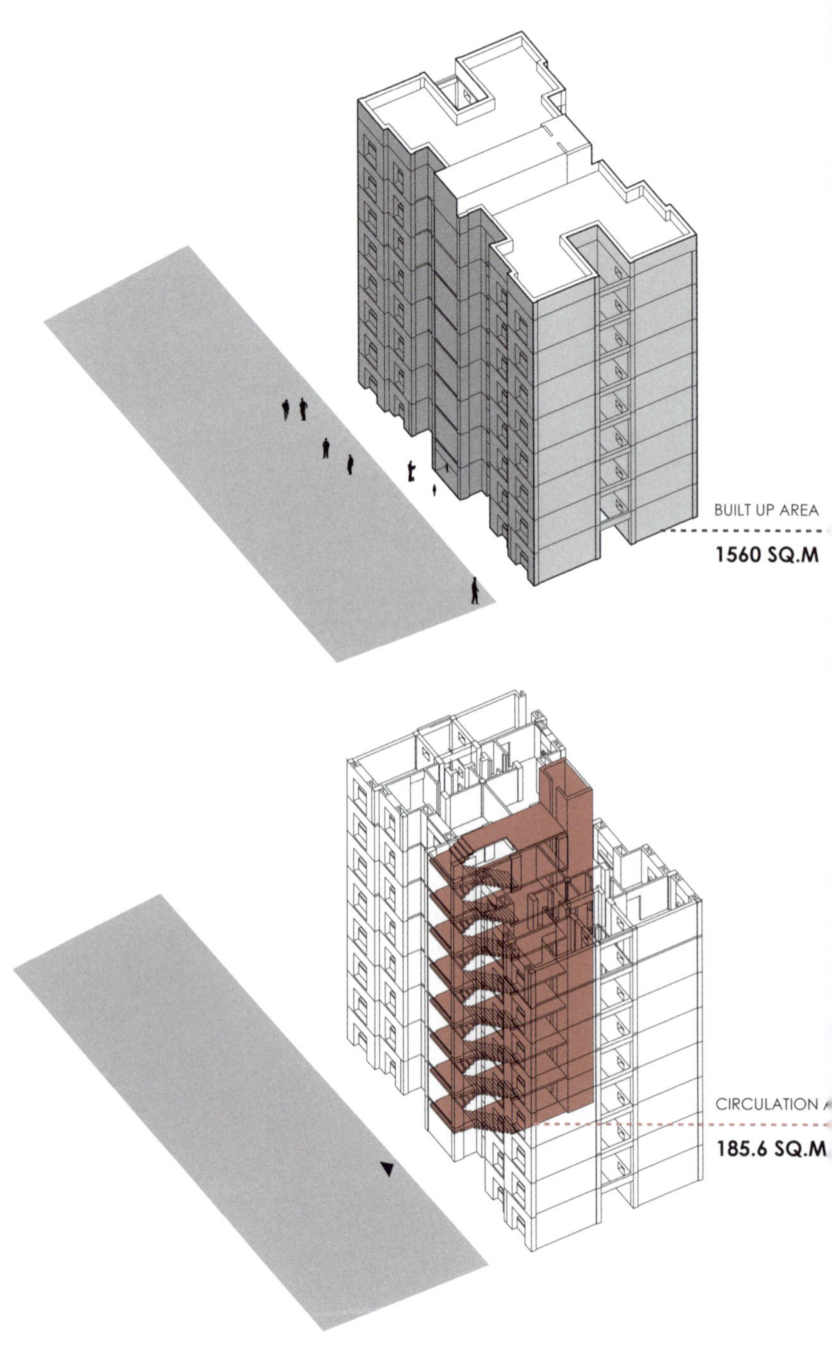
BUILT UP AREA
1560 SQ.M
CIRCULATION
185.6 SQ.M

BUILDING FORM

Like most of the buildings in the complex, the one under study is designed as a block of eight storeys, each with four units on every floor. The buildings are further clustered into a C-shaped plan with common open space in the centre of each cluster.

Each MHADA block is one in a multitude of similar structures that repeat so that the result is a vast sprawl of interlocking buildings. The open spaces in the interstices between buildings are used as gardens and play areas.

BUILT UP AREA PER PERSON

9.83 SQ.M
CONSIDERING 5 PEOPLE PER UNIT

CIRCULATION

The axis of movement – the staircases and lift – based on a typical apartment building plan is clearly defined within the centre of the four units on every storey. There is a very tight lobby space on every floor.

11.9 %
OF B.U.A

CIRCULATION AREA PER PERSON

1.16 SQ.M
CONSIDERING 5 PEOPLE PER UNIT

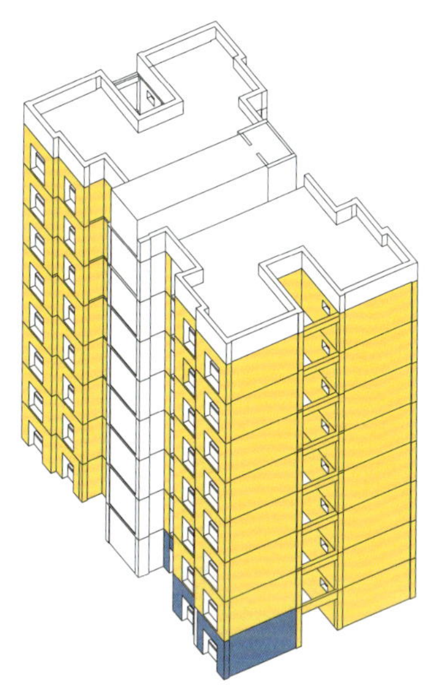

PROGRAMME

One of the 32 units in the building is dedicated to commercial purposes. The unit design for this is identical to that of the residential units.

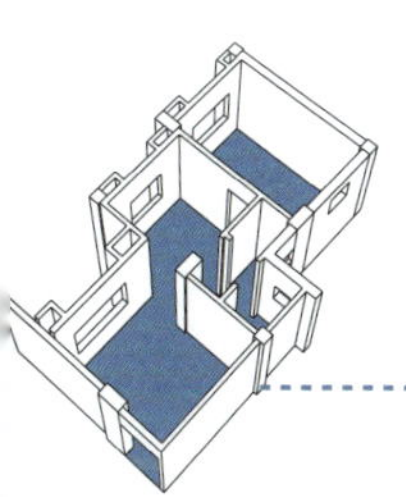

TOTAL COMMERCIAL AREA

36.3 SQ.M

6.3 SQ.M

1 NOS = 36.3 SQ.M

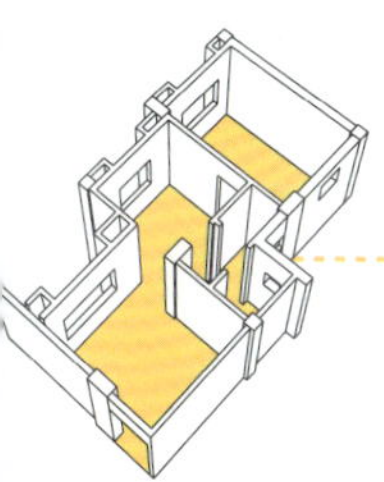

TOTAL RESIDENTIAL AREA

1125.3 SQ.M

.3 SQ.M

31 NOS = 1125.3 SQ.M

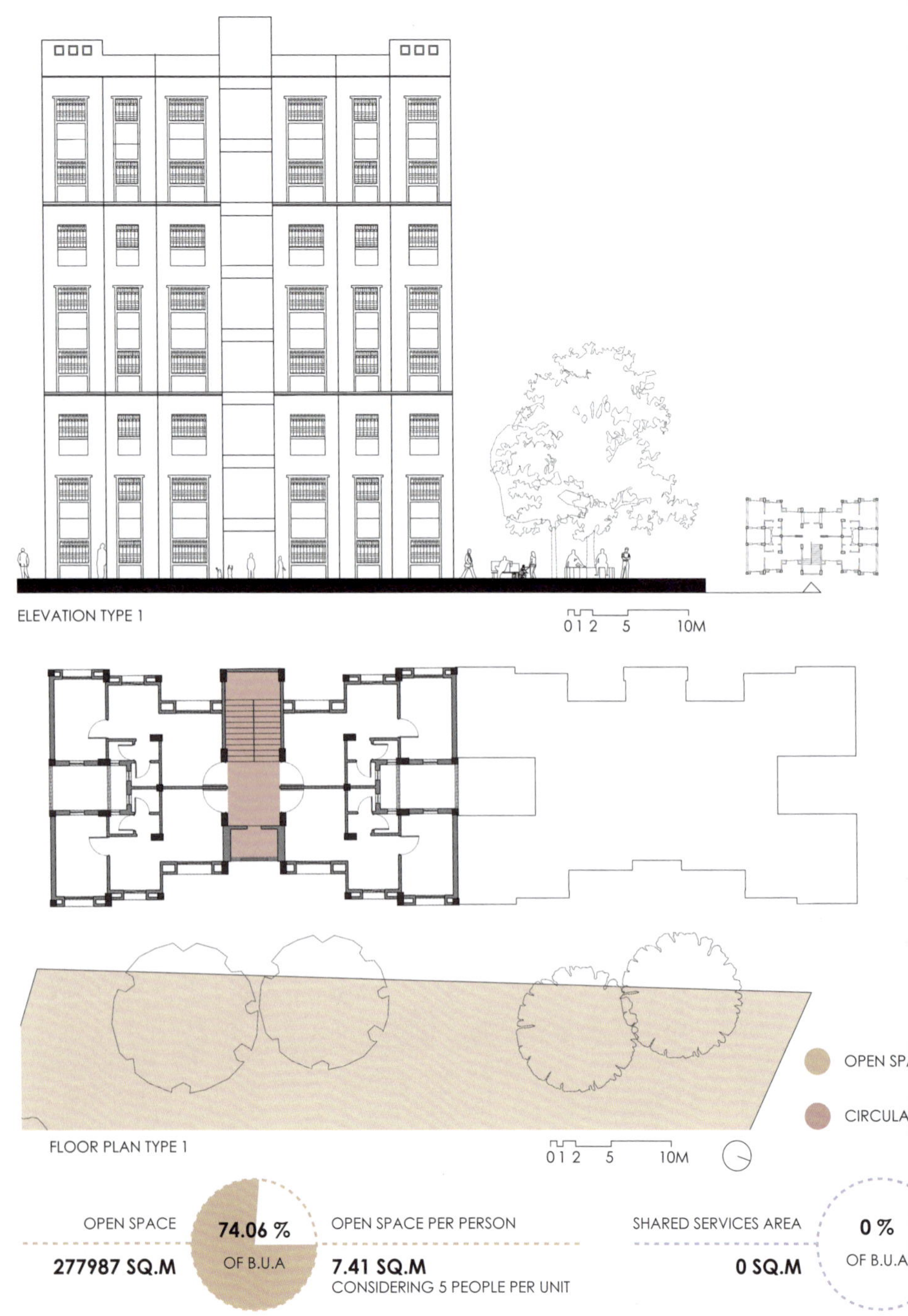
ELEVATION TYPE 1
0 1 2 5 10M
FLOOR PLAN TYPE 1
0 1 2 5 10M
OPEN SP
CIRCULA
OPEN SPACE
74.06 %
OF B.U.A
277987 SQ.M
OPEN SPACE PER PERSON
7.41 SQ.M
CONSIDERING 5 PEOPLE PER UNIT
SHARED SERVICES AREA
0 %
OF B.U.A
0 SQ.M

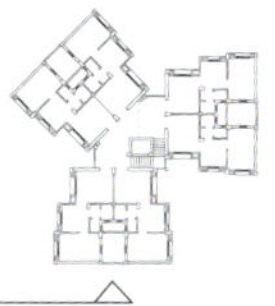

/ATION TYPE 2

ENVELOPE

The building has been constructed out of precast concrete; mechanisation and standardisation of units having enabled speedy construction.

Building exteriors are painted as per the income group they house, colour being the only variety in an otherwise homogenous sprawl.

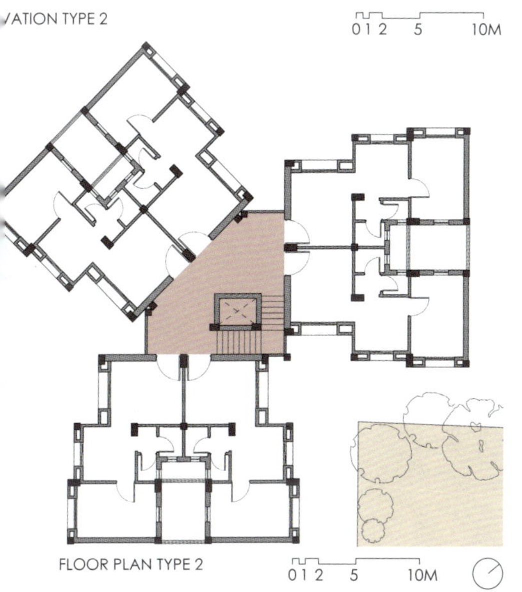

FLOOR PLAN TYPE 2

FLOOR PLANS

Residential units are divided into three spaces – living, kitchen and bedroom. There is also space for a WC, bath and wash basin area and all the spaces are staggered in plan so as to maximise the façade area for windows.

In Plan Type 1, there are four houses on every floor. Where buildings fit perpendicular to each other – as in Plan Type 2 – the specific positioning of individual units negotiates the corner, so that six units surround a triangular lobby on every floor. In both cases, adjacent units are separated by a ventilation shaft that is concealed from view by a *jaali* wall on the façade.

RED SERVICES AREA PER PERSON

Q.M

ISIDERING 5 PEOPLE PER UNIT

CIRCULATION AREA

185.6 SQ.M

11.9 %

OF B.U.A

CIRCULATION AREA PER PERSON

1.16 SQ.M

CONSIDERING 5 PEOPLE PER UNIT

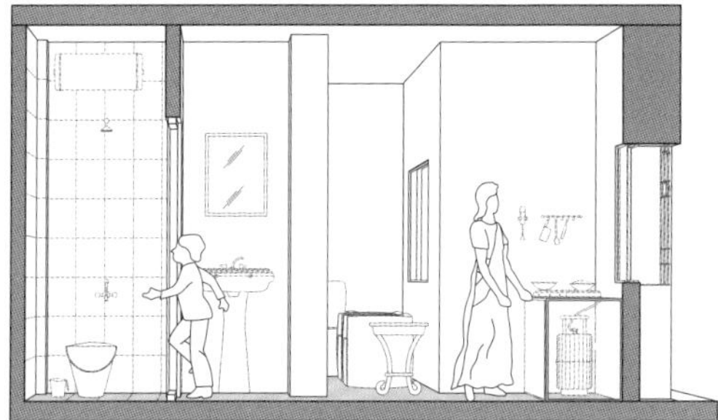

TYPICAL UNIT - SECTION B

UNIT

The unit plan – 36.3 sq.m in area – is divided as per function and movement is clearly defined, with living space on entry, followed by services areas and a bedroom. An attempt has been made to provide adequate light and ventilation to every room, the result of which is a staggered façade that is a product of interior requirements.

TYPICAL UNIT - SECTION A

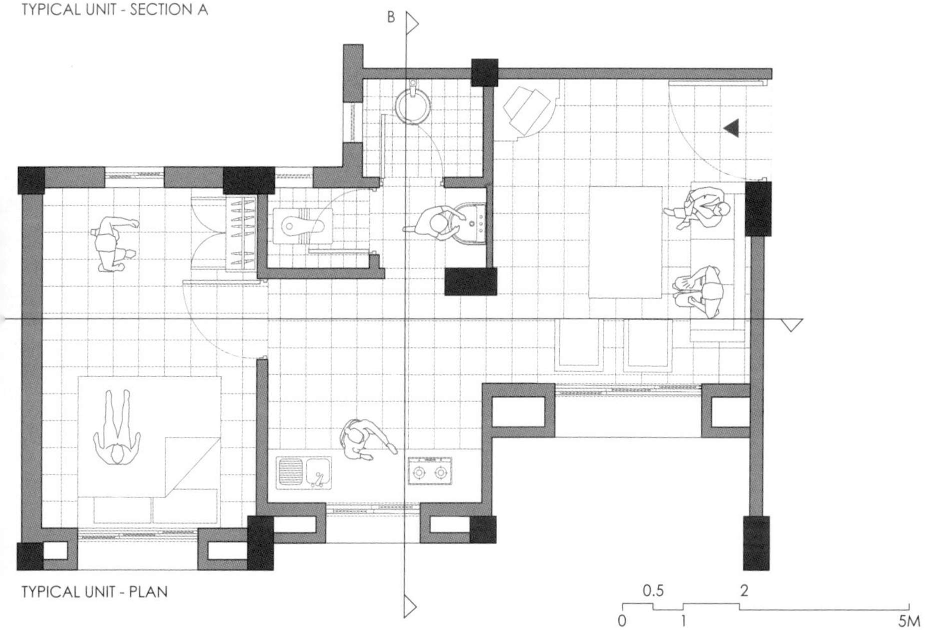

B

TYPICAL UNIT - PLAN

0.5 2

0 1 5M

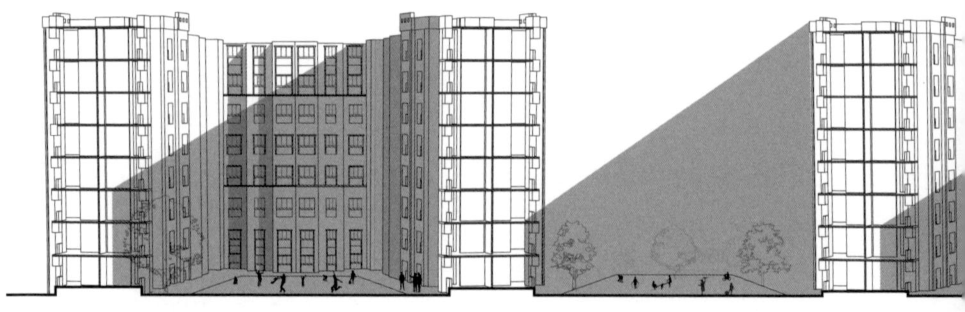

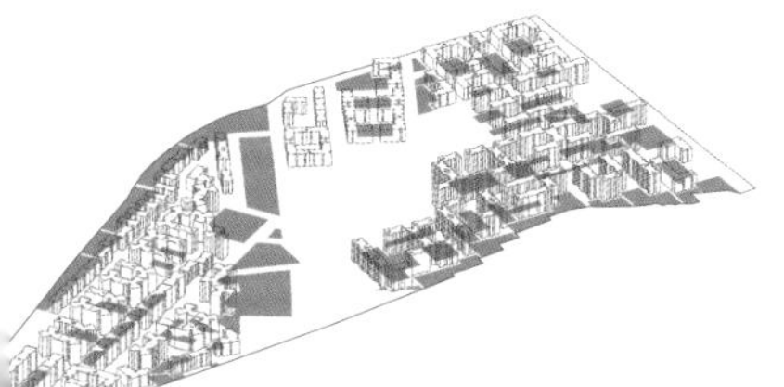

ANALYSIS

There is only one type of housing unit which is repeated in plan, creating a monotony that is further perpetuated by the aggregation of these units at the building level.

The configuration of clusters in the site plan however, allows for open space between and within them. Additionally, each building is eight storeys high and the quantum of open space between them with respect to their height is considerable. This area is used for community interaction and as a children's play area, but at the unit level there is no such scaled equivalent. The common lobby at every floor serves as little more than a buffer space between lift and main door, storing shoes and cycles and eliminating any possibility of interaction between residents.

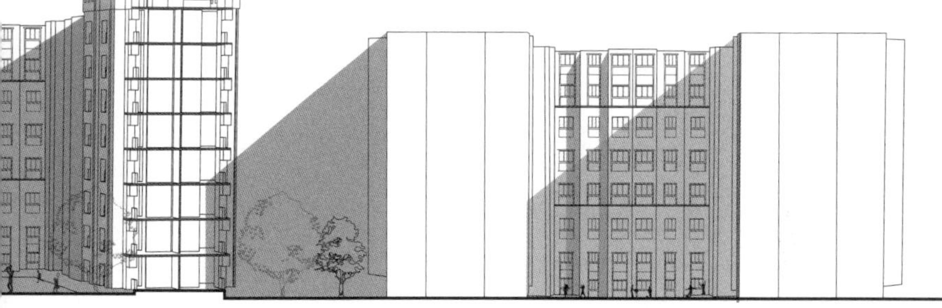

11

AMBEDKAR NAGAR SRA

11 | AMBEDKAR NAGAR SRA

RACKED AND STACKED

2011
LOWER PAREL

In the 1990s this plot was covered by a sprawling informal settlement. The area came under slum rehabilitation and Omkar Realtors and Developers acquired the land in 2007.

By 2010 there were four towering buildings where the settlement had once been, providing free housing to the existing residents under the directives of the Slum Rehabilitation Authority (SRA). The residents of the former slum that occupied the land were granted 25 sq.m (carpet area) units each, free of cost. They have legal ownership of their houses but as per the rules are not allowed to sell or rent out the flats for ten years after construction.

In 2011, a commercial tower was built by the Naman Midtown group, who bought a part of the plot from the original developers. This was part of the builder's free sale component, to earn back the investment made in the construction of the rehabilitation units.

In addition to this building, a small number of flats in the four towers was also allowed for sale in the open market, and a few house families displaced from other areas. All the families that originally inhabited the squatter settlement have been rehabilitated in the scheme.

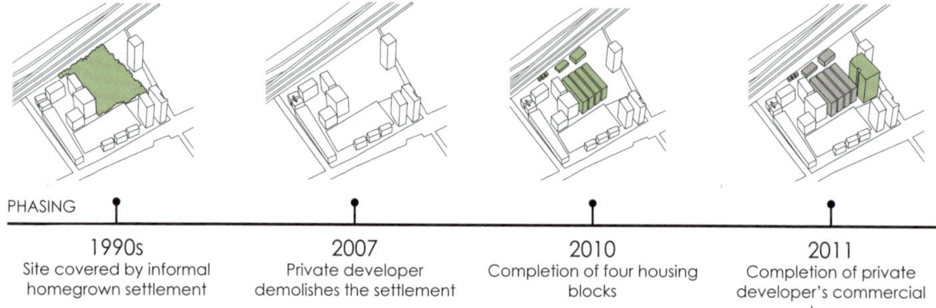

LOCATION

The four towers that comprise the SRA housing lie east of an open ground on Senapati Bapat Marg in Lower Parel. The plot itself does not abut any road and is accessed via an alley that connects to the main road.

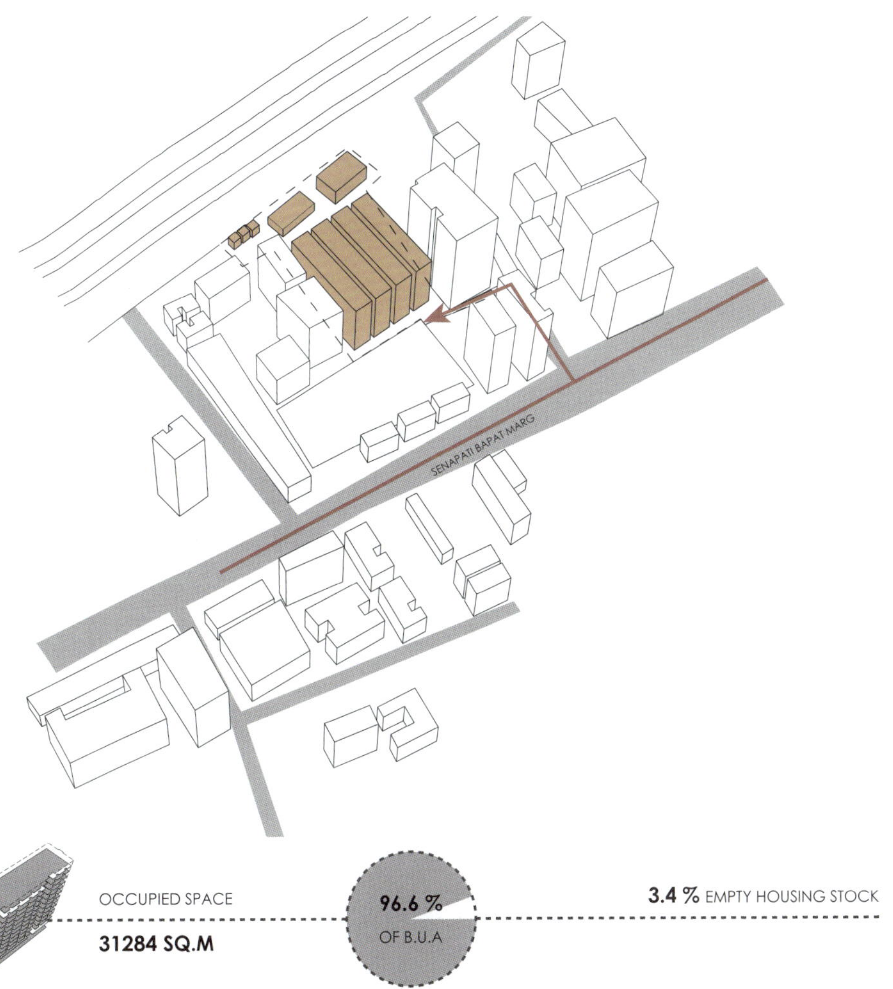

OCCUPIED SPACE

31284 SQ.M

96.6 %
OF B.U.A

3.4 % EMPTY HOUSING STOCK

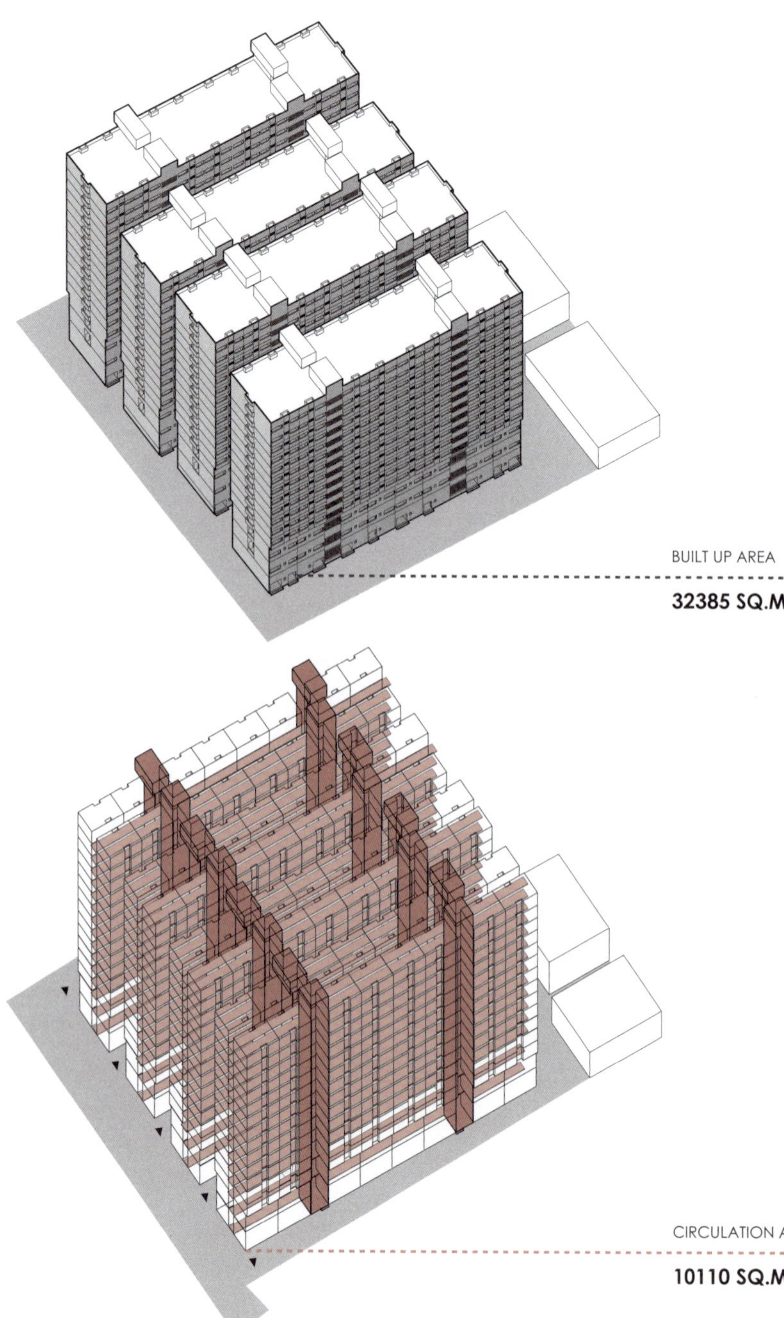
BUILT UP AREA
32385 SQ.M
CIRCULATION A
10110 SQ.M

BUILDING FORM

The housing blocks consist of four identical buildings, each 15 storeys tall. At the ground and first floors, each structure is set at 6 m from the other. From the second floor upwards, the floor plates cantilever out by 0.5 m along the length of the building in the northeast and southwest directions. As a result, the gap between buildings narrows to 5 m for 13 storeys. Building facades are mirror reflections of each other and a slim column of open space is all that exists between neighbours on either side of the divide, creating poor conditions for light and ventilation within these housing units.

BUILT UP AREA PER PERSON

7.69 SQ.M
CONSIDERING 6 PEOPLE PER UNIT

CIRCULATION

Internally each building has a 2 m wide double-loaded corridor running through its entire length. There are two sets of lifts and 1.5 m wide staircases for vertical circulation.

24.19 %
OF B.U.A

CIRCULATION AREA PER PERSON

1.72 SQ.M
CONSIDERING 6 PEOPLE PER UNIT

PROGRAMME

The ground and first floors of each structure contain commercial units, while the rest of the units are residential. Additionally, one of the buildings contains a multipurpose hall on its ground floor and there is also a temple on the site.

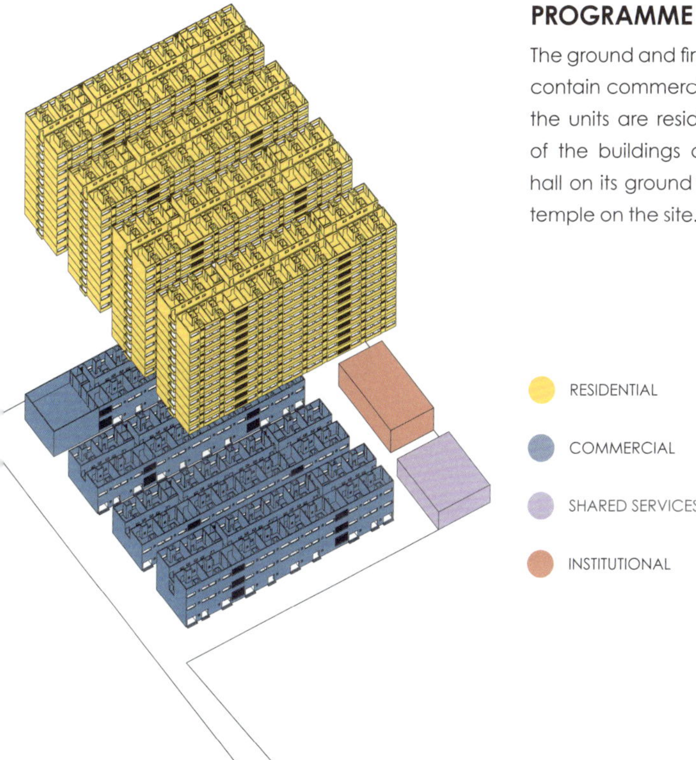

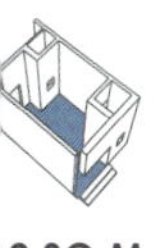

3 SQ.M
NOS = 550.8 SQ.M

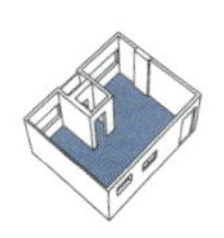

28.3 SQ.M
X 108 NOS = 3056.4 SQ.M

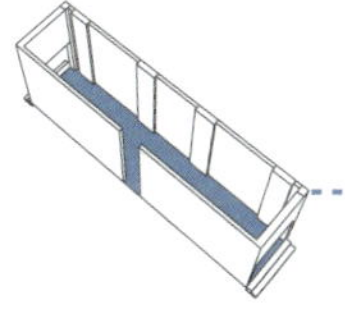

30.3 SQ.M
X 18 NOS = 545.4 SQ.M

TOTAL COMMERCIAL AREA

4152.6 SQ.M

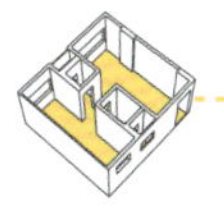

31.4 SQ.M
X 816 NOS = 25662 SQ.M

TOTAL RESIDENTIAL AREA

25622 SQ.M

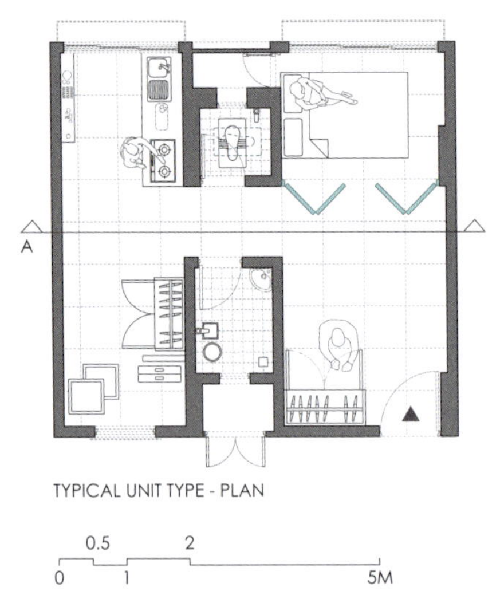

TYPICAL UNIT TYPE - PLAN

0.5 2
0 1 5M

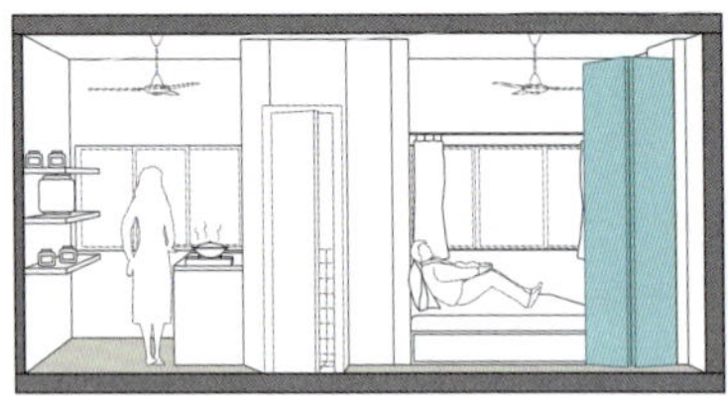

TYPICAL UNIT - SECTION A

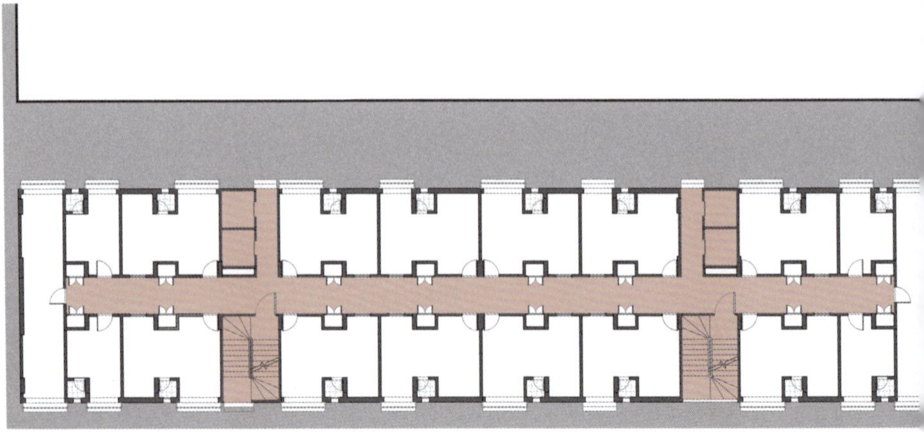

GROUND FLOOR PLAN

2 8 20M
0 4

OPEN SPACE
2949 SQ.M

7.02 %
OF B.U.A

OPEN SPACE PER PERSON
0.50 SQ.M
CONSIDERING 6 PEOPLE PER UNIT

SHARED SERVICES AREA
0 SQ.M

0 %
OF B.U.A

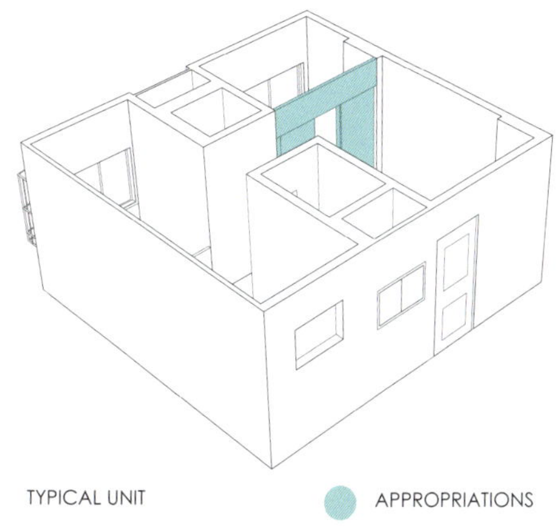

TYPICAL UNIT

APPROPRIATIONS

UNITS

The standard unit size is 31.4 sq.m and is laid out such that living and kitchen spaces are separated by a WC and bath area. This arrangement – as opposed to an open floor plate – inhibits flexible use of the space.

As per SRA rules, beneficiaries are not allowed to make civil interventions in their units for ten years after moving in, and therefore the houses are largely unaltered. Some residents have made minimally invasive additions in the form of folding partitions that divide the living space into two, so that an additional independent bedroom can be accommodated.

FLOOR PLANS

There are 18 similar units on a floor, nine on each side of a double-loaded corridor.

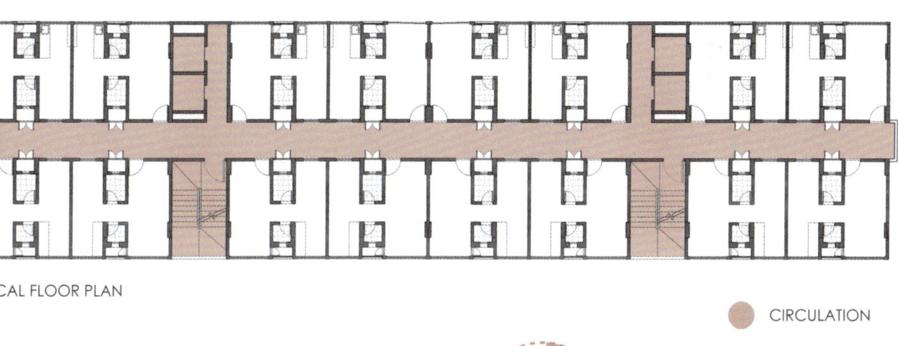

ICAL FLOOR PLAN

CIRCULATION

RED SERVICES AREA PER PERSON

Q.M
ISIDERING 6 PEOPLE PER UNIT

CIRCULATION AREA

10110 SQ.M

24.9 %
OF B.U.A

CIRCULATION AREA PER PERSON

1.72 SQ.M
CONSIDERING 6 PEOPLE PER UNIT

NORTHEAST SIDE ELEVATION

ENVELOPE

The northeast and southwest facades of each of the four towers demonstrate monotony that is the result of a cookie-cutter approach to the design of units. Grilled windows alternate with slatted openings, the latter incorporated to provide daylight and air at staircase mid landings and to toilets. Despite this provision and the ventilators between units and corridors, cross ventilation in the northeast-southwest direction is rendered impossible due to the close proximity of the buildings.

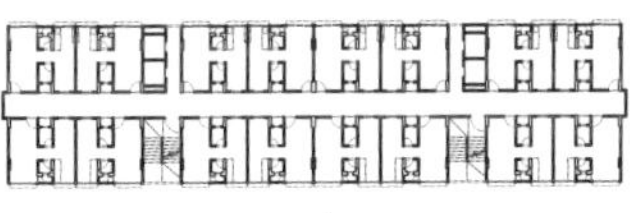

1.5 6 16M
0 3

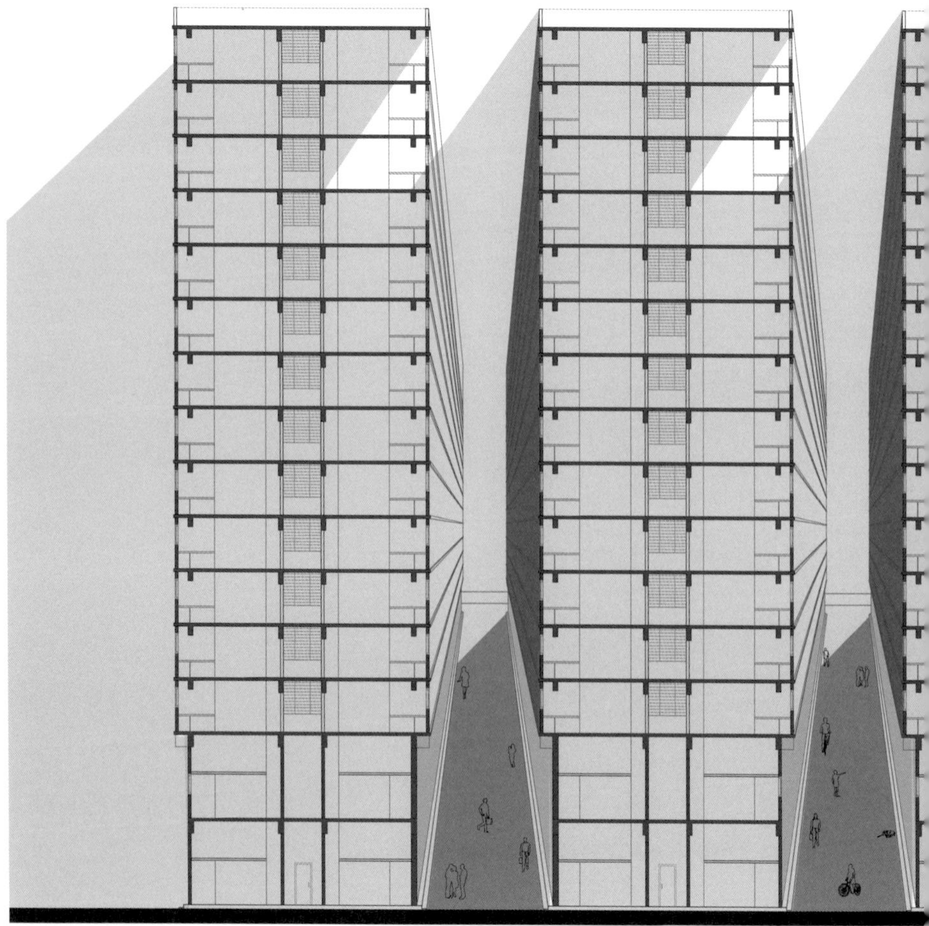

ANALYSIS

The contrast between this complex and its surroundings is only too apparent. Curtain glazed commercial establishments almost double the height of the four SRA buildings surround them, accentuating the sense of skewed development.

At the building level, the quality of architectural space was observed to have impacted social engagement. The corridors between units could have been potential spaces for release, but being poorly lit and ventilated are unsuccessful and used for storage.

Additionally, the external faces of houses are very close to neighbouring windows. This proximity between units in adjacent towers is not only inhuman and physically stifling, but also a safety hazard.

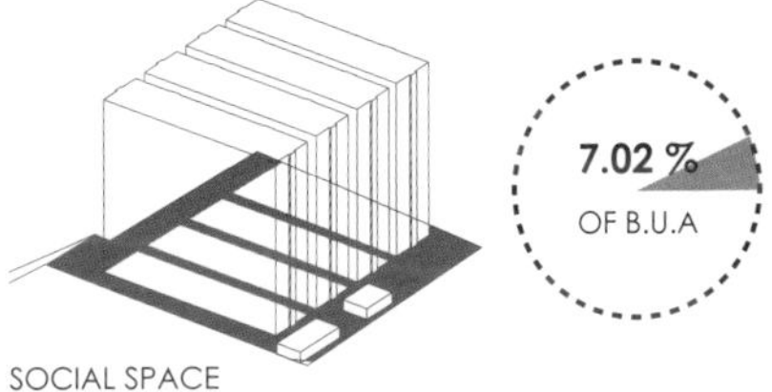

SOCIAL SPACE

NAMAN
MIDTOWN

INFERENCES

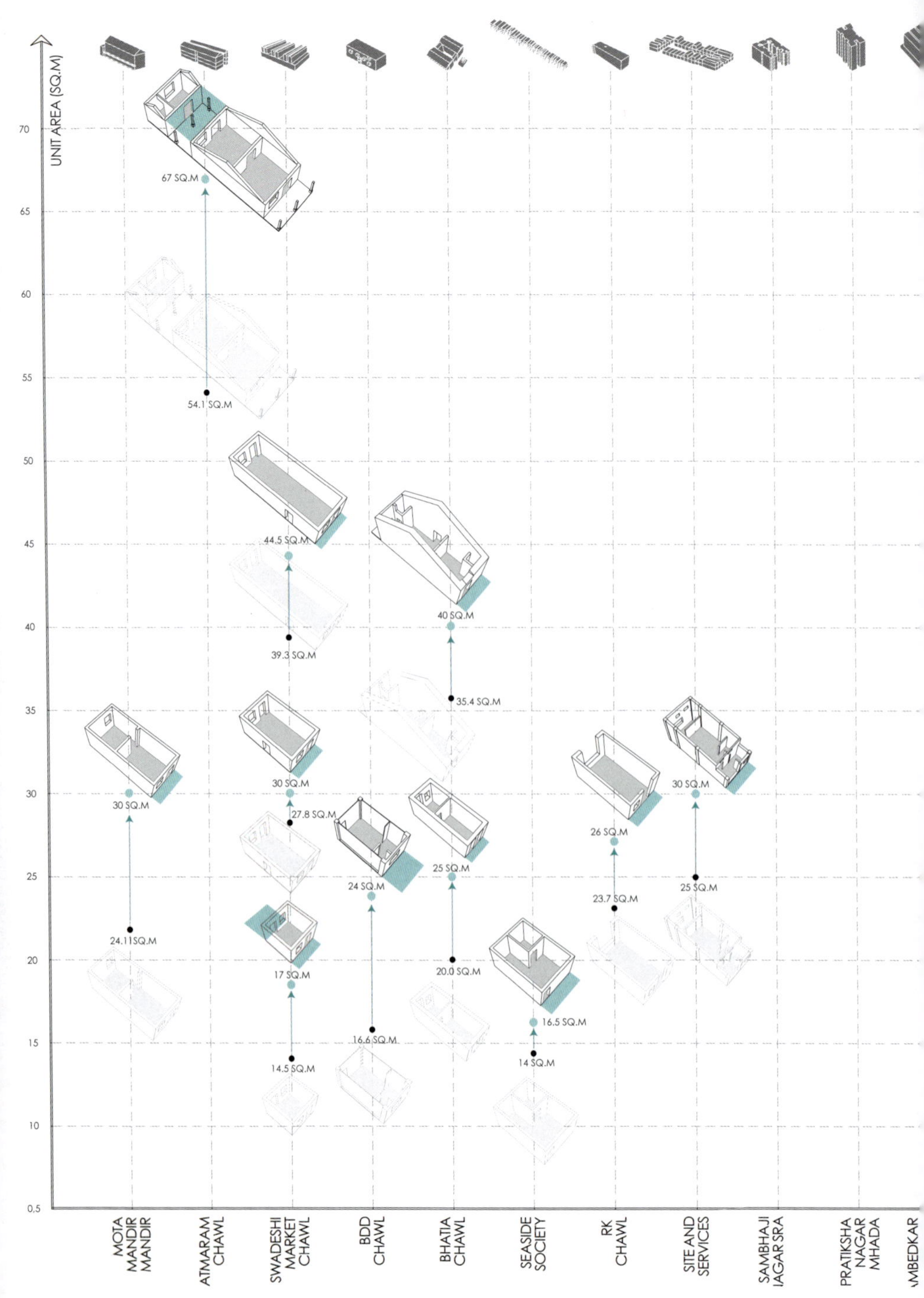

UNIT AREA (SQ.M)
70
65
60
55
50
45
40
35
30
25
20
15
10
0,5
67 SQ.M
54.1 SQ.M
44.5 SQ.M
39.3 SQ.M
40 SQ.M
35.4 SQ.M
30 SQ.M
30 SQ.M
27.8 SQ.M
24.11SQ.M
17 SQ.M
14.5 SQ.M
24 SQ.M
16.6 SQ.M
25 SQ.M
20.0 SQ.M
16.5 SQ.M
14 SQ.M
26 SQ.M
23.7 SQ.M
30 SQ.M
25 SQ.M
MOTA MANDIR MANDIR
ATMARAM CHAWL
SWADESHI MARKET CHAWL
BDD CHAWL
BHATIA CHAWL
SEASIDE SOCIETY
RK CHAWL
SITE AND SERVICES
SAMBHAJI IAGAR SRA
PRATIKSHA NAGAR MHADA
MBEDKAR

EXTENDED DOMESTICITY

This graph is a comparison of the limited unit interior areas, with the amount of space external to it that supports interior programmes.

The measurement of the quantum of these supporting spaces and appropriations forms a useful starting point in understanding inhabitants' aspirations through the space they create for themselves within the constraints of their built environment. At the same time it is also reflective of an architecture that evinces elasticity, offering the potential to be converted temporally and used for multiple functions.

The SRA and MHADA projects are largely free from external appropriations and encroachments and have therefore not been plotted on the graph.

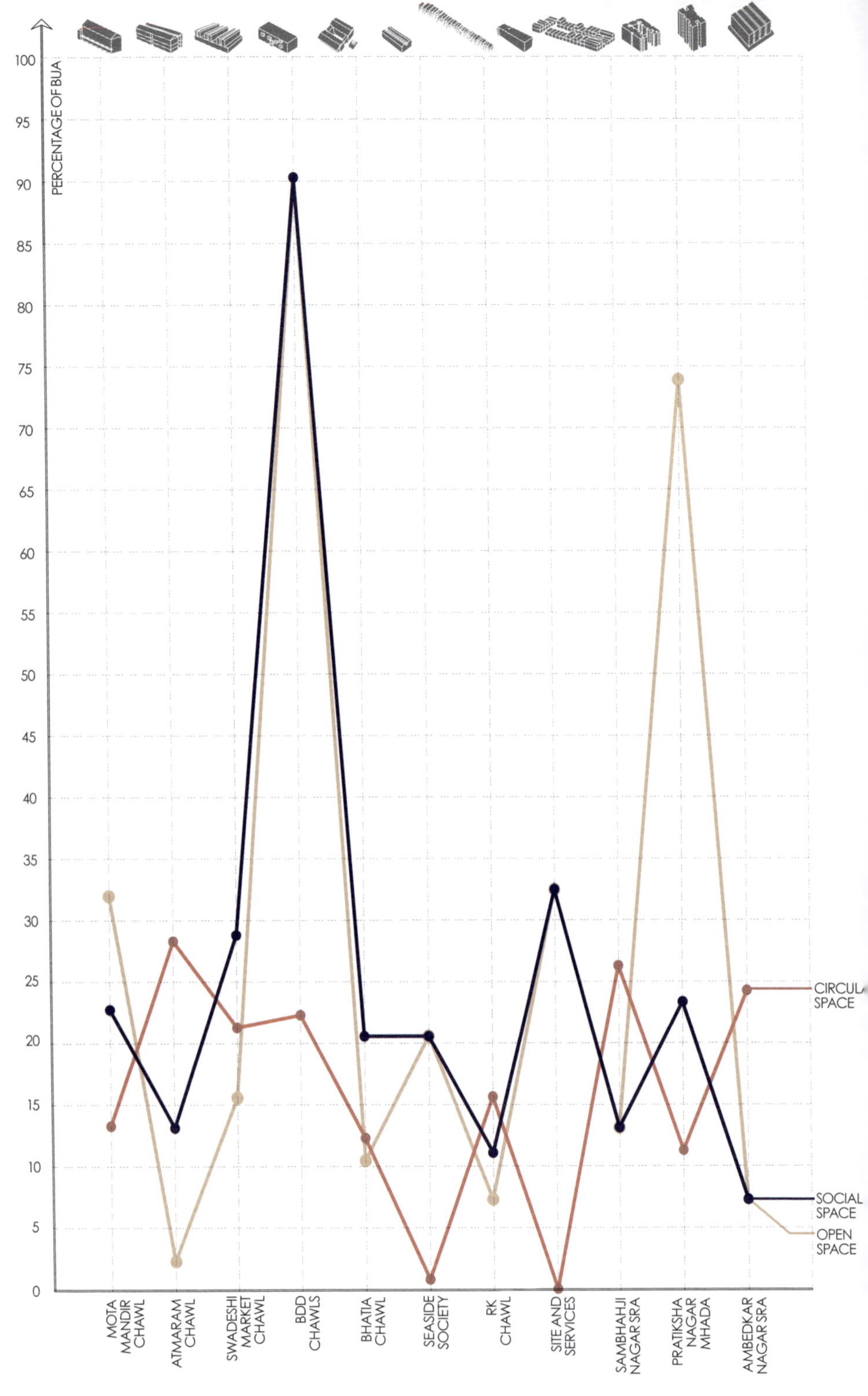

PERCENTAGE OF BUA
100
95
90
85
80
75
70
65
60
55
50
45
40
35
30
25
20
15
10
5
0
MOTA MANDIR CHAWL
ATMARAM CHAWL
SWADESHI MARKET CHAWL
BDD CHAWLS
BHATIA CHAWL
SEASIDE SOCIETY
RK CHAWL
SITE AND SERVICES
SAMBHAHJI NAGAR SRA
PRATIKSHA NAGAR MHADA
AMBEDKAR NAGAR SRA
SPACE
SOCIAL SPACE
OPEN SPACE

SOCIAL SPACE

The graph compares the quantum of social space (based on observation and physical measurements) against circulation and open space in each of these projects.

Swadeshi Market Chawl and Bhatia Chawl are closest to the archetype of chawl housing, arranged as they are, as rows of units along corridors that front a common courtyard. Such architectural elements determine the area of social space, which in these projects is inevitably greater than both circulation and open spaces, as it is accounts for both.

In RK and BDD Chawls, the corridor width is 2.1 m and 2.66 m respectively. Despite the constrained width in the case of RK Chawl, the corridor plays an important role in the social lives of its inhabitants, becoming a receptacle of community interaction. In marked contrast are the BDD Chawls, where the corridor is bereft of activity. This difference can be attributed to the impact of communal demography in the two chawls – the BDD Chawls houses people from various communities, while RK Chawl is predominantly Gujarati. The social space as observed in the BDD Chawls is the result of people interacting in the open space between buildings, and not within them.

In terms of open space, at about 74% and 91% of Built Up Area respectively, the MHADA and BDD projects soar above the rest of the cases in the study, but despite this, spaces in the MHADA project seem to facilitate less social interaction. Based on our observations, we found that single large swathes of open area between buildings though used by children as play areas, etc don't catalyse round the clock social interaction, while tighter clusters with a more intimate scale that enables greater spatial and visual connectivity to common courtyards, was seen to work better.

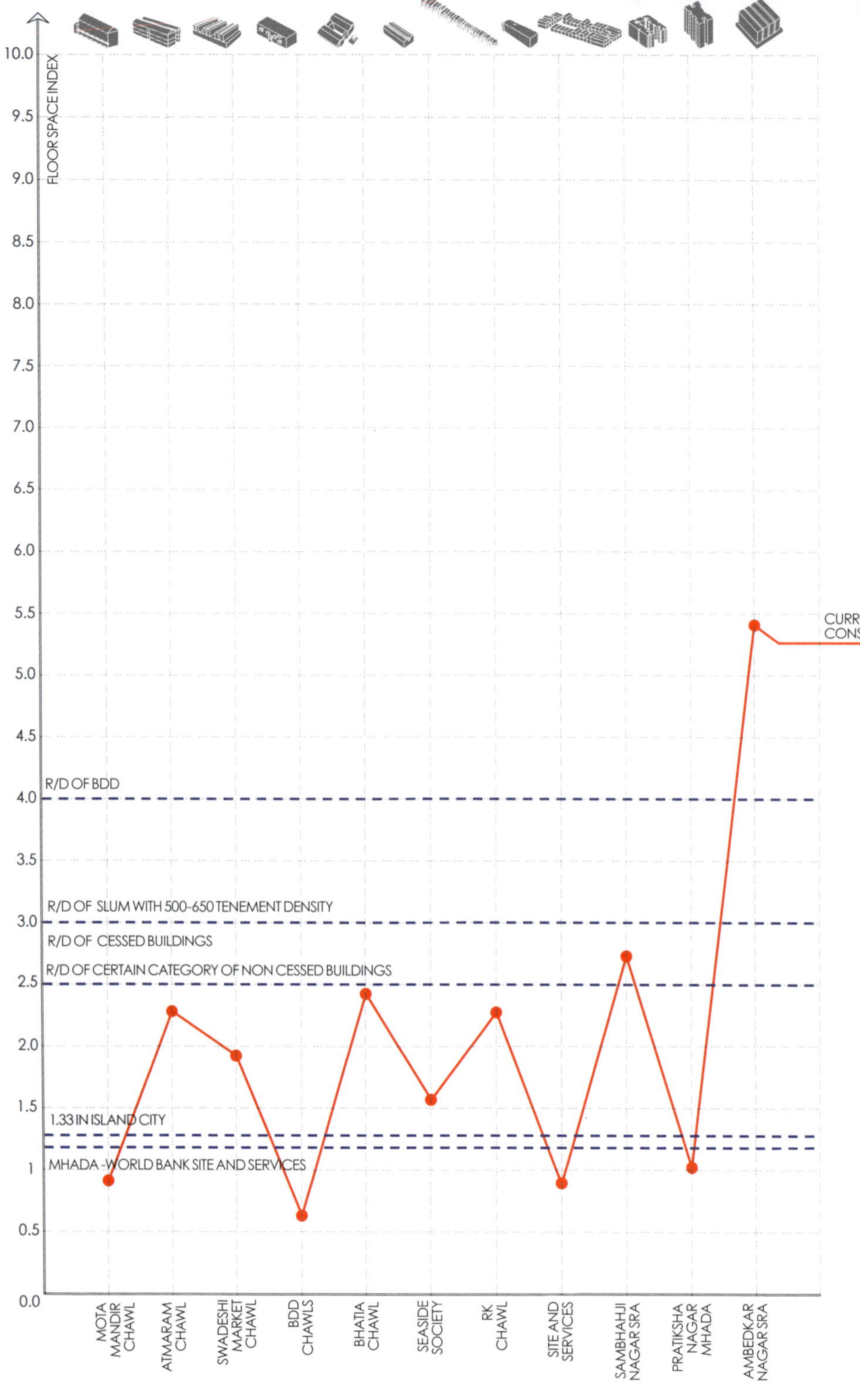
FLOOR SPACE INDEX
10.0
9.5
9.0
8.5
8.0
7.5
7.0
6.5
6.0
5.5
5.0
4.5
4.0
3.5
3.0
2.5
2.0
1.5
1
0.5
0.0
R/D OF BDD
R/D OF SLUM WITH 500-650 TENEMENT DENSITY
R/D OF CESSED BUILDINGS
R/D OF CERTAIN CATEGORY OF NON CESSED BUILDINGS
1.33 IN ISLAND CITY
MHADA -WORLD BANK SITE AND SERVICES
CURREN
CONSUM
MOTA MANDIR CHAWL
ATMARAM CHAWL
SWADESHI MARKET CHAWL
BDD CHAWLS
BHATIA CHAWL
SEASIDE SOCIETY
RK CHAWL
SITE AND SERVICES
SAMBHAHJI NAGAR SRA
PRATIKSHA NAGAR MHADA
AMBEDKAR NAGAR SRA

FLOOR SPACE INDEX (FSI)

The points on the graph indicate the FSI currently consumed by each case in the study, and how they compare with standard FSIs available for redevelopment of these projects.

As a purely academic exercise Seaside Society, as it currently stands on a plot that is in effect a pavement, equates to an FSI of 1.65. That it consumes an FSI comparative to state-mandated figures, forms a valid argument against high rise, high density models like the SRA.

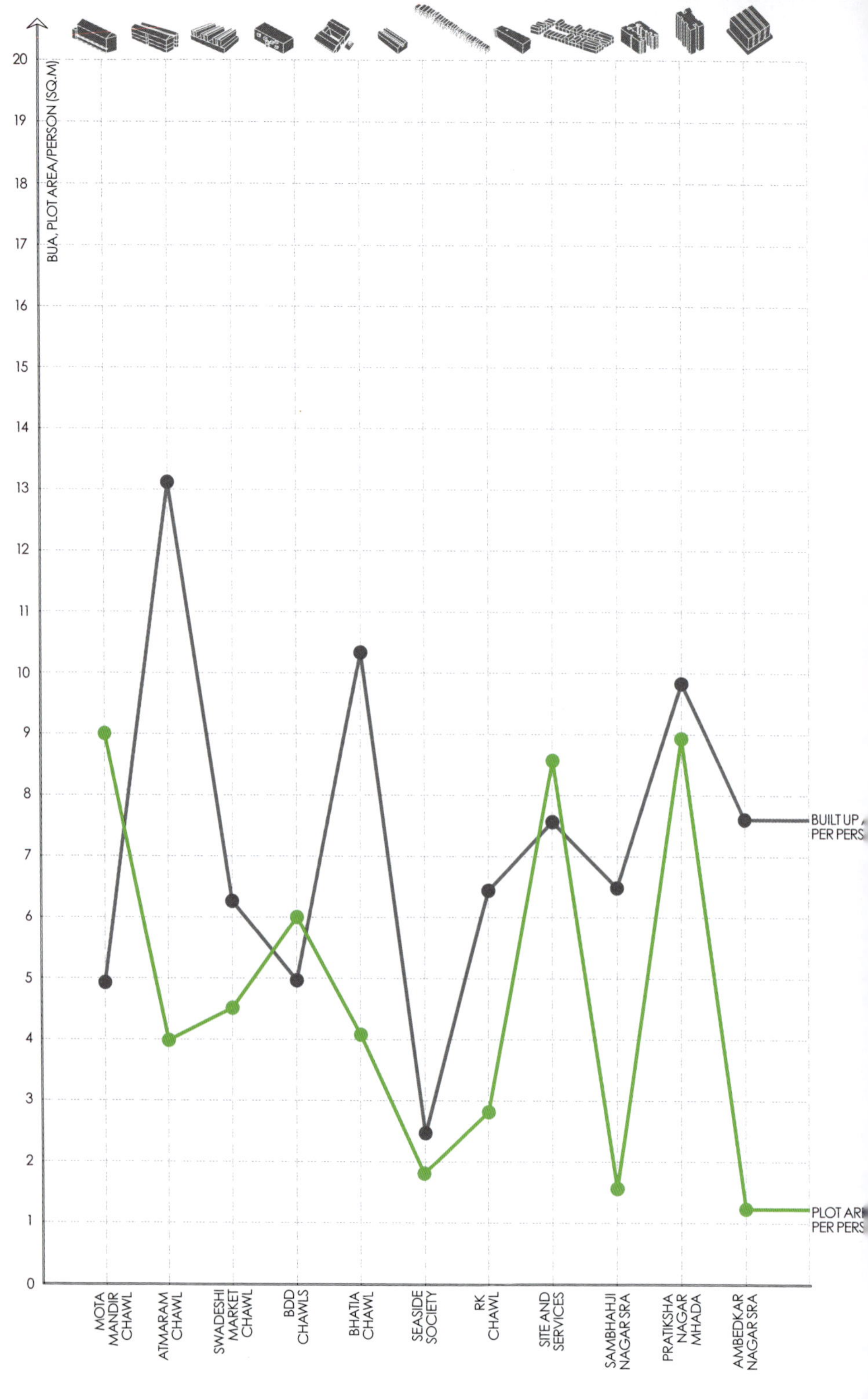
BUA, PLOT AREA/PERSON (SQ.M)
20
19
18
17
16
15
14
13
12
11
10
9
8
7
6
5
4
3
2
1
0
BUILT UP A
PER PERS
PLOT AR
PER PERS
MOTA MANDIR CHAWL
ATMARAM CHAWL
SWADESHI MARKET CHAWL
BDD CHAWLS
BHATIA CHAWL
SEASIDE SOCIETY
RK CHAWL
SITE AND SERVICES
SAMBHAHJI NAGAR SRA
PRATIKSHA NAGAR MHADA
AMBEDKAR NAGAR SRA

BUILT UP AND PLOT AREA PER PERSON

This graph is a function of the square metre area in terms of Built Up Area and Plot Area of each of the 11 projects divided by the number of residents occupying the building.

Atmaram Chawl and Ambedkar Nagar SRA individually show a vast difference between these two areas, with Built Up Area Per Person significantly higher than Plot Area Per Person in both cases. While this would normally be considered undesirable, in Atmaram Chawl, the built form is articulated so as to generate interior spill-out space that compensates for the lack of open area on the ground. In the SRA project, with corridors being poorly lit and ventilated, there is no such alternative to plot area.

In the BDD Chawls and Site and Services projects, the two ratios lie close to each other on the graph, in both cases Plot Area Per Person being higher than Built Up Area Per Person. Both these projects are low rise models of development with either large open spaces as in BDD, or a central courtyard as in Site and Services, adding to their vitality and contributing to a healthy ratio of plot area to number of people. These spaces serve multiple functions and reinforce the importance of open space in planning.

EPILOGUE

In the Name of Housing started as research into the architecture of affordable housing types as background material for a design project in our studio. The more time we spent in the field looking specifically at the form of these projects, the more instructive they became, both through the breadth of their variations, as well as the depth of their spatial and formal engagements. The analytical diagrams and drawings in this book further galvanised our belief that these armatures however unique, still seem to gravitate around certain emergent commonalities. This concluding essay attempts to elaborate on a few of these characteristics and argues for these to be benchmarks while designing the architecture of low income affordable housing. A few of these parameters are as follows:

Networks

Global best practices in planning today acknowledge the importance of transportation networks to affordable housing. Our study furthers this understanding by bringing to light the interdependencies that these projects share with the city, in that their design, while influenced by the larger site context, also impacts the surrounding city fabric.

The two cases of Mota Mandir and Swadeshi Market Chawl both evince the nature of precincts networked within the urban landscape rather than being just isolated housing blocks. These projects within various degrees of adjacencies to street networks show how their built forms accommodate linkages to the adjoining urban fabric, allowing for the city to permeate though their private domains.

Such systems are not limited to physical connectivity alone, but are also part of socio-economic networks as seen in *slim city*, Seaside Society. Symptomatic of all such settlements, residents of Seaside Society work within close proximity of their homes and are enmeshed in various activities servicing the formal city, while also being serviced through various mechanisms, by it.

Social Infrastructure

The importance of social cohesion has been a critical paradigm for the sustenance of these housing types. The role of built form and its elements like courtyards, corridors and staircases in the generation of social connect is significant. This condition challenges the assumptions of regulatory frameworks in a city like Mumbai, which are designed to segregate common space from living space in fear of the former being encroached.

Bhatia Chawl's intimate height to width ratio of the courtyard facilitates communication across its volume, resulting in an extended social fabric that is embedded in the architecture. Residents of the society here speak with great pride about their housing and how, many of them were born and grew up in the building. They wouldn't mind more area being added to their individual units, but are clear that it cannot be at the expense of the common spaces that they share.

This case lies in direct contrast to the SRA project in Lower Parel where corridors, devoid of light and ventilation, are no more than conveyors of people – circulation that offers little potential for community interaction.

Open Systems

Embedded in most projects was the idea of architecture as a systemic framework that allowed a structural logic to coexist with variation and flexibility in unit size, design and programme.

Buildings such as RK Chawl are notable for their ordering of units within a staid repeating grid that allows for four units of varying size as well as socio-economic class. In Atmaram Chawl the alternating plan configuration of access and programme allows for part of the unit to function independently, creating avenues for expansion or monetisation of excess area.

Appropriations

The previous point segues into one of the most pertinent aspects of design of low income affordable housing, this being the ability to allow for expansion and change over time. As capacities and aspirations of residents grow, so does the need for the architecture to allow for this to be accommodated.

While internal reconfiguration of space – such as the conversion of the *mori* to a bath area or insertion of a loft level – was seen to be the norm in all the projects, we found the natures of appropriation differing from project to project, contingent on shared values of community, geographical location as in RK Chawl, or as a result of their absence as seen in BDD.

Detail

It was instructive to see the sophistication of construction and technical detail within these projects, emphasising the lucidity of their construct while being pivotal in the production of extremely liveable spaces.

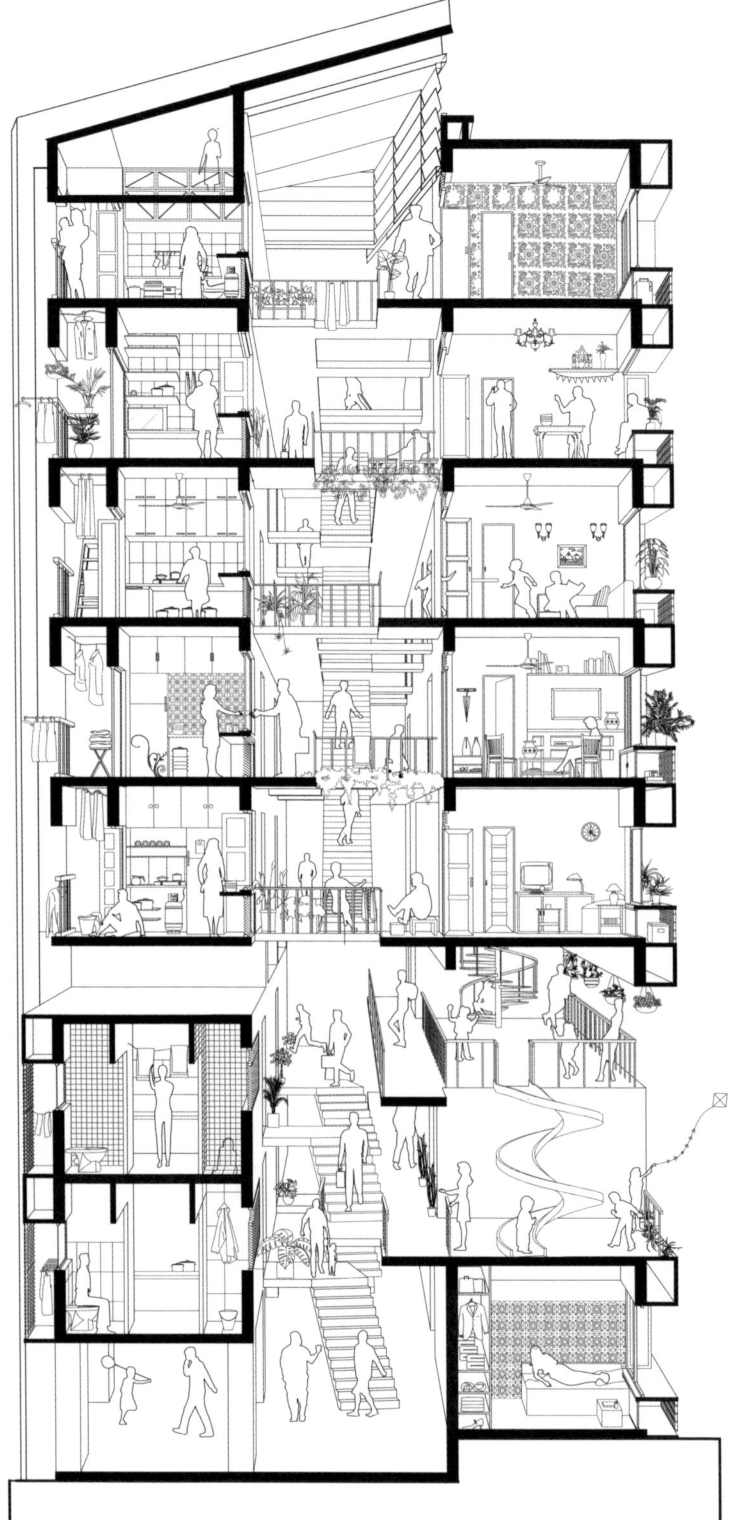

Tight interiors and high densities have given rise to a range of inventive architectural details at every scale, as seen in the louvred stack ventilation of towers of Swadeshi Market Chawl, sophisticated structural engineering in the bulging homes at BDD and tripartite windows for natural cooling at Bhatia Chawl.

Such modifications help position the design details of affordable housing projects, not merely as receptacles of people, but as well thought out functioning systems that hold clues for the design of housing in today's context.

The architecture of low income affordable housing whether state-built or state-enabled developer housing, in most cases lacks imagination and is usually just a mathematical exercise to maximise real estate profits. The above five points are but a few of the many paradigms that can inform the design of affordable housing, since at present, the understanding that such design needs to consider amongst other issues: expandability, systemic openness, live-work scenarios and socio-cultural space, is largely absent.

Our design project in Navi Mumbai is far removed from the geographical and economic constraints of our field of investigation but notwithstanding it attempts to provide fertile ground for the studio to test the projective capacity of our learnings in real time and an authentic context. It is our hope that the presentation of our research as individual case studies in the public realm in the form of this catalogue provides a reference for consolidating these learnings, as well as leaving them open to interpretation by others.

PLANS
UNITS

GLOSSARY

Balwadi: Indian pre-primary schools usually set up for children from economically weaker sections and run by Non-governmental Organisations (NGO) or the government.

Carpet Area: The net usable area within a building or room, excluding that covered by the walls.

Cessed Building: Buildings whose residents pay a cess or tax for their repair to the housing board.

Chajja: Projection at the lintel level of doors and windows that protects the opening from rain or harsh sun.

Chawl: Housing typology that emerged in the early 1900s in reaction to the demand for cheap housing for migrant labourers working in Bombay's mill lands.

Floor Space Index (FSI): The quotient of the ratio of the combined gross floor area of all floors, excepting areas specifically exempted under the Development Control Regulations, to the plot area, i.e. Total covered area of all floors/Plot Area.

Free sale component: The extra portion of FSI granted to developers undertaking slum rehabilitation work, as an incentive that cross-subsidises the cost of construction of cost-free rehabilitation tenements.

Gaothan: Low rise community housing in former village settlements, now surrounded by urban development, and inhabited by descendents of the original residents of the city.

Jaali: Perforated screen or mesh built on the façade of a building to allow air flow.

Leave and License: An agreement that grants permission to the tenant only as per the terms of a contract and involves no transfer of interest of the property, unlike a tenancy/rental agreement in which there is an element of immovability of the tenant by the owner unless evicted under the Rent Act.

Maharashtra Housing and Area Development Authority (MHADA): The body that undertakes housing projects under schemes for various income groups.

Maisonette: Self-contained living unit, usually of two or more floors, having its own independent access and part of a larger structure.

Mori: Originally a floor drain (also known as *nullah* or *nahani* trap), extended to mean ablution/potwash area.

Pagdi: The system of property sale whereby houses coming under the purview of the Rent Control Act, 1947, authorise long-time tenants to sell their tenancy rights provided they give a share consisting of one third of the sale price to the landlord.

Pergola: Latticed surface constructed to form a shaded walkway or work space below it, shielded from sunlight.

Site and Services: Schemes – usually for low-income families – that provide rehabilitation in the form of plots of land – either on ownership or land lease tenure – along with a bare minimum of essential infrastructure needed for habitation.

Slum: Informal settlement characterised by shanties, usually no more than two storeys high, put together with cheap, easily available materials, often lacking adequate infrastructure and inhabited by migrants.

Slum Rehabilitation Authority (SRA): The body instituted by the Government of Maharashtra in December 1995, with the aim of providing free basic housing in place of squatter settlements, through collaboration with private developers.

Venturi Effect: The phenomenon by which an interior space is cooled by means of air movement through the walls of a narrow – usually louvred – tower above such a space.

WC: Acronym used for 'Water Closet' – the term for a room containing a toilet or the toilet itself.

DEFINITIONS

BUILT UP AREA (BUA) : This is the area covered by a building or room, including walls and circulation spaces. Unit areas indicated in each chapter are BUA.

OCCUPIED SPACE : Many of the projects were observed to have vacant rooms. This area is a measure of the currently inhabited space in each of the projects.

OPEN SPACE : This area includes setback space and area within courtyards.

SHARED SERVICES AREA : A feature of all chawls is the common toilets and bath areas. Shared Services Area is useful in gleaning information on the ratio of toilet space to the number of people. Cases in the study that have inbuilt toilets have a Shared Services Area of zero.

CIRCULATION AREA : Corridors and external staircases and ladders constitute Circulation Area.

SOCIAL SPACE : This area is a cumulative of spaces used for socialisation between inhabitants outside the dwelling unit. It has been quantified based on observation and measurement and in most cases includes parts of open and circulation space.

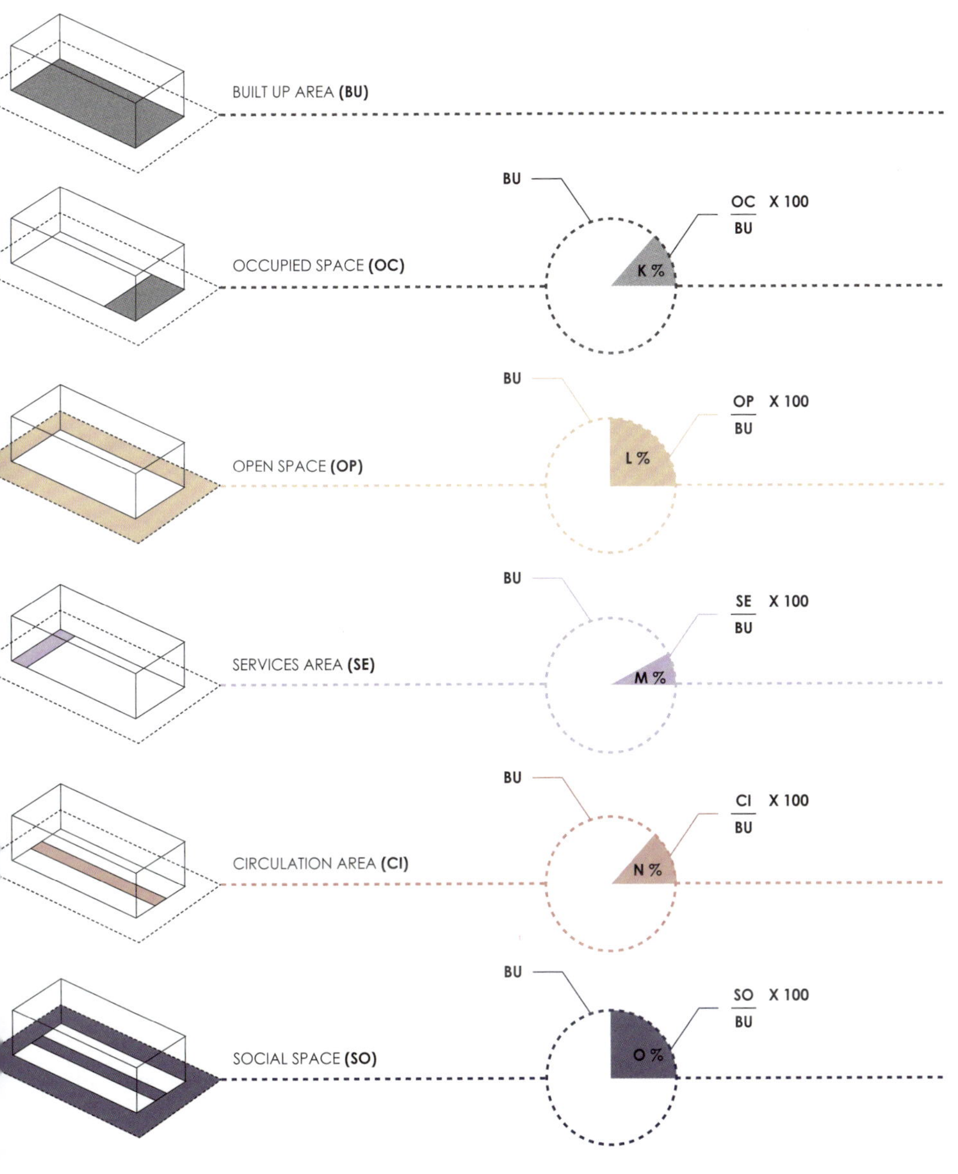

areas are measured in Square Metres

BIBLIOGRAPHY

Books and Essays:

Dwivedi, S. & Mehrotra, R. (1995). *Bombay: The Cities Within*. Mumbai, Maharashtra: Eminence Design Pvt Ltd.

Prakash, G. (2011). *Mumbai Fables*. Princeton, New Jersey: Princeton University Press.

Correa, C. (2010). *A Place in the Shade*. Gurgaon, Haryana: Penguin Books India.

Fernandes, N. (2013). *City Adrift*. New Delhi, Delhi: Aleph Book Company.

Iyer, K. (2014). *Boombay: From Precincts to Sprawl*. Mumbai, Maharashtra: Popular Prakashan.

Urban, F. (2011). *Tower and Slab: Histories of Global Mass Housing*. Abingdon, Oxfordshire: Routledge.

a+t research group. (2015). *Why Density?*. Vitoria-Gasteiz, Alava: a+t architecture publishers.

a+t research group. (2013). *10 Stories of Collective Housing*. Vitoria-Gasteiz, Alava: a+t architecture publishers.

Mehrotra, R. (2011). *Architecture in India: Since 1990*. Mumbai, Maharashtra: Pictor.

SPARC & KRVIA. (2010). *Re Dharavi*. Mumbai, Maharashtra: Self-published.

The Royal University of Fine Arts, Art and Architecture. (2009). *Dharavi: Documenting Informalities*. New Delhi, Delhi: Academic Foundation.

Adarkar, N. (Ed.). (2011). *The Chawls of Mumbai: Galleries of Life*. New Delhi, Delhi: imprintOne.

Campana, J. (Ed.). (2013). *Dharavi: The City Within*. Noida, Uttar Pradesh: HarperCollins Publishers India.

Mehta, K. (2008). Alice in Bhuleshwar: navigating a Mumbai neighbourhood. New Delhi, Delhi: Yoda Press.

Patel, S. B. (2006). Housing Policies for Mumbai. In R. Mehrotra, P. Joshi, P. Shetty & B. Menezes (Eds.), *Mumbai Reader 06* (pp. 222-235). Mumbai, Maharashtra: UDRI.

Newspaper Articles:

Srivastava, R. & Echanove, M. (2014, November 28). 'Slum' is a loaded term. They are homegrown neighbourhoods. *The Guardian*. Retrieved from http://www.theguardian.com.

Singh, V. (2015, May 25). 1-BHK flat in Sion is MHADA's most wanted. *Mid-day*. Retrieved from http://www.mid-day.com.

Nair, M. (2000, August 22). Bhuleshwar temple in unholy mess. *Mid-day*. Retrieved from http://archive.mid-day.com.

Mehta, R. (2012, October 12). Maharashtra Housing and Area Development Authority plans rehab for slumdwellers on its land to create hsg. *The Times of India*. Retrieved from http://timesofindia.indiatimes.com.

Phadke, M. (2014, July 4). MHADA yet to fully evacuate 3 of 8 most dilapidated cessed buildings. *The Indian Express*. Retrieved from http://indianexpress.com.

Pandit, S. (2015, July 23). Around 500 people have lucky escape as portion of two-storey chawl collapses in Kalbadevi. *Mid-day*. Retrieved from http://www.mid-day.com.

DNA Correspondent. (2015, July 24). Part of Swadeshi market collapses. DNA. Retrieved from http://www.dnaindia.com.

Pinto, R. (2016, January 7). Parts of Mangaldas Mkt, some cessed SoBo buildings likely to lose heritage tag. *The Times of India*. Retrieved from http://timesofindia.indiatimes.com.

DNA Correspondent. (2015, January 6). Mhada buildings crashing despite high construction cost. *DNA*. Retrieved from http://www.dnaindia.com.

Express News Service. (2014, May 24). MHADA sets aside Rs 10 crore as insurance for occupants of oldest buildings in city. *The Indian Express*. Retrieved from http://indianexpress.com.

Abedi, S. S. (2015, July 24). Mumbai: Lucky escape for 500 as staircase collapses in Kalbadevi. *Mid-day*. Retrieved from http://www.mid-day.com.

Times News Network. (2011, November 24). Many old city bldgs to get 2.5 FSI for redevpt. *The Times of India*. Retrieved from http://www.timesofindia.indiatimes.com.

Suryawanshi, S. (2015, December 27). Mhada shortlists 13 architects for BDD chawl redevelopment. *DNA*. Retrieved from http://www.dnaindia.com.

Team DNA. (2014, December 12). Charkop – a model of planned development. *DNA Syndication*. Retrieved from http://dnasyndication.com.

Khan, T. N. (2009, November 28). Bhang Wadi Beckons. *DNA*. Retrieved from http://www.dnaindia.com.

FPJ Bureau. (2013, July 21). Stop-work notice: Court grants relief to builder. *Free Press Journal*. Retrieved from http://www.freepressjournal.in.

Awatramani, T. (2010, May 4). Girgaum: The forgotten heart of Mumbai. *CNN*. Retrieved from http://www.cnn.travel.com.

Srinivas, H. (n.d.). *Urban Squatters and Slums: Sites and Services*. Retrieved from http://www.gdrc.org.

Blog Posts:

Choudhury, C. (2011, April 15). On Neera Adarkar's anthology *The Chawls of Mumbai* [Web log post]. Retrieved February 24, 2016 from http://middlestage.blogspot.in.

airoots. (2014, May 9). Mumbai Modern: Revisiting BDD Chawls [Web log post]. Retrieved March 4, 2016 from http://urbz.net.

Ravi, V. (2013, August). Walking through Kalbadevi, Mumba Devi temple in Mumbai [Web log post]. Retrieved February 26, 2016 from https://pixelvoyages.wordpress.com.

Reports and Other Publications:

Chiplunkar, G.D. (Ed.). (2011). *Development Control Regulations*. Mumbai, Maharashtra: Urban Development Department.

Municipal Corporation of Greater Mumbai. (n.d.). *Landuse and Growth Management*. Retrieved from MCGM Website: http://www.mcgm.gov.in/irj/go/km/docs/documents/MCGM%20Department%20List/City%20Engineer/Deputy%20City%20Engineer%20(Planning%20and%20Design)/City%20Development%20Plan/Landuse%20and%20Growth%20Management.pdf

Praja. (2014). *The State of Affordable Housing in Mumbai*. Retrieved from Praja Website: http://www.praja.org/praja_docs/praja_downloads/Report%20on%20The%20State%20of%20Affordable%20Housing%20in%20Mumbai.pdf.

The World Bank. (1985). *Staff Appraisal Report, India, Bombay Urban Development Project* (Report No. 4794-IN). Retrieved from World Bank website: http://www-wds.worldbank.org/servlet/WDSContentServer/IW3P/IB/2000/02/09/000178830_98101901065028/Rendered/PDF/multi_page.pdf.

Shetty, P., Gupte, R.,Patil, R., Parikh, A., Sabnis, N. & Menezes, B. (2007). *Housing Typologies in Mumbai*. Retrieved from CRIT website: https://critmumbai.files.wordpress.com/2011/10/house-types-in-mumbai-final.pdf.

Mumbai Transformation Support Unit. (2009). *BDD Chawls: Surveys, Findings and Redevelopment Strategies*. Retrieved from Vision Mumbai website: http://www.visionmumbai.org/images/projects/bdd%20chawls_final%20report_aug.pdf

Web Pages:

SRA.gov.in. (n.d.). Retrieved February 8, 2016, from http://www.sra.gov.in.

MHADA.Maharashtra.gov.in. (n.d.). Retrieved February 24, 2016, from http://mhada.maharashtra.gov.in.

Girgaon.in. (n.d.). Retrieved April 22, 2016, from http://girgaon.in.

ABOUT

sPare, launched in January 2016, is the research arm of sP+a (Sameep Padora and Associates). Its intent is to investigate the seen and unseen relationships between architecture and the city and contribute to the discourse on the built environment through rigorous documentation and analysis.

sPare's maiden study, *In the Name of Housing* is an ongoing research project. The work was first displayed in a month-long exhibition at the Somaiya Centre for Lifelong Learning, Mumbai, January-February 2016. The exhibition – an allied event with *The State of Architecture: Practices & Processes in India* – later moved to the Kamla Raheja Vidyanidhi Institute for Architecture, Mumbai. This book is a result of the exhibition and sPare's maiden publication.

sPare is also currently finishing work on it's second research project entitled (re)CODING that analyses the evolution of Mumbai's housing form seen through the lens of historical emergence of Mumbai's building code. This study along with the others is representative of sPare's larger interest in understanding the role of design with respect to the intersections between architecture, community and history.

ACKNOWLEDGEMENTS

This book, a part of our continuing research on affordable housing types, is a documentation and analysis of 14 housing projects in the city of Mumbai. While the catalyst of this study was an affordable housing commission from a private developer, the research pretty much took on a life of its own.

The documentation of these projects was a mammoth effort fronted by Diane Athaide and Saloni Parekh and would have been impossible without their commitment, perseverance and belief in the validity and need for such research. Marsha Silgardo, Larika Desai and Niharika Kannan toiled tirelessly on the production of the analytical drawings and diagrams in this book along with a group of fantastic student volunteers, who unstintingly contributed their time and effort. I would like to thank Shreyank Khemalapure for helping us with resources, as well as the student volunteers, namely Ankit Shah, Chintan Shah, Goldie David, Jemin Mehta, Juzer Furniturewala, Mit Sheth, Monali Suryavanshi, Nishriti Shetty, Rhea Pejavar, Rishabh Suvarna, Sanjana Shah, Shrutika Parkar, Saurabh Bhayaje, Sayalee Chavan, Sweta Kandari and Vishal Udeshi.

Additionally, Maitri Dore's assistance in writing the text for this document and Mythili Shetty's editing were invaluable, as was Nupoor Monani's help with data on Swadeshi Market.

As the studio's first formal research project we depended heavily on the studio's resources; Aparna Dhareshwar, Mythili Shetty and Vami Koticha, supported by the office staff including Anil Dhulap, Sumit Pendhari, Hriday Sharma and Sudama Baudh did an incredible job.

I am delighted that through nai010 publishers the international edition of this book will now find a global audience. Many thanks to Marcel and Carlien for making this happen.

I am deeply grateful for Dirk van Gameren for his unflinching support in bringing the accompanying exhibition to the TU Delft and for the publishing of the international edition of the book. I am indebted to Rahul Mehrotra for his advice and support throughout the process of making this catalogue, as also for his mentorship and assistance.

I would also like to thank Pinkish Shah for his constructive comments on the final draft and Vikas Dilawari for readily helping us with information on the heritage status of some of the projects. Kunal Bhatia shot the photographs published in this book many times over until we had just the right frame. These form an integral part of the study without which the narratives of these projects would be incomplete. I would also like to thank photographers, Steven Athaide and Karan Arora who documented some of these projects beautifully for our exhibition.

None of these narratives would have been possible without the generosity of the residents in every project we studied, who welcomed us into their homes, allowing us access to document their private spaces – extensively and often repeatedly. Many of these conversations have been hugely informative in our understanding of the lifestyle that accompanies certain housing types. Further, private trusts and societies, developers and officials, granted us permission to enter their building premises; for this I am extremely grateful.

I would also like to thank Neera Adarkar, Kamu Iyer, Rupali Gupte and Prasad Shetty for all their wonderful work and publications on housing types in the city of Mumbai. Their work became the bedrock for us to build our study on, giving us an overview of historical and contemporary housing models and enabling us to launch our research into the architectural specificities of the same. I also owe thanks to my instructors PK Das at the Academy of Architecture, Mumbai, Reinhard Goethert at MIT and Professor Yves Cabannes at Harvard, for piquing my interest in housing through electives during my days as a student.

More recently, many conversations with Rahul Srivastava and Matias Echanove of URBZ, during our collaborations on the Dharavi and Shivaji Nagar projects have been pivotal in informing my understanding of the complex issues that govern urban housing.

I'd like to end by thanking my parents Neelu and Maharaj for their unflinching support, Nikita and Prateek for their indulgence, and my wife Ritu and son Avirath for being patient with the incessant hours and holidays spent at work.

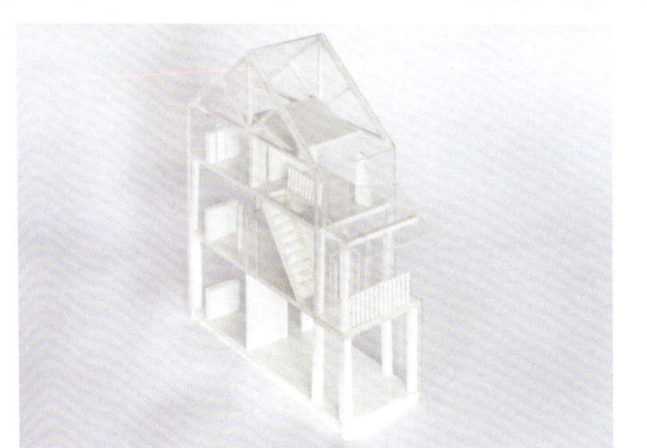
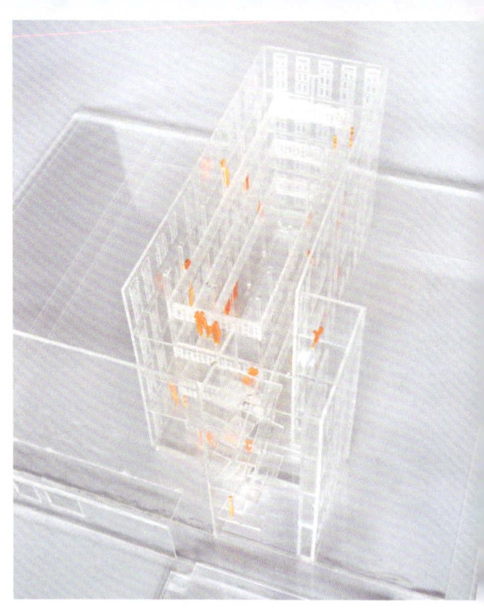

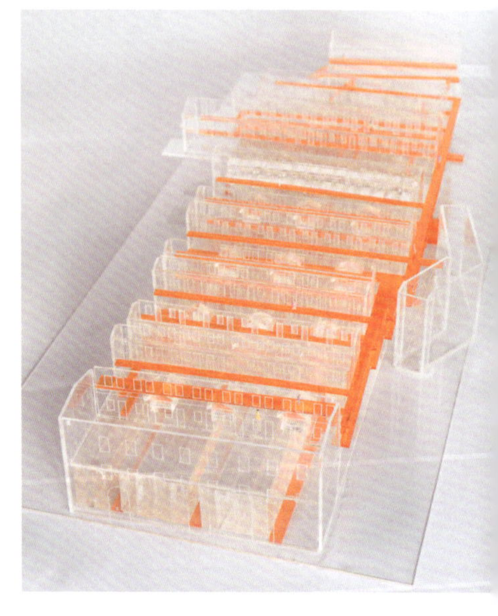
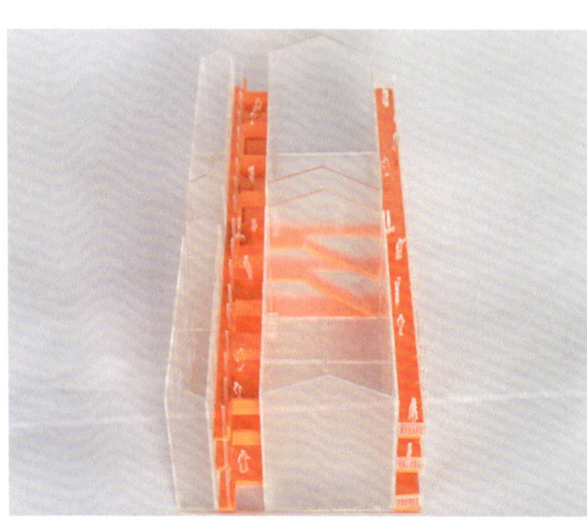

THANKS

Studio

Aditya Sharma
Akhila Arakkal
Aniket Umaria
Anil Dhulap
Aparna Dhareshwar
Diane Athaide
Harshat Verma
Hriday Sharma
Kanika Sharma
Kriti Veerappan
Larika Desai
Mansee Doshi
Maitri Dore
Manasi Punde
Marsha Silgardo
Mythili Shetty
Niharika Kannan
Pranav Thole
Sachi Mavinkurve
Saloni Parekh
Sameep Padora
Sandeep Patwa
Sanjana Purohit
Saurabh Suryan
Shravanthi Kumar
Sidharth Somana
Sudama Baudh
Subham Pani
Sumit Pendhari
Surabhi Dahivalkar
Vami Koticha
Vishal Jayan

Volunteers

Ankit Shah
Chintan Shah
Goldie David
Jemin Mehta
Juzer Furniturewala
Mit Sheth
Monali Suryavanshi
Nishriti Shetty
Rhea Pejavar
Rishabh Suvarna
Sanjana Shah
Shrutika Parkar
Saurabh Bhayaje
Sayalee Chavan
Sweta Kandari
Vishal Udeshi

Photographers

Karan Arora
Kunal Bhatia
Steven Athaide

Special Thanks to the Residents and Officials

Mr Allwyn Das
Ms Asha Katale
The Dandekar Family
Ms Maimuna Ansari
Ms Manjula Shah
Mr Manoj G Pandya
Mr Manoj Kumar Yadav
Ms Mayuri Merchant
Mr and Ms Mrugesh K Shah
Mr and Ms ND Parmar
Mr Otaram
Ms Reshmi Magdun
Mr Ravindra Akela
Mr Sachin Bhowad
Mr SB Navle
Ms Surekha Pandit
Ms Vidya Vilas Chavan
The Siemens Management

CREDITS

Author
Sameep Padora
with a foreword by Rahul Mehrotra
and an introduction by Dirk van Gameren

Editors
Maitri Dore, Mythili Shetty

Text
Maitri Dore

Translation
Maitri Dore

Layout and Design
Marsha Silgardo, Diane Athaide,
Larika Desai

Photos
Kunal Bhatia
www.kunalbhatia.net

Lithography
Saloni Parekh

Printer
Wilco Art Books, Amersfoort

Production
Carlien Korpel, nai010 publishers

Publisher
Marcel Witvoet, nai010 publishers

sPare
Sameep Padora, Saloni Parekh,
Diane Athaide, Marsha Silgardo, Maitri Dore,
Larika Desai, Niharika Kannan

This publication was made possible by financial support from:

TATA TRUSTS

nai010 publishers is an internationally orientated publisher specialized in developing, producing and distributing books in the fields of architecture, urbanism, art and design. www.nai010.com

nai010 books are available internationally at selected bookstores and from the following distribution partners:

North, Central and South America - Artbook D.A.P., New York, USA, dap@dapinc.com

Rest of the world - Idea Books, Amsterdam, the Netherlands, idea@ideabooks.nl

For general questions, please contact nai010 publishers directly at info@nai010.com or visit our website www.nai010.com for further information.

Printed and bound in the Netherlands

ISBN 978-94-6208-553-4
NUR 648
BISAC ARC003000, ARC025000

How to Build an Indian House is also available as e-book:
ISBN 978-94-6208-565-7 (e-book)

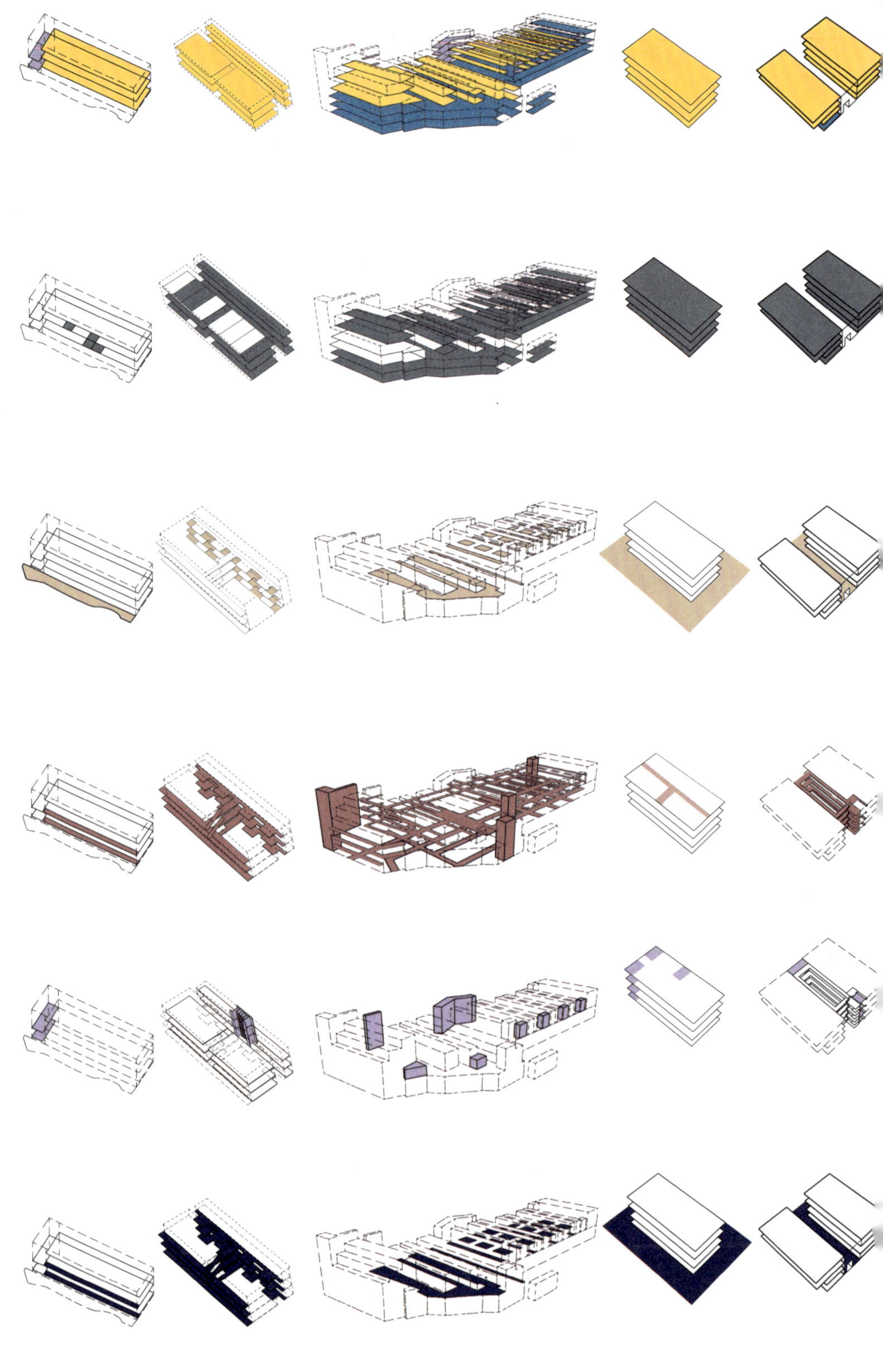